DOWN THE TUBE
The Northern Line

Carole Blacher
Judy Worham

Best wishes from

Carole + Judy.

Worbler Press

WORBLER PRESS

Published in the United Kingdom by:
Worbler Press,
Brookwood,
Homedean Road,
Chipstead,
Sevenoaks,
Kent TN13 2RU
www.worblerpress.com

This book is a work of non-fiction.

The rights of Carole Blacher and Judy Worham to be identified as the authors of this work have been asserted by them in accordance with the Copyright, Designs, Patents Acts 1988.

A CIP record of this book is available from the British Library.

First printed in October, 2011

Cover design by James Watson watsonprimeadvertising@gmail.com

Content copyright ©Carole Blacher and Judy Worham 2011

Typset in 13/14pt Garamond
Printed in the UK by Reyvis Design Print, Bromley BR2 9NS

ISBN   978 0 9570317 0 8

Dedicated to the staff of the Northern Line, with special thanks to those encountered on our journey and referred to in this book, even the man at Tufnell Park.

Acknowledgements

With grateful thanks to Debbie at Reyvis for all her help and support. James Watson for his excellent cover design and the Worbler logo. Carl Heydorn for his technical expertise in setting up our website. Geoff for his technical help and unfailing good humour. Katherine our marketing manager for her exemplary administrative and organizational skills who has been such a help in promoting our book. Our thanks to Harry Beck whose map inspired us along the way and to Transport for London for producing the mapettes that show not only the local streets, public toilets and places of interest, but also onward bus routes. Finally, our grateful thanks for the many members of the general public whose unsolicited offers of help gave us a picture of the cheerfulness and generosity of the people of London.

Table of Content

INTRODUCTION

'What are we going to do now Yogi?' A question often posed by Boo Boo, that hapless bear, and now Carole and I were asking each other. Retirement loomed large, how to stave off senility, keep us focused and amuse ourselves. Gardening was just not an option. We both needed to escape from our grandchildren, twelve between us. We could easily spend all our time babysitting.

'And then there's the husbands,' Carole said. We have two, one each that is. They needed to be escaped from too.'

'We could easily spend our time making nice little meals and ironing their underpants,' I said.

'What about extreme ironing,' Carole suggested, 'flatten their jim-jams on the top of Snowdonia.'

'It's been done before.'

'What about or starting up a flea circus?' she suggested.

'They might get into the underpants.'

'No, that's ants.' I nodded. She had a point

'Something original,' Carole said and her little face lit up with a beatific smile. 'If we need to escape, how better than a tunnel?'

'I've seen that film, I'm not filling my trouser legs with dirt, or jumping over a wooden horse whilst you do.'

'It's already dug for us,' Carole said. 'The tube. We could travel a line, get off at every stop, pop up to the surface to sample the delights of the locality, visit places we've only ever passed through.'

'Under,' I said. 'And we could write about it.'

'We'd be like mole reporters,' she said enthusiastically.

And so the project was born. Partners in crime at the FE College, we had sat through interminable meetings being told what to do and how to do it. The only way to survive the tedium was to adopt the maxim 'silliness is next to godliness,' so we'd collaborated on the staff magazine and enjoyed making fun of our *seniors and betters*. Carole, always the ringleader with her pink hair and her audacious attitude to authority was just the companion for me, a timid conforming Archers fan.

'We'll start with the Northern Line,' she said. The adventure began on 4th June at London Bridge Station.

CHAPTER ONE

London Bridge

'London Bridge, a place known world wide, not a bad place to start,' Carole says so we dive down to the platform to begin our momentous journey. This is the first of the fifty stations on the Northern Line.

Our first impression is a striking one. The ads are obviously in the process of being removed giving the opposite wall a messy Jackson Pollok effect in contrast to the rest of the pristine, recently refurbished surroundings. The passenger side walls are of brilliant white enamel and the floor is tiled with what looks like marble. The ceiling is stainless steel with a rail running along the centre which holds the bright fluorescent lighting, speakers and CCTV cameras. Even the electric rail is clean and supported on white, upside down pudding basins. The platform is wide with a raised section at one end for wheelchair users and the whole place gives the impression of a modern and efficient station. Of course we have been here many times before being seasoned London travellers, but here's the real difference between then and now, we have never really taken much notice and now we're looking about us.

A location which is all buzz and bustle during the rush hours is now relatively quiet so on leaving the station to go above ground, Carole and I decide to have an escalator race. This involves both of us stepping on to the two parallel escalators at exactly the same moment and then shouting words of encouragement in the hope that one's chosen vehicle will arrive before the other. Of course they arrive simultaneously but by standing as far forward as possible and thrusting out her chest Carole claims a photo finish victory.

'That's cheating,' I exclaim indignantly.

'No it's not, it's *gameswomanship*,' retorts Carole. 'At least I didn't take drugs or lubricate my escalator with surreptitious squirts of WD40. Anyway you're much better endowed than I am and it's hardly my fault if you choose to hide your boobs under a bushel.' I'd never quite thought of my Marks and Spencer bra in those terms before.

As we leave we count the entrance/exit barriers. There are 14 on the Northern line side and 15 on the Jubilee line side – grossly unfair if you ask me. The Jubilee line may be newer but the Northern Line has character and history and we're just the women to explore it. Going through the barrier we wander around the spacious concourse with its ticket office and pillars in strange places. Carole is fingering the leaflets on offer whilst my attention is drawn to the magnificent sight of a Scottish gentleman in full regalia. I point him out to Carole.

'He's probably a busker with his bagpipes in that case so let's get out of here before he launches into *Amazing Grace.*' I agree. We share a dislike of bagpipe music (if you can call it music;) we beat a hasty (silent) retreat out on to Duke Street. Walking down Tooley Street past the London Dungeon Carole suggests we visit Hay's Galleria since I have never been there. A converted wharf this is now a delightful, architecturally impressive shopping arcade with many small craft shops as well as restaurants and bars. At the entrance we find a Christmas shop. Now there is something incongruous about Christmas shops at the wrong time of year. We go in and wander around looking at the usual – and some quite unusual – paraphernalia that needs dark nights, cold weather and seasonal music to put one in a purchasing mood. We leave empty handed without so much as a backward glance at the rainbow coloured tinsel wondering whether a glass of mulled wine might have persuaded us to buy our Christmas decorations several months in advance of the event.

So it's into Hayes Galleria on Carole's recommendation; her main reason for loving this place is the giant 60ft bronze sculpture of a ship, The Navigator, which is almost surreal and she says always reminds her of that wonderful film *The Time Bandits.*

'The sculpture used to move – the oars would row, water would squirt out of various orifices and a bell would toll,' she muses wistfully, 'but I haven't seen it do that for many years now.'

'Maybe the mechanism is broken and the Ship Sculpture Repair Committee haven't yet reached agreement on who's responsible for undertaking and paying for the work,' I suggest.

'More likely a victim of Health and Safety legislation,' she replies sadly.

'Yeh, can't have people being hit by flying oars, drenched and deafened by the tolling of a ship's bell,' I add, but the day is too sunny and the surroundings too engaging for us to waste time on *a grumpy old women* rant about how things were better in our day.

Emerging on to the riverside and looking out over the Thames I am awed by the view. To our right there's HMS Belfast and across the water we can see a huge modern tower and the distinctive Gherkin looming up behind the classical buildings that line the waterfront. The magnificent Custom House rebuilt in 1814 using Wren's original design, provides a classical contrast framing the modern city developments which rise up behind it. Leaning over the parapet and looking to my left I can see London Bridge and to the right, Tower Bridge. The sun is shining and the river sparkles with reflected light. It's just lovely. Carole starts to sing *Maybe it's because I'm a Londoner.* I appreciate the sentiments expressed, if not Carole's singing.

We wander downstream past HMS Belfast and Southwark Crown Court toward More London, a development of new shiny offices which positively ooze prosperity and optimism. Between the gleaming silvery glass and steel edifices, or *monuments to capitalism* as Carole dismissively calls them, and the river, is a weird modern amphitheatre cut into the ground called *The Scoop.* This is used to put on free events for the people of London and anyone else who wants to see them. Today there is nothing to see apart from a few individuals sitting on the steps eating their sandwiches, so we proceed to City Hall, the new *seat* of Mayor Boris. It looks very odd – intuitively wrong – as it leans backwards, away from the river and we want to go round its sloping edge and push it up straight. This tilted glass

sphere of a building was designed by Norman Foster and opened in 2002. Now if his other famous London edifice, 30, St Mary Axe, is known as *the gherkin*, this should be called *the pickled onion.*

We go inside and are greeted by polite and helpful security staff who inform us about the public areas and offer us plans of the building. It seems that we can walk up to the second floor via a spiral walkway which goes around the outside of the building where we can see The Chamber.

'Sounds like something out of a Hammer Horror film,' quips Carole. 'Just the place for a bloke called Boris.'

'It says here that it's a "flexible space for public debates and meetings" which is open to the press and public,' I say consulting my plan.

'Does that mean it's got rubber walls?' Carole grunts as we start our ascent. 'Flexible space my ....'.

Reaching the second floor we find a place to sit and a free booklet entitled *Inside City Hall.* We take our ease and read and learn about the building's ecological design features, which include an explanation of why it is such an odd shape.

'Here look at this,' says Carole pointing to a paragraph in the booklet. 'It says this building was funded by the developers of More London and is leased to the Greater London Authority for twenty five years.'

'So what happens in 2027 when the lease runs out?' I ask. 'The taxpayers of London will doubtless have to cough up humungous sums of money to renew it. Told you it was a monument to capitalism,' she adds smugly.

'The Chamber might have lost its flexibility by then so they'll have to move anyway,' I suggest. 'Happens to us all with age, although 25 isn't very old for a building. You could install a very whizzy Stannah stairlift round the outside of this spiral walkway.' I point out the section in large letters which says that the building is glass so that Londoners can see in demonstrating the openness of London's government.

'Believe that and you'll believe anything,' mutters Carole under her breath.

Leaving the spectacularly empty chamber we walk back down towards the café, stopping to press buttons on a screen display showing the development of this area of London over a thousand years. We move on again and stop to admire a map/aerial photograph of Greater London which is spread out on the centre of the floor beneath us. Carole spends ages trying to locate her road and eventually manages after putting her glasses on, finding the M25 and Biggin Hill Airport. This keeps her amused for a good five minutes while I edge slowly towards the café, more interested in reading the menu than a map.

Over coffee we speculate about the likelihood of seeing Boris, and if we did, what we might say. *Would you like to borrow my hair brush*, is our favourite, but it's unlikely we'll run into him so we content ourselves with admiring the view of the Thames before wending our way back to the station via some intriguing demolition and rebuilding going on behind it. We pause and join the knot of observers looking through a window at a building site where a vast excavation is underway. Various men in hard hats are shouting, gesticulating and industriously driving cranes and diggers. This, we now realize, was the foundation of *the shard*. How people can conceive of and execute such projects is a constant source of amazement to us. Why buildings stand up, especially giant distorted pickled onion shaped ones, is as much of a mystery to us as how all these workers can possibly know what they should be doing amid the muddy chaos. Men may not be much good at sharing their feelings and they can't wash up for toffee, but they do know how to build stuff we conclude. We're moving on south, so make for the station, next stop please.

Borough

Carole is humming 'don't sleep in the subway darling' as we alight on to the paved platform surface which is buffed to a satisfying silky shine by what could be an army of Southwark's finest youth offenders on community service. This is just one of the many delights of this underground station. Subsequently we're both singing, 'don't flash in the lift shaft darling,' but more of that later.

Seated on the platform, we look about us. The platform empties quickly and only a few people arrive, none of them appears to be in a hurry. On the wall opposite the advertisements look tatty but they serve a necessary function; they hide some of the dirt that is stuck there like grubby Artex. As we sit on the regulation metal seats, four in a row, there's that familiar noise, starting like a giant tummy rumble as the next train approaches. We wait, all breathless expectation, then it bursts into an impressive roar as it belts out of the tunnel, all patriotic red, white and blue. The train comes to a halt and we scrutinise it carefully.

Carole says, 'Have you ever noticed that each carriage has its own number?' Well I hadn't, so she goes on, 'and, how do the train operators choose which one goes where?'

'I don't know,' I reply.

'Once the train has been constructed, much like a string of sausages does it ever change?' she asks, not waiting for an answer. 'Would a fat carriage controller say, "Take off 52657, and put on 53528." Incidentally, how would he say that?'

'I don't know,' I reply impatiently, 'but sausages aren't constructed like that. Wouldn't a string of beads be a better analogy?' She ignores me, and keeps on about those blasted numbers.

'Would it be fifty two thousand, six hundred and fifty seven?' She pauses, shakes her head and carries on. 'Nah, too much of a mouthful. Perhaps he just says the numbers, 5 2 6 5 7, or 526 fifty seven?' None of this can I answer so I stand and turn towards the exit. Carole walks in the opposite direction towards the far end of the platform and I think she's muttering,

'How can we find out?' We – I don't think so, but even so I follow her protesting. 'But the exit's this way,' I indicate, pointing over my shoulder.

'I know, I'm just taking a walk on the wild side....to the end of the platform as we know it,' she responds jauntily. We have come to six wooden doors mysteriously marked *Private* and a seventh bearing the sign *Pump Room Cleaner*.

'Do you think she lives in there?' asks Carole

'Who?'

'The Pump Room Cleaner. Not much of a job. I wonder where the others go,' she muses pointing to the other six doors. 'We could end up in a magical underground kingdom or somewhere like Narnia,' she continues grasping one of the handles.

'We could end up getting arrested,' I reply turning back towards the exit. 'C'mon lets go.' I walk steadfastly in the direction of the Way Out arrow hoping that Carole will follow and we will not end up being banned from the Northern Line before we have even started.

I point out the metal boxes that are fixed to the wall and house various notices and ads. They are curved at the back to fit the curve of the tunnel wall and flat at the front so that the posters they display are flat.

'I think they're a waste of money. I can read a notice even if it's slightly bent,' Carole says disparagingly

Carole is thrilled to find that the southbound platform is above the northbound platform as we go up some steps, and across a little bridge with wire netting allowing us a glimpse of the platform and line below. I don't know why she finds it

so pleasing, but her squeals of delight and pointing are very embarrassing. People are looking.

Making our way to the lift we encounter another source of joy for Carole. She's easily satisfied today, probably it's the novelty value of our project. There's a notice. It says:

The station is exit only between 8.00 – 10.00 hours and 17.00 to 19.00 hours. Whilst we replace the lift.

Carole says,

'What do you think they're going to replace the lift with?' I'm too busy trying to work out what the message means to reply. 'A fireman's pole, a rock climbing wall, an abseiling experience?' she offers warming to the subject.

Carole pulls out her camera and takes a flash photograph of the notice board. We are about to learn our first lesson regarding security on the tube. The CCTV cameras are everywhere! Taking the one serviceable lift in an upwardly direction even though the notice has suggested we cannot exit this station at this hour, we are met at the ticket barrier by a very irate man. Before we are allowed through he informs us in no uncertain terms that we are **not** to use flash photography anywhere on the underground. Should a train driver experience arc eye when coming out of the tunnel he could be dazzled and miss his stopping spot which would have serious implications for his safety, the safety of the passengers and world peace. (I made that last bit up about world peace). To question what a driver and his train might be doing in a lift shaft a considerable distance from the line occurs to both of us, but we remain silent hanging our heads in shame, whilst desperately trying not to catch each other's eye in case we giggle.

We are sorry, not very sorry, but sorry about the flash photography and his disapproval, but not at all sorry to meet him. He is very easy on the eye, tall dark and handsome, and we both watch as his broad shoulders and manly figure disappear into his office to study the CCTV screens in search of more miscreants.

'Lovely shirt,' I remark.

'Pristine,' Carole observes.

'White enough for a Persil ad?' Carole nods in agreement.

'Could be a hazard for drivers, wouldn't it blind them, coming out of the darkness of a tunnel?' We chortle discreetly.

Having taken our punishment and adopting a suitably contrite demeanour whilst hiding our guilty sniggers, we look round the small foyer and find a wall map. It's a miracle! Every station has one, we soon discover, showing the surrounding streets, places of interest, and distance to the next tube. The map details toilets, libraries, churches, (of which there seem to be an abundance which is surprising given the reported decline in religious observance), places of interest and bus routes. We are thrilled to find that this large map is available in the form a mapette, a small handy free take away paper version we can pick up in the foyer of every station thanks to the bountiful generosity of the ex-God of London, Lord Livingstone. Will Boris replace them with stirring tracts from the Conservative Party Manifesto or extracts from Pliny minor, or will they fall foul of the cuts? Only time will tell.

Our interest lies in the refreshment area so we leave the ticket office, crossing the road so that Carole can take a picture of what she says is *the cool curve* of Borough Station, which is built on a road junction and fits neatly into the space. Now let's look on the positive side of Borough's tube station, don't be afraid to come here if you are hungry. Within spitting distance of the foyer there's Café Riva, The Trinity, Galapagos Net Internet Cafe, Café Chantilly and if you can be bothered to cross the road, there's Starbucks with comfy chairs and newspapers.

One coffee and a waffle later we decide to explore now we are replete and have admired the quality of Starbucks' toilet paper which is embossed with a very tasteful leafy pattern. So nice.

Close scrutiny of the mapette reveals that we are close to Marshalsea Road, the site of Dickens' Marshalsea, the prison that changed his life and informed much of his writing. The surrounding roads refer to his novel *Little Dorrit* and I start to tell Carole about the picture of the debtors' prison painted by Dickens. She listens politely and then says,

'I know. I saw the TV adaptation. The character I liked was the loser with the big ears – the son of the gatekeeper who fancied Little Dorrit but she rejected him and broke his heart.'

'John Chivery,' I chip in.

'Can't blame her though. I mean you wouldn't want your children having ears like that now would you, and there was no plastic surgery in those days.' I tell Carole about Dickens' intense sense of shame when his father was sent to the prison and he was sent to work in the Blacking factory but she is more interested in the psychology of the man rather than his life and literature. Well what do you expect from a woman who doesn't appreciate Shakespeare?

We decide to visit Winchester House which contains the London Fire Brigade Museum since, in his prime (whenever that was) my husband was a fireman. I'm drawn to a blue plaque on the wall that mentions the name of *Captain Sir Eyre Massey-Shaw,* and point it out to Carole telling her he was the founder of the London Fire Brigade. A friendly man in a suit on his way into the building stops to tell us that Massey-Shaw was a great self publicist who enjoyed this sumptuous house as his home. He also enjoyed the friendship of the Prince of Wales (later Edward VII) and they used to ride to fires together. He tells us that the real architect of the London Fire Brigade, then called the London Fire Engine Establishment, was the first Chief Officer called James Braidwood who served in the post for 28 years. He was killed at the Tooley Street fire of 1861 when a wall collapsed on him. We learn that Tooley Street fire is still the biggest in the capital since the Great Fire of London.

'Believed in leading from the front then, rather than swanning about in a carriage with royalty,' comments Carole. Man in suit nods approvingly, we've grasped the point.

The Museum is open but we learn that we can only visit by appointment, however, we are allowed to go upstairs and look around the shop. The shop is on the left at the top of an elegant staircase but on the right is another door which is open revealing a striking painting of a raging inferno. I am about to step in for a closer look when a young man  comes down the stairs and asks me to shut the door because the room is not open to the public. He is very nice about it causing me to reflect upon the difference between my treatment when perpetrating an infringement, and that of Carole. I think I'm better at getting away with it than she is because she looks naughty and I don't. The man in the shop is called Ashley and he invites us to join the 2 o'clock tour of the museum but we have to decline as we must press on to the Elephant and Castle. On the way back to the station I attempt to give Carole *not looking naughty* lessons but she lacks the necessary humility and only manages to look nonchalant.

Back at the station we run into the irate London Transport man again. It transpires he is the station manager and he's now outside his domain enjoying a fag. He isn't cross with us any more so we have a chat. His name's Dave and he's been working for the London Underground for 20 years. He finds the shift system very tiring but is enthusiastic and knowledgeable about his job. He's very safety conscious and says with evident pride, and just a hint of superiority, that the 'fail-safe system on the underground is foolproof, unlike overground trains.' We don't really know what he means so we nod approvingly.

'I bet there are some nasty accidents though,' Carole says.

'Not as many as you'd think but there is the occasional drunk falling onto the line.' Warming to his subject he tells us about *coconuts*. 'They're usually men, they put their briefcase between their legs and stand too close to the edge of the platform. The train comes in and they bend down to pick up their case just as the train passes them and it takes the top of their head off.' We all laugh. Dave has to go back to work. It's a shame, he really is gorgeous, oh, and well informed.

Being one of the older stations there are no escalators here. The alternative to the lift which we came up in, is a spiral staircase encased in an iron tube around eight feet in diameter. At the top and bottom are notices informing us of the number of steps.

'We'll walk down,' I suggest to Carole.

'And avoid walking up,' she says establishing a founding principle of our tubing. She understands me. We dawdle rather than sashay down the steps to the platform. Next station please.

Elephant and Castle

On alighting we sit on the platform and drink in the scene. There are no ads on the walls, they've all been scraped off. The effect is striking. It is just like a work of modern art. Carole says that it would be difficult to create something as good and takes a photograph of it - without flashing of course.

'That could win the Turner prize,' she comments.

'Nah, too good,' I say

The walls are being replastered in places and this station has its roof covered in that metaly mesh stuff, pleasingly curved to fit the tunnel. The station is busier than Dave's manor, but it is really clean. This time we notice a safety strip before the yellow line of raised dots, obviously a non-slip device to prevent us intrepid travellers from sliding onto the line. Oh, the thought just gives me shivers. Having been picked up as misbehaving at Borough, we notice the proliferation of security cameras. Has our handsome station manager e-mailed ahead? Watch out for two mad women brandishing a flashing camera I suggest to Carole? 'Probably not,' she says, deflating my flight of fancy.

We couldn't work out why but the trains appear slowly from the tunnel, not in a rush like other stations we could name (and no doubt will.) We come to a notice which says 'WAY OUT'. Clear enough you might think, but at each end of the notice there is an arrow pointing, yes, you've got it, in opposite directions. What to do? We ponder and then another helpful member of the underground staff advises us which is the quicker of the two options. We stop at the exit to the street in the foyer and chat to yet another London underground employee. He too is willing to pass the time with us and explains that the men who sit behind the darkened glass windows are the ones watching the CCTV cameras for trouble. This time we leave unscathed, no bad behaviour here.

The Elephant and Castle tube station takes its name from an 18th century pub which stood nearby. Before it was a pub it was the site of a sixteenth century playhouse called the Newington Theatre which used to put on Shakespeare's plays. The pub was demolished in 1959 in order to create something so much more up to

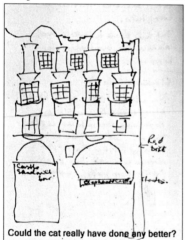

date, and now constitutes the concrete urban nightmare that is the sight before us. The pub's sign, comprising an elephant with a castle on its back, was preserved and can now be seen in the local shopping centre.

The station exterior is rather charming in sharp contrast to the surrounding area. I

Could the cat really have done any better?

attempt a drawing. It isn't rather charming, in fact it's a total mess.

'My cat could have done better,' remarks Carole. My drawing feebly shows the rows of windows and curves of the facing at the top of the building. It details the windows, pillars and semi-circular windows above the entrance. All of these features are set against deep dark red tiles. It's old-fashioned in appearance and Carole takes a picture, so sensible, to be using 21st century technology.

We look out over a hideous huge roundabout with an incessant flow of fast moving traffic and modern wide straight roads radiating off in several directions. The middle of the roundabout is occupied by a weird giant silver rubic cube.

'What's that?' I ask. Carole consults her map.

'It's supposed to be a monument to Michael Faraday.' We look at it critically.

'It lacks the grandeur of Nelson's column, don't you think?' she says and I nod in agreement. 'But then, Faraday was only a gifted scientist and inventor who improved the quality of people's lives,' she continues. I think she might be being sarcastic.

'Oh yea, enabling them to produce large carbon footprints.' We are going to argue, I can feel it coming on.

'Well, he wasn't a swashbuckling adulterous one-eyed admiral who led men into battle, was he?' I want to go, ooooh, but I don't, it'll only annoy her.

'So Horatio's contribution was helping to keep down the population of drunken lecherous sailors.' She gives me a withering look. We break into song, *What shall we do with the drunken sailor?* People passing give us a wide berth.

We pull ourselves together and quietly stare at our mapettes. A kindly lady mistaking us for two elderly and rather confused tourists offers to give us directions and help us across the road. Well, she had the first two things right, but we're not owning up to being tourists. We politely decline her help.

'Where do you fancy going?' I ask Carole.

'Look at this,' she says, 'the nearest and largest place according to our map is the London College of Communication. The LCC! Let's see what they have to say.'

In the spirit of our adventure, I agree. We set off to circumnavigate the Michael Farady rubic cube experience, negotiating half a dozen green man crossings and subterranean tunnels. Farady wins the mole and badger underground navigation award, Nelson can't compete.

At the London College of Communication it turns out they have quite a lot to say to us. It is open day and we are warmly greeted by a pleasant young lady, given literature about courses and, much to our surprise, ushered in to a lecture theatre. Carole whispers in my ear as a man starts a PowerPoint presentation about the college, its courses and facilities.

'He looks like a fugitive from a 1970's OU programme.' I giggle into my tissue and see that she's right, he's got a ponytail, a scraggy beard and suede shoes. Carole's phone goes off during his talk. Typical!

The PowerPoint is good with lots of attractive pictures but we aren't going to become undergraduates no matter how enticing the courses and facilities are—we've already done that. After the lecture we are offered a tour of the college but skip it in favour of a look round the exhibition of surface design. I'm in front of Carole as we tour the students' display of their final year's work. It's then that I see it and run back excitedly.

'Come and see this, you'll love it.' I lead Carole to the display by Andrea Halls. She has a long swathe of material printed with a flamingo pattern.

'Wow, I must write her name down,' Carole says scrabbling in her pocket for her pen. I look on fondly knowing she has a real affection for flamingos, identifying with them for being elegant, slim, pink, graceful and for being able to stand on one very thin leg for a long time. Her house has a distinct flamingo theme so I know she'll buy some material and have it made up into a parachute or a hang glider's wing or something quite crazy.

We have coffee amongst the exhibits and there is an opportunity to draw on a tablemat. I resist since my previous efforts have hardly met with aesthetic approval.

Returning to the station we lose our way a bit as there are multiple entrances and exits, and finding our way back in, proves a lot more difficult than finding the way out. We end up in a street market and have to ask for directions. Finding the station Carole nearly has a nasty flashing accident on the way down to the platform whilst attempting to photograph the interesting tiled stairway of 111 steps. We mingle unobtrusively with other passengers to avoid detection.

'Put your hood up,' Carole mutters, 'and keep looking down.'

'Don't worry I whisper,' as I finger my mini water pistol in my pocket. 'They'll never take us alive.' I show it to Carole who bursts out laughing as we board the southbound train.

Hay's Galleria: Named after its original owner, Alexander Hay, it was originally a brewery in the seventeenth century and transformed into a wharf in 1851. At its height 80% of the dry goods arriving in London passed through Hay's Wharf. Badly bombed in the second World War it was redeveloped in 1987, renovating the warehouses to provide shop and office space, raising the former dock area and covering it with a domed glass roof. There are plenty of places to eat and drink and it opens out on to the embankment.

City Hall: Weirdly magnificent building with very 'green' credentials which you can visit any weekday between 8.30 and 5.30. If you have enough money you can even hire the function suite called 'London's Living Room' on the top floor which has fabulous views of the city.

Dickens and the Marshalsea: The Marshalsea had been a prison since medieval times and was a debtors prison when it closed in 1842. Now all that remains of it is a length of wall in Angel Court bearing a plaque. For more information on the Dickens links in London along with sightseeing routes go to: www.walksof london.co.uk/little-dorrit-marshalsea-.shtml

London Fire Brigade Museum: Located in Winchester House on Southwark Bridge Road, home and workplace of London's chief fire officers between 1878 and 1937. It traces the history of fire fighting in London from the Great Fire of 1666 to the modern day. Visits are by appointment only and there is a small charge. Call them to book on: 020 8555 1200 ext:39894 or email: museum@london-fire.gov.uk They welcome school visits and produce a Teacher's pack.

Elephant and Castle: The site of the coaching inn from which it takes its name was formerly occupied by a blacksmith and a cutler. The coat of arms of the Worshipful Company of Cutlers features an elephant with a castle on its back which was used because of the use of elephant ivory in handles. The underpass, described by Boris Johnson as 'disgusting and dangerous', has multiple, well signposted exits decorated with some very colourful tiling and murals. Exploration late at night is not recommended.

London College of Communication: Has a long history dating back to 1883 but moved to its present site in 1964 as the London College of Printing. Combining with various other communications related schools and colleges it became the London College of Communication after the completion of a new, modern extension in 2004. It now offers a range of FE, HE, Postgraduate and short courses. For more information go to their website: www.lcc.arts.ac.uk

CHAPTER TWO

Kennington

We get off the train to what sounds like someone strangling a fractious child. Clearly something needs oiling. The train disappears down the tunnel still complaining loudly, this time like a stiffly jointed serpent. The train's absence reveals blank tatty walls, remnants of old ads clinging obstinately having escaped the scrapper this time, but we are informed by a large notice that the area is awaiting 'site maintenance.' To compensate for the mess the non-slip bobbly Braille safety slip along the edge of the platform is coloured a bright sunny yellow, as are the 'Mind the gap' warnings.

Kennington station has wooden benches attached to the wall and Carole and I sit on one and look about us. There's an old-fashioned wooden surround station clock with roman numerals displaying the time.

'Its' three forty,' Carole says. I'm taking notes so I don't look up, just nod. 'It's three forty twice a day on that clock. It's three forty twice a day, every day.' Carole warms to her subject as I continue to ignore her. I'm not going to encourage her. 'It's interesting because it will be three forty seven hundred and thirty-two times this year. Normally it would be seven hundred and thirty times.'

'But this year is a leap year,' I jump in. 'and look, it's now three forty-one.'

'Ah,' she sighs, 'the glory of three forty has past, but I shall remember this moment until I forget it.'

What's she like? She has time to think of this nonsense as the trains come in and linger with their doors open before leaving. I encourage movement before she gets worse so we take the lift. We could have taken the stairs, all seventy-nine of them. As we emerge from the lift Carole says 'Look, there are two entrances and exits.'

'You'd need to know that if you arranged to meet a friend at Kennington Underground Station,' I say. Carole disagrees,

'Not in the age of the mobile you wouldn't,' and we forget our mission in a discussion of life before this handy little invention. I'm brought back on stream as a drunk with a dog on a lead pushes past me shouting. He's not shouting at me or anyone else, and his dog doesn't seem bothered. No one seems to notice him.

I become absorbed in the interesting facts posted up in the original parts of the foyer. Now, did you know that last year there were 1,024 injuries on escalators? I also look at the heritage plaque celebrating the opening of this station in 1896. I wonder if drunken men shouted in the station in 1896?

Leaving the station we cross the road in order to admire its facade. Like Borough it's situated on the corner of the road but has none of Borough's gracious curves.

It does have a little dome on the top of the station building.

'Oh!' exclaims Carole, ' a mini St. Paul's Cathedral.'

'I think it looks a bit like a toddler's hat.'

'Either way, this is our first domed station experience,' she whispers in a voice of awe and wonder.

'It's used to house the lift mechanism.' My prosaic explanation takes all the excitement from her little face, so dropping that topic we look about us. We are in a pleasantly situated wide road and take our trusty mapettes out.

'Where to?' Carole asks.

'Here,' I say stabbing my finger vaguely at one of the landmarks. 'Let's go down Braganza Street. It's a great name, sounds a bit romantic, with a hint of swashbuckling.'

'Yea,' says Carole, 'where will that take us to?'

'Walworth Farm.' It beckons us, so off we go.

Braganza Street has none of the qualities of its name so I'll gloss over it, but it does lead to a pleasant oasis of calm amongst the urban sprawl of London. The farm, is situated right on the corner of two roads, and is enclosed by a high wire mesh fence, but the gate is unlocked and we step into a little bucolic delight. Whoever planned it out intended to use every single nook and cranny and the place is a riot of plants and flowers. Bees hum and do whatever bees do when they're not after your jam sandwiches. Roses hang from garlands of rope, flowers spring from raised beds. There are two poly tunnels, one full of cacti. A monkey puzzle tree grows in the middle of it all and blooms drop from the Jubilee pergola.

Judy interviews Ken, the scarecrow at Walworth Farm.

'No animals,' Carole says frowning.

'No room for them. Don't be picky.' We wander amongst the vegetable patch and find some very wild parts which Carole admires.

'You know Capability Brown?' she asks.

'Not personally.'

'You're being pedantic. This messy bit of the garden was designed by his brother, Incapability.' She smiles at her own joke.

'I suppose that's his statue over there', I say indicating a drunken looking scarecrow by the shed.

'Could be. They say he worked under the influence of a particularly fine claret.'

And so talking nonsense to each other we wend our way slowly trying to take in the riot of growth. It's quite delightful, until we reach the pond.

There's always a snake in the grass as Milton very well knew, you know, the Milton who wrote about *Paradise Lost* where nasty things happened in the garden. Something nasty happened to me. Gazing down into a murky pond and admiring the way the old railway sleepers have been arranged around the edge like the rays of the sun, Carole points out a dead frog. My reaction is one of horror and total revulsion.

'What's wrong?' Carole asks, noting my deadly pallor.

'That,' I gasp. 'That terrifying frog.'

'I think they're rather sweet.' Well, she would.

'You've never been attacked by one, have you?'

'No. I've never kissed one either', she responds unsympathetically. Undaunted by her disbelief I launch into my frog horror story.

'There, there,' she murmurs. 'It's over now. You could have therapy to rid you of this phobia you know.'

'No. I'd have to think about their horrible pointy fingers. I know they want to use them to leap at me and cling on to my warm skin, and I tell you, I just can't stand it. It's only nature I hear you say. They can't harm you. That's just where you're wrong.'

Carole is coughing into her handkerchief, but really I know she's laughing at me. I choose to ignore her. She sits me on a bench where I watch anxiously for signs of amphibian invasion whilst she buys a couple of plants and then it's time to leave this paradise with a mummified frog lurking in the undergrowth and return to the safer confines of the underground.

Oval

Alighting from our train onto a long thin platform we take the regulation wooden benches with yellow armrests and gaze about us. The platform floor is tiled and the walls are clad in plastic looking white panels. The walls opposite the platform have too few ads to hide their scabbiness, and those that are there, are dirty and tatty. 'Mind the gap' has a faded air and there's no  overhead digital display, except for the time. That reminds me, it's coffee time.

16

Looking up as we leave the platform Carole says,

'The station lies.' I think about what she's just said. 'But then, if it were oval we'd never get out. We'd just go round and round.' I nod sagely and wonder what's coming next. 'So they'd have to issue passengers with a 'Get out of the Oval free' card.' She's off on one again. 'There's no cricket stuff here either. Not a wicket or a hector protector in sight.'

'What's a hector protector?' I ask. Carole sniggers,

'An abdominal protector,' I stare blankly.

'A box.'

'One of those, thingummy bobs' I say gesturing vaguely toward my genital area.

'A protective cover, for the goolies, against the googlies.' We snigger.

We travel up the escalator and come to a gleaming green tiled foyer decorated with white cricket vignettes in various batting and bowling poses. It's just what we've been expecting from such an illustrious station. Carole looks at the figures and touches the tiles gently murmuring, 'Lawn green,' almost to herself.

'Stand there Carole.' I've got my camera out. She moves to the place indicated, but goes far too much to the left. 'A bit to the right.' She moves even more to the left. 'No, right, not left.'

'It is right.'

'No, my right, not yours.'

'Well that's not right,' she says.

'Yes, it is, my right, I'm taking the picture, do as you're told.' She moves following my pointing finger and stands to attention as I snap.

'You flashed,' she shouts accusingly.

'Shhhh,' I whisper as I secrete my camera furtively in my bag.

'Why do you always get away with it?' Carole demands looking about her seeing the complete absence of interest in my action. 'Where's the irate member of the station staff ready to tear you off a strip?'

'Ah, how I wish that Dave were here, he can tear me off a strip any day,' I sigh.

'Do you remember Lorne Greene?' she asks, looking once more at the figures depicted on the wall.

'Wasn't he that actor in that series on the television?'

'Yea, it was a western.'

'It was set on the Ponderosa Ranch.' She nods. 'And once when we were in Cornwall.....'

'Bonanza,' Carole says ruining my story. I was only just at the beginning.

'Exactly.'

'You're losing focus,' she says. 'Concentrate on the station.' Carole draws my attention to the enlarged station foyer. We agree that it has been refurbished to accommodate and impress all the cricket enthusiasts who pass up and down its escalators and through its electronic turnstiles. A large window to the right, looking for all the world like a ticket office sports a sign saying; *This is not a ticket office*, and another saying; *Assistance and Information*.

'Most frequently asked question?' Carole asks.

'Where's the ******* ticket office?'

Carole starts laughing and points out a sign that says; *The last northbound train has gone*.

With Bonanza still on our mind and humming, *Dum diddly, um diddly, um diddly, dum, da, dum dum*, we gallop out of the station.

Emerging into the sunlight we take in the view of a pleasant leafy suburban area give or take a few hundred cars and a rather noisy ambulance speeding along the wide open road. Opposite there's a grand looking church and a large park with three small fountains on the corner. Once the ambulance has gone it has all the ambience of the English country garden situated by an arterial road. Next to the station there's a flower stall. Nearby Oval Shoe Repairs waits to take care of all our oval footwear needs. Next door there is the Oval Snack Bar where we have coffee, in round cups; oval ones would have been a nice touch.

Whilst sipping our coffee we look out over a busy junction controlled by traffic lights and I watch a black man cross the road. He catches my eye because he has the most superbly toned body. He's dressed in casual slacks and has a sleeveless white top which clings to his magnificent torso. The café is a chippy and chirpy sort of place and the service is fast and friendly. The chips look and smell great, but it isn't anywhere near lunchtime so Carole drags me away with a dismissive,

'You can't possibly be hungry yet!' She doesn't understand me.

Leaving the café we admire the trees and the general leafy-greeness of the district.

'While we're here I suppose we should go and have a look at the cricket ground,' I muse consulting my mapette.

'Never been a great one for cricket, all that rubbing the ball on their trousers to make it shiny. Bet they wouldn't wear white if they had to do their own washing,' Carole says.

'I don't mind cricket but I think it goes on for too long.'

'I was always more of a football fan.'

'I spent much of my childhood playing it, on the beach or in the back garden.'

'Expect that's because you've got brothers.'

'You're right. I might even have liked it but I hardly ever got to bat.'

'My dad played in goal for Sydenham Gas,' Carole says.

'When I was allowed to bat, I was always out after two or three balls and had to cry and make everyone's life a misery to be allowed another go.'

'Didn't have women's football teams in my day. Hockey was the nearest I got – but it's not the same with a stick and a little hard ball is it?' Carole says but I'm too immersed in past injustices to respond.

'Made the school second eleven though'.

'I ended up being able to bowl reasonably well for a scrawny girl.'

It's quite easy to find the cricket ground which is not very far from the tube station. We arrive at the wrought iron Hobbs gate dedicated to Sir Jack Hobbs Surrey and England cricketer.

'Do you know he scored 197 centuries and was reputedly the most complete batsman,' I announce smugly.

'Did the others have leprosy then and bits dropped off them?' responds Carole dismissively. Sir Jack could gain entry at the Oval were he alive, but it appears that Carole and I cannot. We are refused entry by a polite, but firm security guard. A delivery man draws up to the gates in a white van. He is going to be allowed in.

'Will you smuggle us in?' Carole asks the driver who laughs and shakes his head. The doorman also laughs good-naturedly.

'You could look the other way,' I suggest to the doorman who shakes his head. I think he's getting a bit fed up with us, we're not moving on so he says we can walk round to the main entrance and perhaps go to the shop. We move off.

'He just wants to get rid of us,' Carole says sagely as we move off.

'That's what women do isn't it? Shop?' I say bitterly. 'Not allowed to bat, or be in the first team, so go shopping.' Carole nods in assent.

We find that walking round to the other gate is a long trek, halfway round the perimeter of the Oval and it's hot and dusty. We can't see anything because the ground is boarded up.

'Lawn green,' Carole says, not for the first time today and stops to admire the green stockade that hides the cricket ground from view. She runs her hand admiringly over its pristine surface. I'm worried, she's been told no defacing the fence and that always spells trouble. She fumbles in her bag and produces an indelible board marker.

'That's graffiti,' I gasp. She smiles wickedly and the job done sheaths her weapon of choice. She's written, *The Oval*. I grab her arm and hurry her away before some official tries to put her on the naughty step, or, since we're by the road, on the naughty kerb.

We pass Archbishop Tenison's school and watch the pupils playing a game of cricket in the playground.

'How appropriate,' I murmur in approval.

'Shouldn't they be playing tennis at Tenison's? Did he give his name to the game of tennis?'

'No. Come on, stop dawdling.' I'm anxious to get on before she does the next dreadful thing. We arrive at the Surridge entrance to the ground.

'It sounds like waste from Surrey,' Carole says. From outside we can peek through and see the concave structure that covers part of the main entrance with green plants growing up it, or down it? Either way it looks attractive.

Here we meet our next Dave who has a sense of humour and considerable charm as well as being smartly dressed and beaming with friendliness. We both want to marry him. Not only does he let us in to the ground, he takes us up two flights of steps where we can gaze in awe at the hallowed turf. It's quite a sight, an oval sight, strange because it's all overlooked by a huge magisterial gasometer. Odd or what? Carole wonders if they have the pavilion end and the gasometer end. Dave tells us it's the Vauxhall end. Disappointing. Dave points out the chief groundsman so we give him a wave.

'Wicket looks a bit brown,' says Carole. I nod my head.

'Why do they do that, when the rest is all green?' I ask.

'Yea,' she agrees, 'it should be the same colour as the rest of it.'

'I was going to ask him for a few tips about my grass, but now I've seen how he keeps the wicket I'm glad I didn't bother,' I say.

'Isn't the wicket and the state of it the most important part of the pitch?' Carole asks.

'Yea, so how come he gets away with keeping it nearly bare of grass? I've got a bit of grass that isn't doing too well in my back garden, but even that's better than his wicket.'

'You could give him a few hints,' Carole suggests.

We descend from the edifying sight of the venerable pitch and make our way to the shop. There must be something we'd like to buy. On the way we stop and watch a lady artist painting an advertisement for NatWest on the wall. She shows us the picture she's going to draw. It will look as if a cricket ball has burst through the bricks when she's finished. We talk about wall art, her life and then leave her alone having bothered her enough.

The shop's a bit of a mess. It's got a central pillar which means that visually you get no real sense of what is on offer as you walk in. There's stuff all over the floor waiting to be unpacked and it's very cramped. By the till there's a large television. I presume that when there is a match on it shows what is happening on the pitch so that no part of the game is lost by shoppers. Carole pulls a face.

'More likely so that spectators don't miss Eastenders when one of those interminable five day test matches is being played here,' she mutters. Back to the merchandise. I buy a leisure shirt with the England logo on it for my son-in-law who is an enthusiast for the game he spends hours playing.

In the ladies, and yes, there is one, we find a hand dryer called the Dyson Airblade. It has all the properties of a wind tunnel operating at gale force. It gets our hands dry while testing the aerodynamic qualities of our fingers. We wash our hands several times just to try it out.

It's time to leave cricket behind us. We kiss our new friend Dave goodbye. What a smasher. Wending our way through back streets Carole looks about her.

'These have seen better days.'

'So have we.'

'Yea, who are we to criticise.'

Not content with one visit, we are now on a mission to find the Charlie Chaplin Adventure Playground in Kennington Park. Flanked on one side by an exceedingly high-rise block of flats, this is one of London's well used but less manicured parks. It has wonderfully mature trees and open spaces, a sports area for basketball, tennis. The adventure playground looks a bit unkempt to me.

'That's a bit of a mess.' Carole gives me one of her looks,

'Children don't like tidiness, they like hiding, making dens and finding things.'

'OK, but isn't it sad that the playground is like a prison compound.' We look at it entirely enclosed in wire mesh.

'I think kids would have a great time here, all they need is imagination and most of them have that in abundance.'

This park is full of both character and characters, including several supine sleepers and many dog walkers. Carole grabs my arm and points towards a lady in the distance who appears to be swinging two anorexic purple squirrels in alternating circles attached to strings.

'Can you see what I can see?' I nod. 'Do you think she's allowed to do that?' I shrug my shoulders, palms up in a *don't ask me* gesture. 'Those poor creatures. Wouldn't you think the humiliation of being dyed purple was enough, without being swung about like that?' It was necessary to investigate further. The squirrel torturer turns out to be a friendly woman pursuing her hobby. The purple squirrels are in reality scarves tied to the end of a long piece of string which is weighted at the scarf end. The contraption, or sport, or pastime is called *spiral poi*.

'It sounds like an oriental skin disease,' Carole mutters under her breath as we walk away.

We find Café Café Kennington Park which is bursting at the seams with people wanting to buy a snack and sit in the sunshine. When we come to pay for our comestibles we have to rummage through purses and pockets to find change as they don't do credit cards this far out of town. Sitting out on the decking we people and dog watch. An interesting procession of canines and their owners pass by.

'Look,' says Carole. She points to a feisty little dog, a Jack Russell who appears to be out for a walk on his own. He's trotting along jauntily heading straight for a puddle. He carries on expecting it to be shallow, and disappears into an invisible hole in the middle. When the dog emerges his face expresses first surprise and then embarrassment.

'They're so like people in some ways.'

'I think he's blushing,' I say to Carole.

'Yes, he's looking round to see who noticed his gaff.' The dog looks so sheepish we both avert our eyes.

Two cappuccinos and a couple of sandwiches later we wander back through the park in the direction of the station. We notice little unkempt corners where the local alkies have marked their territory with empty Fosters cans, cigarette butts and urine.

'And sometimes people are more like dogs,' Carole remarks.

In the station foyer we notice the board carrying the thought for the day. It reads: 'Nothing is too small to know, nothing too big to attempt.' William Van Horne. We think about its meaning in relation to Jack Russells and gaining entrance to closed cricket grounds as we descend back into the tube.

Stockwell

This station platform is well presented with a new looking roof in white. The ads are up-to-date and the seats are wooden with bright steel handles. The lighting strip is different from anything we've seen before, it's neat and unobtrusive. We listen to an announcement over the tannoy system.

'What did he say?' Carole asks.

'Search me.'

'He sounded as if he was in the middle of a very tasty peanut butter sandwich.'

'It didn't make for clarity, did it.'

At the top of the escalator we are greeted by a substantial police presence. There are five of them on our side of the barrier and another six or seven on the other side, including a man with a large black police dog.

'What's going on here?' Carole asks a policeman.

'Normal routine surveillance,' she is told.

'Yea?' is her reply, in a questioning, I don't believe you so tell me more sort of way. No dice. I try to distract Carole's attention before she asks if they are expecting a sudden influx of Brazilians, or does something I'll regret. It doesn't work. She whips out her camera ready to take a picture.

'No photography Miss,' says a burly officer.

'Miss eh? Whose looking young today?' I say steering Carole towards the open exit. Quick as a flash, except fortunately she doesn't use flash, she raises her camera and takes a surreptitious picture.

'You're so naughty, you'll get us in trouble,' I hiss pushing her into the street. What's she like? She's even looking at the picture she's just taken.

'It doesn't really do them justice does it,' I say as I peer over her shoulder.

'Police and justice are not always compatible.'

The view of the station from outside is of an unimpressive brick box-like structure, but the fruit stall which sits against the empty brick wall shows a glorious riot of the fecundity of nature. Looking at the mapette of the area we are somewhat unimpressed – the *Bunnies on the Green Day Nursery* being the only place which arouses even the faintest interest, but not enough to warrant a three hundred yard walk.

The murals on a round structure next to the

Clocktower and decorated entrance to the former air raid shelter beneath the station

Clock Tower brighten up the area considerably. We learn they were painted by a local Primary school and that the structure is the entrance to a purpose built air raid shelter constructed below the existing tube platforms in 1942. It is still used as an archive – but it has to say something about a place when what is below the ground is of more interest than what is above it.

Time to move on.

Walworth Garden Farm – *A registered charity, the farm was created by local residents on derelict land and opened in 1987. It provides education, training and resources in organic horticulture for the local community. The garden is open from, 9.00-4.30 pm Mon-Fri and 10-2pm on Saturday*

The Oval – *Owned by the Duchy of Cornwall and originally a market garden, the Oval was leased to Surrey Cricket club in 1845 and is still their home ground. The cost of turfing it was £300 and the turfs came from Tooting Common. In 1868, 20,000 people saw England play the Aboriginal cricket team on the first ever tour by a foreign side. Currently known as the Brit Oval (it changes its name according to current sponsor) information about fixtures, ticketing and ground tours is available on their website: www.britoval.com*

Kennington Park – *formerly Kennington Common, site of public executions until 1800 and of the Chartists 'monster rally' in 1848, it became a public park in 1854. It now offers a wide range of sports facilities including tennis courts, basketball and netball and all-weather floodlit football and hockey pitches. The Adventure playground is free to all 5-16year olds and trained staff supervise and organize various activities. The **Charlie Chaplin** adventure playground caters for children with disabilities*

CHAPTER THREE

<u>Clapham North</u>

The platform here is scary, and so too, we later find, is Clapham Common station. The platforms are identical. Both are about eight feet wide with only two old wooden benches in the middle spaced far apart. There are trains coming in from opposite directions on either side.

Not so bad like this

'Persons of a nervous disposition should avoid this station,' Carole says looking anxious. 'I feel myself inexorably drawn towards the edge.'

'It would only need a slight stumble,' I say.

But pretty scary like this!

'Or a vertiginous veer,' she offers, 'and I'd end up reading between the lines.' Feeling distinctly vulnerable and not wishing to linger, especially given the absence of platform furniture, we walk briskly towards the exit stairs avoiding even a wayward glance at the magnetically alluring rails.

We ascend the steps from the platform then take the escalator. A new and melodious sound greets our ears. We can hear stirring, inspiring music playing. We go to the information desk to ask for an explanation.

'It's an experiment,' we are told by a smiley man. 'If passengers like it, we'll have music playing at all stations.' We give a thumbs up to the Northern Line Opera experience.

We give the thumbs down to places of interest at Clapham North looking at our mapettes.

'I'd like to see the Cavalry Impact Church. I wonder if there is evidence of charging men on horseback?' Carole asks

'There's only one way to find out,' and so in the spirit of enquiry and seeking after novelty, we set off to see this church with its equine connections. We make our way in eager expectation; fortunately it's not far. There's no evidence of the impact of charging men on horseback at any point on the flat, dull, windowless wall which is the front of the church.

'Maybe it's inside,' suggests Carole making for the door. I look again at the map.

'Carole, did you have your glasses on when you were looking at the map?'

'No, I don't think I did.'

'If you had, you would have noticed that we have come to see the Calvary Impact Church, nothing to do with horses at all.' Carole looks abashed until she sees the funny side of it and bursts out laughing.

'Cavalry is a misleadingly similar anagram of Calvary.'

'The mistake is pardonable,' I say loftily.

'It's a very boring looking church isn't it,' Carole says.

'Yes, a few hoof prints on the wall would improve it no end.'

'Look at the number of churches there are around here.' Together we study the map and see we could visit St. John the Evangelist, St Peter's, Clapham Methodist Church, The Bible Truth Church of God, Kenyon Baptist Church, not to mention Ahi Ul Bayt Islamic Centre.

'No public toilet at all.' I point out.

'If God didn't want us to wee, why did he give us bladders?' Carole asks.

'He works in mysterious ways.'

Walking back towards the station Carole grabs my arm to arrest my attention pointing to some washing hanging on a line.

'The cheek of it,' she gasps.

'It looks all right to me. Nicely pegged, crisp, white. What's your problem?'

'Look at the towel,' Carole splutters.

'Oh yes.' I can see what she means. 'Not only have they had the cheek to nick the towels from their holiday hotel, but they're exhibiting them in the front garden.'

'Barefaced, that's what I'd call it' she says.

'Those policemen lounging about at Stockwell should get down here and so some detective work.'

'Vila Nova Gaia would be so grateful.'

Clapham Common

Stepping down from the train our hearts sink to find an identical platform arrangement as Clapham North. Our second experience of an eight foot platform is no improvement, we are still very nervous.

One of the escalators is being refurbished which has given the underground authorities the opportunity to share a few salient historical facts displayed on the boarded up wall as informative posters. I take notes on the way up. I can see that Carole is not busy with her notebook. Good. At the top of the escalator I regale her with questions.

'Do you know who Bumper Harris was?' It's a rhetorical question, I know she doesn't know. She shakes her little head. 'He was a one-legged man who was employed by the underground authorities to reassure nervous passengers that escalators were safe when they were first introduced in 1911.'

'Hopped on and off, did he?'

'Yes, he was paid 4d a day for his trouble.'

'How did he lose his leg? Not in an escalator accident I presume,' she asks. She's plumbed the depths of my knowledge, I have no idea how Bumper Harris lost his leg. In order to keep the advantage, I press on.

'There are 413 escalators in operation on the underground and they carry 580 million people.'

'That's more than a million each,' she pauses, 'I wonder how many people you can get on an escalator at one time?'

In the foyer we have to ask for our mapette telling us what is of interest in this area. Jennifer a London Transport employee informs us with a cheeky grin that they cost 5p.

Clapham Common Station JUN 4 20

'Get outa here' quips Carole.

We are both very taken by the collision avoidance convex mirror installed for the convenience and safety of those exiting and entering the station steps which has a particularly perilous sharp corner.

'No danger of cavalry impact here,' says Carole.

'Not even in the rush hour.'

From the outside we can see that the station has retained its original glass dome. The place is fair buzzing with people. We consult our mapettes.

'Five churches, and a monastery,' I tell Carole.

'Two public loos. The good people of Clapham are doing something right.'

'Yea, perhaps they leave the hotel linen behind when they come back from holiday.'

Coffee is our first priority so we drop into a small local café called *Greenbag* selling only organic products. There are books, pamphlets and broadsheets so Carole and I sit and read. Carole takes *Discovering Clapham* and learns that Captain Cook's widow lived in a house overlooking the common. I look at *The History of Clapham* and learn that Turner's patron, Doctor Munro lived here. He met Turner in his role as a specialist in mental health when Turner's mother was treated in Bedlam. The site of Bedlam is now occupied by the Imperial War Museum. Well I never knew that, and the coffee's good here too.

Carole moves on to the *Clapham Society Newsletter*. She reads an extract to me.

'Permission has been refused to a developer proposing to replace an idiosyncratic building with a modern office block.'

'That's good, isn't it, but what does idiosyncratic architecture look like?' Carole thinks.

'Perhaps Gaudi made out of Lego?'

We both look at the magazine called *Edge* and agree it's somewhat posey design speaks volumes about the people who frequent the café.

'Clearly an elitist demographic,' Carole murmurs.

Leaving we make for Cock Pond which is a large paddling pool that is shut for cleaning. There is one toddler and a selection of rebellious crows blissfully unaware of the large *keep out* signs. The toddler's Mum sits and watches from behind the fence.

'I wonder how long it will be before the paddling pool reopens.'

'Each paddler will probably have to complete a risk assessment and undergo a rigorous foot inspection before being allowed to dip their toes in the water.' Carole has, in a long career in teaching had too much of bureaucracy.

'This must have been a pit used for cock fighting in the past.'

'Probably, but this has got to be a better use than watching a couple of chickens ripping each other to pieces.'

'No risk assessment for chickens in the middle ages?'

'None today either,' says vegetarian Carole waspishly, and I hang my head in shame remembering last night's delicious Thai chicken green curry.

We wander about a bit, admiring the idiosyncratic shops which form a line opposite the common. We are walking along the road called the Pavement heading for the historic part of this area, Old Town. We're in a pleasant part of town with the common to our left. We come upon the house of Doctor Munro which is one of three really lovely old Queen Anne houses. Sadly much of Clapham Common is neither idiosyncratic nor of architectural interest.

Retracing our steps, we happen upon a fabulous butcher's shop with a large old-fashioned shop window which contains a breathtaking display of carnivorous delights. Carole pulls a face. She fails to appreciate the beauty of the sight in front of her.

'I'll stay outside whilst you go in.' Carole's vegetarian status precludes her from admiring the range and the quality of the meat on offer. Inside it's even more impressive and I'm spoilt for choice. A pound of pork chipolatas and a Clapham pasty later, (bought ironically from a Cornishman,) I leave M. Moen & Sons' establishment. In a vain attempt to regain a modicum of moral standing I show Carole the blue plastic bag containing my comestibles, holding it up for her inspection.

'It says it can be reused, has been made from 100% degradable polythene and will biodegrade harmlessly under landfill conditions after disposal.'

'How about the sausages and the pasty?'

'I have my own biodegrading system for those,' I reply smugly, patting my tummy.

Clapham South

It is with some relief we find we're back to normal here as regards platform arrangements. The trains only come in on one side and the platform is the regulation decent size, other than that, there is little to excite the northern line aficionado here. There are no ads on the grubby white walls, and the benches are bog standard. Searching for something of interest, I find it.

'Now that's a first isn't it,' I say pointing to the 'Mind the gap' sign which is alternately the right way up or the wrong way up, depending if you're getting on or off the train. Whichever it is, there's one that's the right way up for you.

'If you can read then surely you can see the gap,' says Carole, 'unless you suffer from aperture blindness.' We hear the distant rumble of an approaching train which gets louder to the point of deafening as it thunders into the station.

'Shouldn't they have a 'mind the loud scary noise' warning?' suggests Carole. It's time to move on, and that means moving up.

At the bottom of the escalators there are some strikingly large mahogany double doors. They say 'Danger High Voltage'.

'I don't believe a word of it,' I tell Carole. 'I think these are the station staff's cupboards and they don't want us passengers messing with them so they threaten us with imminent death.'

'It works for me,' says Carole.

The foyer is far more salubrious than the subterranean sections of the station with more mahogany doors, two octagonal domes and a third dome that has been filled in so we ask, why and when, that sort of stuff.

'That happened when the flats were built on top of the station, in the 30s,' an obliging London Transport man tells us. Outside we see what he means as we gaze up at four stories of very 30s looking flats.

'Advertised as handy for the northern line,' Carole suggests. In the entrance or exit, depending on your direction, there's a round hanging light fitting which looks very medieval like the sort a swashbuckling hero would swing from. It strikes an incongruous note in spite of being fitted with low energy bulbs rather than candles. We look around and make notes eyed suspiciously by the station staff. If they came and asked us what we were up to we'd willingly say, but they don't.

The station entrance opens out to reveal a florist called *Dover* having a door inside the foyer which takes one through to the road outside allowing for a substantial display of flowers on the wide pavement. Carole is more taken by a fishmonger which is next to the florist.

'Look, wild salmon and turbot all on proper tiled slabs.'

'Very traditional, rather than idiosyncratic.' It's pleasant to be above ground, the sun is out fitfully, but warm when it appears. We wander across Clapham Common and happen upon Eagle Pond which is very small and is tastefully landscaped with a miniscule island with ornamental tree. We admire the sight but find a big heap of litter that mars the scene.

'Ducks and geese are busy,' Carole says.

'It must be the mating season for water fowl.'

'There are a lot of children playing. Why aren't they in school?' I ask. Walking on towards the park café, we admire the recently renovated bandstand.'

'Very Trumptonish,' says Carole.

'My Dad loved that programme. He knew all their names. Do you remember the fire brigade's roll call at the beginning of the programme?'

'Pugh! Pugh! Barney McGrew! Cuthbert! Dibble! Grub!' Carole recites effortlessly. She would.

We eat our lunch on the café's terrace and fall once more to dog watching. There are several pugs frolicking prissily in the grass.

'They're French,' Carole says. I'm so intent on the pugs I think she refers to them.

'I thought they came from China.'

'The children, not the dogs. That's why they're not in school.' Carole is right, the café is full of French people, they must be having an outing here there are so many of them.

The owner of the pugs leaves and our attention is drawn to miscellaneous mongrels chewing sticks, begging for food and laying panting in the sunshine. One in particular takes my eye as it has that hopeful look of a dog anticipating casual food. It wanders about a bit trying to catch the attention of each of us as we lift our food to our mouths. I know what it's thinking. One of them will weaken. I can look really appealing in a pathetic 'I'm hungry and my owner doesn't understand me' sort of way.

'He's a bit fat,' Carole says, and that's why he hasn't a chance of scrounging food, no one gives him a morsel.

'Hey! There's a man with a unicycle,' I point excitedly. 'I always wanted to try to ride.' Carole cuts across my jabbering.

'It's a measuring device. A wheel with a stick, the sort used by surveyors.' I'm crestfallen so to cheer me up Carole takes me to investigate. The man with the stick explains that he's measuring out where to put up barriers for a forthcoming event *Picnic in the Park*. It's being put on in order to benefit a worthy charity so we are sorry we'll miss it, but walking away Carole points out a fatal flaw in the plan. People will be able to hear the music outside the barriers and enjoy the music for free.

Ambling over the grass in the direction of the station, enjoying the air before descending back down underground, we stop by Mount Pond, and watch a man who is paddling his hands in the water. The fish seem particularly friendly all gathered round the edge to greet him. Our closer inspection reveals them to be in some distress and the man with wet hands tells us that the problem is blue algae which is fatal to fish and no one can do anything about it.

'See Clapham South and die,' Carole says sadly. We beat a hasty retreat.

Clapham Common – One of London's largest open spaces, situated between Clapham, Balham and Battersea. As common land it was mentioned in the Domesday Book but acquired by the Metropolitan Board of Works from the Lords of the Manors in 1877 and protected for present and future generations. Of its three ponds, Eagle and Mount ponds are used for angling and Long pond traditionally used for model boating. The bandstand was built in 1890 - the largest in London and a Grade II listed building – and restored in 2005-6, including landscaping of the surrounding area. It is the venue for various events but can also be hired for performances, exhibitions and classes.

CHAPTER FOUR

Balham

For the first time we are on a platform that curves so in order to see both ends we have to sit in the middle. Apart from an old clock with its wooden surround and Roman numerals, there's little remarkable here. We listen to an announcement.

'What did he say?' I ask Carole. I think her ears are better than mine.

'Search me, it sounded like Shane McGowan reciting Shakespeare having consumed a litre of Glenfiddich.'

'He was born in Tunbridge Wells.'

'I'd always been told it was Stratford-upon-Avon.'

'I mean Shane McGowan.' She's a mischievous grin spread across her face and I realise she was teasing me.

'No, surely not Tunbridge Wells.'

'Yep, it's true, he was at school there until he was six.'

Ascending the escalator we again have to ask for our mapette of the area. Outside there's a station building opposite and the over-ground station is just round the corner, now isn't that handy?

'Janus like' is Carole's comment.

'Two faced. Looking in opposite directions?'

'Yes, that's right. He's the god of gates and doors.'

'Bill Gates and Dianna Dors?' She gives me a withering look.

'Jimmy Hill was born here,' she says obviously still miffed by my Shane McGowan birth location information.

'Anything else of interest that you know?' I ask.

'Yea, it's had a Sainsbury's since 1888.'

'Lucky Balahamites!'

Having consulted our mapettes we find no encouragement to move deep into

Balham and there's a stiff breeze blowing and the day is none too warm. Feeling lazy we visit The Exhibit which is a bar with a restaurant and cinema on respectively, the ground, first and second floor just around the corner from the station. Our eyes are drawn to the four bas-relief sculptures stuck on the wall of the over-ground station. To the left of us there's the bus terminus so all forms of transport are within spitting distance.

'That's interesting,' Carole says taking a closer look at the bas-reliefs. 'I wonder who created them.' We ask at the main-line station as they are attached to their wall. No one knows. We ask in the book shop which overlooks them. The proprietor doesn't know. Carole looks a little down so I suggest a saunter along Balham High Road.

We encounter a treat. We come across Bertie and Boos. We pass Starbucks and Café Nero and I suggest you do too because a trip to Bertie and Boos is a real treat. Outside there are bright blue awnings and two lovely wide curved windows as the café sits snugly on the corner of Balham High Road and Ramsden Road. Inside there are bright red sofas and small old-fashioned school desks to sit at. I take one and Carole gets the coffee. I open and shut the desk, and put my finger down the hole where the inkwell should be. Over a delightful cup of coffee Carole and I recall our past, the times we sat at such desks in our youth. We remember the smell of the ink, of making blotting paper pellets soaked in ink which we flicked around the class on the very rare occasions we were left unsupervised. Happy days. We read the information about Bertie and Boos' grandparents who were stage performers and they have followed in their footsteps. The place has atmosphere and we soak it up but then, sadly, it's time to move on.

It's busy and crowds are pouring into the station and riding the escalator as we go back down into that tunnel under the ground. People move urgently and dodge past us as we shamble along. According to the town website over six million journeys are made to and from Balham every year. Our advice? Visit Bertie and Boos but don't try to find out who sculpted those bas reliefs.

Tooting Bec

'We're not going to linger here.' Carole is in imperative mood as we alight from the train, and I'm not going to argue. With barely time to notice the total absence of digital display and few ads bunched in the middle opposite the entrance, we hurry along the rather unremarkable platform to the exit. Travelling up the escalator I can see that Carole's head is nodding. What's she up to? She's not wearing blue trousers, red shirt and a pointy hat with a bell on it. At the top she turns her face to me, big smile, eyes sparkling.

'I've had brilliant idea.' My heart sinks, her ideas usually lead me into areas way beyond my comfort zone. 'You know we can judge the depth of the platform from the station foyer by counting the ads as we go up the escalator.' My mind reels. This is a stroke of sheer inspiration, but I have to have my moment of caution.

'Are the ads evenly spaced on all escalators?' I ask.

'Probably not, but it'll be a great rule of thumb don't you think?' I look at my thumb which is likely to be quite different from other thumbs, and with it signal my enthusiasm for her idea.

'Much better than looking at all those annoying ads.' I'm warming to the idea.

'Yea, who wants to be told how to banish wrinkles.'

'You could end up looking like Angelina Jolie,' I suggest

'Nah, I don't believe in miracles.'

'How many then?' I ask

'23. This is a 23 APE.'

'What's an APE?'

'Ads per escalator.' She's a genius. It's official.

Immediately outside the station, which is of a very similar design to Tooting Broadway and Balham, there are white metal boxes full of free papers. It's easy to see who lives in this locality as we pick up a copy of *The South African, New Zealand Times* and *Australian Times*. I would have picked up a copy of *New Zimbabwe* but the space where the papers should have been was full of rubbish, perhaps a comment on the sad state of the country. I also pick up a glossy magazine called *Welcome Stranger* which seems very warm and friendly. Inside this glossy there are ads for the cheapest way to call home, home being Australia. There are networking sites for travellers, details of events going on mostly in London, but also in other parts of the UK. Carole and I look at one particular page.

'Gosh,' she says looking at a picture of Wayne. I too exclaim over several other dull photographs of readers who have willingly sent pictures of themselves for publication.

'They're not doing anything remotely interesting.' Carole agrees. 'They're not even in interesting locations.'

The best article in the glossy magazine informs the stranger about the only way of getting into some key events if you don't have a corporate ticket. There's a whole page devoted to Wimbledon and thanks to it, I now know what I'd do if I wanted to go. I've never been yet, but one day I will.

'Look Jude, Club Tropicana is giving away free cocktails on Saturday nights to ladies for the first hour, 10.30 to 11.30,' Carole says.

'My goodness, however will they wake up in the morning to listen to the Archers omnibus?' I wonder.

There are lots of travel ads and opportunities for medical research. The medical research turns out to be acting as a guinea pig for pharmaceutical companies. Do they remember the Northwick Park Hospital trials which left six healthy volunteers in intensive care?

Flicking through the *Australian Times,* I am horrified by an article about paid maternity leave. It seems that Woolworths have only just offered to pay maternity leave to their employees and they are the first company in Australia to do so. I'm amazed that it's not a right already.

'Haven't they gone bust?' Carole asks.

'Woolies Australia is a supermarket chain, nothing to do with our now defunct F. W. Woolworths.'

'I miss the pick and mix,' Carole sighs. It's surprising that she's so slim. Me, I never touch the stuff and I'm the size of a small house. A brief perusal of the numerous freebies reveals that, although aimed at different populations, many of the articles are actually the same.

'There's a big article on Wellington which is differently presented in each paper, five pictures in one, two in another, different type faces but identical text.' I announce like a self styled Chief Inspector of the secret freebie fraud police

'The price is right though isn't it. But the best things in life aren't always free and you can't expect *Sun* standards of journalism in a local rag.'

'No, they'd probably have Wellington topless on page three alongside an expose of his three-in-a-bed romp with King George's two illegitimate daughters, all information gained via phone hacking.'

'Now that *would* be a scoop!'

We've spent too much time on the papers loitering around outside the tube station. Looking at the mapette we see the enticing London Sewing Machine Museum and ten churches and a convent. As Carole observes, places seem to get holier as we go south.

We both admit to an insatiable curiosity. It has to be done. The problem is it's off the mapette so strictly it's out of bounds and it's not a warm day. But we have to see it and if we go and visit, perhaps we can find out why people find it so compelling. We set off a brisk walk along Tooting Bec Road. We are on our way to Tooting Bec Lido, the outdoor pool that is open to the general public from May to September, but to members of the South London Swimming Club it is open all year round. Brrrrr. It's unheated, and as we enter through the new entrance we can see it's enormous.

There's a bit of a breeze as we wander about and we're both glad we're wearing coats but there are hardy folk swimming up and down and only two of them wearing wet suits, or as my brother calls them, wimp suits. On one side of the pool there are boards giving information about the history of the pool. Opened in 1906 we learn it took four months to construct and was a project originally devised by the Rector of Tooting, the Reverend Anderson as both a means of tackling local unemployment and a lack of hygiene. The pool is 100 yards long by 33 wide and contains a million gallons of water. It's original name was Tooting Bathing Lake, changed to Lido when they became fashionable in the 1930s.

The changing rooms are striking having alternating red, yellow and green doors and a nice big gap at the bottom for the wind to blow in. This is a place for the hardy. Carole and I manage another coffee from the very pleasant café and take in the art deco architecture, but we are oh so glad we don't have our cosies with us.

Returning to the station we reflect on our visit; we didn't get to see Jimmy Hill or even Sainsbury's, but we've done justice to the environs of Tooting Bec.

Tooting Broadway

On the train from Bec to Broadway, Carole says,

'These carriages are just like people doing a conga.' She pauses in that, I'm going to say more way. 'They cling on to each other in motion in a curious bouncy joggling way.' I nod: it's the only thing to do. 'Do you think that when they get to the end of the line, Morden, High Barnett or Edgeware they form a circle and celebrate with the Okey Cokey?' I just know she's going to sing and look about me in trepidation before covering my face with my hands. The other passengers are blissfully unaware.

'You put a passenger in, a passenger out, in out, in out, you shake 'em all about. You open doors, close doors and mind the gap, that's what it's all about.' No one looks, but it is with some relief that we arrive on the platform, Carole needs distracting.

'Look, I'm wearing pink shoes.' She looks at my pink shoes which are leather boat shoes, with leather laces. She doesn't say anything which is disappointing; I only bought them to impress her.

Now I don't know why but some stations just seem to have trains arriving and leaving more frequently than others, and they're in and out here like Peter Mandleson's political appointments. I suspect bunching. This is an ordinary station with an overhead digital display. I look at the walls

'The ads at this station all crowd together in the middle,' I point out.

'Oh yes, leaving vacant dirty white walls at each end of the platform. Nasty.'

'I do like the retro clock,' drawing Carole's attention to the one pleasing feature of the platform.

'Retro, sounds as if time goes backwards. Wouldn't that be good, I'd never be late for anything.'

'You might be late leaving.'

We ride up the 21 APE escalator singing *Only four stations to Morden* to the tune of *24 hours from Tulsa*. At the top we are greeted with stirring music and two domes that let the light into the foyer, but this simply lulls us into a false sense of well being. Our good humour and optimism are dashed by the news that THERE ARE NO MAPETTES AVAILABLE AT THIS STATION. We have become so accustomed to popping up from down below and grabbing a mapette to give us an idea of what's in the locality, picking on some poor unsuspecting place to visit and we're off. But here, we have to look at the map on the wall and we can't take it away with us.

'Why does every other station so far have maps ready and available and Tooting Broadway doesn't?' I don't even pause for breath. 'Who is to blame for this oversight? Heads should roll ....' I'm interrupted.

'Oh get on with life and stop over-reacting,' Carole advises, so I do as I'm told, but my neck aches from staring up at the large map affixed to the wall as we seek out the various local attractions. We plump for Waterfall Road reasoning that we had not anticipated a cascade in Tooting, but decide to do coffee first.

Outside the station there's a bronze statue of Edward VII erected by public subscription.

'Why?' I ask, not waiting for a reply, 'Why erect a statue to that fat monarch, that bon vivant, that lover of girls, gambling and gluttony. What did he ever do for Tooting Broadway?'

'You're ratty today,' Carole says mildly, which makes me even more bad-tempered. 'Perhaps he gave it a royal charter or something.'

'Look, the statue refers to Alderman Archibald Dawnay who was the Mayor of Wandsworth for eleven years. I hope he did things that were more useful than plonking down a statue of a fat man who had to wait 59 years before coming into his inheritance.' Carole's a bit bemused, she's usually the ranter. 'Terrible name Archibald. I'd rather be called Wally Jumlat.' One of my shoelaces has come undone and I stoop to retie it. So much for the pink shoes.

In a reversal of our usual roles Carole takes my arm and steers me across the road to Café Nero to placate me with coffee. We sit by a large picture window that looks out on a busy crossing. Now we've done that before, but this is by far and away the most vibrant ever changing view. Looking out at the traffic lights there's a constant stream of people crossing or waiting to cross the road. There are mothers with pushchairs and babies in prams (or what passes for prams these days), the elderly tottering along on their sticks, young men and women striding out and those of an indeterminate middle age going at a sensible speed. There's white, black and brown-skinned people, some in coats, some in short sleeves, some brightly dressed in flowing robes, some looking dowdy and down at heel. A group of girls in school uniform pass giggling fit to bust, women in Muslim dress with their robes billowing out in the wind catch my eye. There are men in jackets, joggers, jeans, jumpers, immaculate white shirts and trousers. I feel as if all of life is here and the movement and excitement of it calms me.

'How's your cake?' Carole asks as I bite into it. She's said, no lunch until Morden so I have to stock up.

'All right,' I mutter through a mouthful of sugary crumbs.
'It was more than I can eat though and I feel a bit sick,' I say when I've finished it all.

'We seasoned travellers must become accustomed to the temporary digestive discomforts which may arise in the process of immersing ourselves in alien cultures.'

'What!' I splutter, 'I've just eaten a piece of Victoria Sponge.'

'You need a small adventure,' Carole says, 'It's time for Waterfall Road.'

Now the spirit of the whole Northern Line excursion is that idle curiosity has to be satisfied. We are in the middle of an urban environment and it occurs to us, why is there a road so named? We set off to find the answer. It proves to be easy to locate and we have a piece of great good fortune. Coming out a tall metal gate fencing off an enclosed area with big yellow metal railings, sharp and pointy at the top, clearly signalling 'don't come in,'(it actually says, 'No unauthorised persons beyond this point,') we meet two men. One is young, the other not so, but young to us. They both work for the Environment Agency, and Terry, the older one, is willing to show us what lies behind the intimidating yellow bars.

It is a storm drain. Hardly Niagra falls but

Carole and I find it fascinating. There's so much work that goes on all around us that we seldom see, and often don't know about; people like Terry and his mate are the unsung heroes who contribute to our daily lives, making our existence better, safer, and in this case, dryer. Walking through the gate on the forbidden side of the railings, we peer down into the storm drain which is no more than two steep bricked walls that form a narrow channel, and we watch as the water flows from left to right. It's constant, steady and quick. It falls over a series of very small weirs sending it on its way to join the River Wandle.

We look at the gauge fixed to the wall which shows how high the water can go after a heavy fall of rain. I'd like to see it after a cloud burst as it would be a terrific sight. Terry talks with enthusiasm and interest about his work around the borough. He also tells us that an Indian lady whose garden is next to the storm drain appeared with rice and curry for him and his mate. She cooks for the homeless every Wednesday. I like hearing stories of others' altruism, it warms my cockles, at least I think it does, because I'm not too clear where exactly they are. Bidding our new found friend good-bye we walk away.

'It's great being retired,' says Carole, 'having the time to talk to people.'

'We take a lot for granted don't we,' I add.

'Yea, without that storm drain this area would become an extension of the Serpentine after a heavy downpour.' Bring on global warming – we have Terry on our side!

Jointly we make some awards. Terry becomes an honorary Dave. So too does the un-named Indian lady. My shoelace becomes untied.....again. Carole's dodgy freedom pass decides to work perfectly and she claims that the witches of Wandsworth called up a mystic wind.

'Tosh,' is my take on it. Time to move on before she spouts any more nonsense so we jump onto the 21APE escalator well satisfied with our visit.

Balham – subject of the famous comedy sketch: Balham – Gateway to the south *written by Frank Muir and Dennis Norden and performed by Peter Sellers. As a gateway it is of note only as a portal one passes through on the way to somewhere interesting*

Tooting – also in the London Borough of Wandsworth it boasts two commons, one of which is home to **Tooting Lido,** *the largest swimming pool (by surface area) in the UK – 100yards long by 33yards wide. It was opened in 1906 and managed to survive the financial cutbacks of the 1990's thanks to the efforts of the South London Swimming Club. Now open to the public between May and September.*

River Wandle *– 9miles long and flowing through south west London the Wandle flows into the Thames on the Tideway at Wandsworth. It even has its own fishing club, the Wandle Piscators.*

CHAPTER FIVE

Colliers Wood

For the first time on our journey arriving at the station, I feel jolted as if the driver had to put the brakes on a bit hard. We sit on the customary bench and look about us. The platform curves, the yellow line is fresh and pristine. Mind the gap is offered up for those getting off and on. What draws our eye is the display that shows we are only one more stop away from Morden. I notice Carole looking furtive.

'What are you up to?' My tone is sharp.

'Erm, I'm just singing in my head.'

'What?'

'Well, it's best for someone with little musical talent don't you think?'

'What are you singing?'

'Almost there.' I sincerely wish I hadn't asked as I start singing 'almost there' in my head, as I will for the rest of the day.

The escalator is 29 ads long.

'Deeper than Balham or the Tootings,' says Carole, interrupting me just as I've got to 'close your eyes, close your eyes.' Now I can't remember how the song goes next without going back to the beginning so I ask Carole.

'I'm not singing the Andy Williams version, I'm singing the Michael Jackson song.' I think that rather sums up the difference between us.

It is with much relief that we ask for, and get, a map. Having discussed the River Wandle with Terry over a friendly storm drain, we determine to make our way to the River Wandle Heritage Site.

Outside the safety of a familiarly laid out tube station, we are confronted by a monstrosity. I do not exaggerate. I defy you to leave this particular station and not notice the hideous tower block, unimaginatively named, *The Tower*, except the letter T has fallen off and it has become *The ower*. Carole grabs my arm.

'That's the sort of place Darth Vader might have erected as a rest home for evil

Vader and wader

retired ex-masters of the universe.' We stand in awe at its ugliness, its hideous emptiness and air of neglect.

'Perhaps Davros is lurking in there,' I whisper.

'It's derelict, nothing lives in its dark foreboding interior,' she whispers back.

'Please, see sense, pull it down. Plant roses in its place. It's an eyesore, something to recoil from.' I address the empty air, but Carole's listening and agrees.

This is an inauspicious start for Colliers Wood as we subsequently learn it was voted London's ugliest building in 2006, however, things are about to get no better. Hiding in its shadow is a collection of prefabricated warehouses of the *Allied Carpets* variety fronted by something called the *Kiss me Hardy Wacky Warehouse*.

'Poor Nelson,' Carole murmurs, 'don't you think he'd have been a bit more careful about his last words had he known they'd end up on this tacky warehouse?'

'They do food,' I tell Carole and we go and look at the menu.

'I bet it's the variety that Jamie Oliver wouldn't give to his pigs.'

We walk along the side of the River Wandle. On one side of us there is a busy main road. To the left of us there is a charming river which is flanked by a huge shopping centre combining the retail might of Sainsbury's and M&S. A man is wading in the river rod in hand, casting his fly. We wonder what on earth he thinks he might catch. We ask in general terms about his success, and he shakes his head dolefully saying he's hoping to catch some trout. I am reminded of Dr. Johnston's words about second marriage: 'A triumph of optimism over experience.' I think the aphorism applies here.

'We could buy a couple of trout and chuck them in the river, only dead fish don't bite,' says Carole, identifying the fatal flaw in her plan.

Further along we escape the ceaseless flow of traffic and walk through a short path to find two more fishermen sitting on the bank of the river, this time hoping to catch chub. So far they've caught several plastic bags, a non-matching pair of socks and a brick. They have a cheerful optimism about them, no doubt fuelled by the cans of lager they're knocking back and rather lack the depressing dignity of our first angler.

'The allure of fishing as a sport has completely evaded me,' Carole confesses as we continue to wander riverside. I have to agree.

'Especially sandwiched between Merton High Street and a Savacentre,' I add.

'I'd like to own a pair of waders to paddle about without getting wet.' Note to self, a possible birthday present for Carole. 'But the idea of all that messing about with hooks, lines and maggots and sitting on a bank in the rain staring at a little float all day is sheer masochism if you ask me.' I don't need to ask her, I'm getting the picture. 'I read somewhere that more people in this country fish than play football,' Carole offers.

'Where did you read that?'

'It was in the Angler's Digest.'

'Well they would say that wouldn't they.'

In pursuit of more cultural attractions we follow the footpath alongside the river, past the Tiger's Eye adventure playground in search of a spot on the map called Merton Abbey Mills. Crossing the busy and industrial looking Meratun Way we enter a wooded area.

Merton Abbey Mill

'We could be in the middle of the countryside,' I say in admiration.

'It's an oasis in the midst of an industrial desert.' Carole smiles as she looks about her at the current Merton Abbey Mill which is situated next to the river and has a mill wheel on its side. There are trees that fringe both sides of the river except where they make way for old buildings, shops and a restaurant. We are disappointed to find that the small shed that houses the River Wandle Heritage Site is shut. Established in 1114, the abbey was closed in 1538 and subsequently dismantled during the dissolution of the monasteries, but had, in its time, been responsible for the education of St. Thomas Beckett and Nicholas Breakspear, the only Englishman to become pope. All of this we read on a plaque on the wall.

'I didn't know we ever produced a pontiff,' Carole says.

'Changed his name though. Didn't stick with Nicholas, became Adrian IV.'

'Yea he pontificated if that's what popes do, under the name of Adrian, I imagine it saved him being referred to as *Old Nick*.' Carole chuckles.

'Mm, not a good name for a pope.'

'He died aged fifty-nine. Is that a good age for someone living in the twelfth century?' Carole asks.

'Didn't matter for him, death meant promotion, the only way he could get holier was to be sent to heaven,' I say.

'Look Jude, it says here he came from Abbots Langley and they were so impressed they had a Nicholas Breakspear week in September 2000 to celebrate his memory.'

'Pope celebrations, for a week. What would you do?'

'Issue a few Bulls, pontificate, go to mass perhaps?' Carole suggests.

'Dress up as medieval people and eat boars heads and suckling pig.' Carole shudders at the thought. 'I can't imagine that anyone was vegetarian in those days.'

'Socrates was vegetarian and some monastic orders abstained from eating meat,'

Carole says loftily, so I pipe down.

We move on to read about the silk mill which was on this site from the seventeenth century. William Morris worked here from 1881. Much of the cloth produced was sold to Liberty. Carole likes Liberty prints but I've always felt that the prices they charge are the liberty. The area had also been a centre for the arts and craft movement and there are still shops selling art and craft products. There's also a tiny theatre and an interesting looking restaurant. It felt like a perfect place to spend a sunny Sunday afternoon, but we're here on a drab Tuesday so we don't linger. It is however a wonderful antidote to the near-by incessant traffic, and rampant consumerism of the gigantic shopping complex.

On the way back to the tube we notice a pub called Colliers Tup. Now as I understand it, the word tup has a very clear meaning and it means a ram mating with with a ewe. Carole says it also means the head of a pile driven steam hammer. We debate whether the area gets its name from a settlement of mining sheep shaggers, or if there was a mine here that used a pile driver. Further investigation suggests that the name is derived from the occupation of charcoal burners, how very disappointing.

South Wimbledon

The platform is curved, but its curve is the opposite way to that of Colliers Wood. This is the penultimate station, and then we arrive in Morden. I feel like Frodo Baggins at the end of a long and arduous quest about to ascend the Mount of Doom so I tell Carole. She's unimpressed and thinks I'm exaggerating. She might have a point, but Morden does sound similar to Mordor.

Having ascended the 28 APE, we ask for and get a map. The man behind the counter is so courteous, he's a potential Dave. With our mapettes clutched firmly in hand, we spy the maps located just beyond the barrier. We could have found them ourselves, but if they are outside the barrier and we go through that's fine, but if they are inside the barrier and we miss them, we have a problem Houston. We can't get back. We need team work I decide. One to stay one side of the barrier whilst the other goes through to look.

We look at our mapettes revealing places of only mild interest with no obvious connection to tennis. Ignoring the obvious allure of the Patrick Doody Clinc and Merton Technical College Annexe, we decide to visit the film set of The Bill which is marked on our map. This turns out to be a mistake: it's not even a programme that I've watched and Carole's quite luke- warm about it saying she used to watch it if there was nothing else on. Neither of us mind that it's been axed.

We walk for what seems like miles through a dull, uninspiring industrial estate, past uniform rows of modern houses and then we arrive. We almost miss it, it looks so very ordinary. The flat roofed two storey building is only identifiable by the police vans parked outside. The sign that says *Sun Hill Station* is modestly covered up by a large green tarpaulin. I'm not even sure we're at the right place so Carole offers to peek under the cover whilst I wait nervously on the safe side of the road. I've promised to keep cavey as I anticipate another embarrassing moment when an irate man comes out and tells her off, this time for interfering with ITV's property. She's so bold and carelessly walks across the road, straight up to the sign. She lifts the cover revealing the name and gives me the thumbs up.

There's are a few men unloading stuff from a van. Now I don't suffer from shyness very often, but it comes over me now, perhaps because I've never been a fan of this long running series and I wouldn't recognise any of the stars. I don't approach any of the people occupied with setting up lights or unloading props. Carole and I have so far accosted total strangers with complete confidence but we can't bring ourselves to ask to be shown round the set.

'They may well have told us to bugger off,' Carole says, but on reflection, I can't help thinking we missed an opportunity here. 'What would Shakespeare have written for the Bill?' Carole asks trying to cheer me up.

'A Midsummer Night's ASBO?'

'Much Ado About GBH?' Cheered, we slink away for once strangely mute.

The trudge back to the station is quite depressing, except for the thought that Morden and lunch beckon. If you're looking for tennis or excitement, try one of the other two Wimbledon stations which are not on the northern line. You won't see Roger Federer or Rafael Nadal round this neck of the woods. Carole regales me with a story about a friend of hers who claimed to have seen the ghost of Fred Perry on a staircase, and so we pass the time.

This is it, the final frontier, we board the train with mounting excitement.

Morden, the final frontier.

We're going south for the final time and in celebration before we get to the platform, we emerge into daylight.

'Isn't this odd,' I say.

'What is?' says Carole,

'To be on the underground above ground, if you get my drift.' She does.

'Like the wombles, overground underground.' I can feel a song coming on and am glad that at that moment the train pulls up at the station and we step off.

'This station is a refreshing change,' Carole observes looking about with pleasure. 'Different from those subterranean mole holes we've been burrowing our way through.' She's right, the platform is a modern light and airy affair with stainless steel much in evidence. We are standing under a wide arched roof with light pouring in through the glass paneling. Modern gantries display tube information and the lifts from each platform are very new additions. There are platforms one to

five and all have steps up to the entrance/exit with stainless steel hand rails to keep us in check.

Taking the steps to the foyer, we find the information point and I talk to a man behind the glass window about the end of the line.

'Do the trains turn around?' He smiles at my naivety.

'No,' he says, 'the driver gets out of one end and walks up to the other end.'

'You'd need a space the size of several cricket pitches,' Carole murmurs amazed at my innocence. I should have asked her, but I plough on heedlessly.

'What about the train that came in from the opposite way whilst we were on the station?' I ask.

'That's come from where the trains go to bed.' Now he's being funny. I can be funny too.

'Do you tuck them up at night?' I ask, and then of course he starts to exaggerate wildly and we're laughing and it's getting very silly. I know the trains don't have pillows and duvets.

As we walk away Carole muses on all the passengers that disembark leaving their flotsam and jetsam to be picked up.

'I bet it's mainly copies of the Metro and discarded McDonlad's wrappers.' I can see she's warming to her theme. 'The trains are a bit like a 'push-me-pull-you' in being able to go in either direction. I bet they get a wash and brush up and a medical check then they have their well deserved rest, before they delve back into the labyrinthine tunnels of the Northern Line.' I agree, and hand her a copy of the map.

Walking out of the station Carole says,

'Your tummy is making noises akin to that of a train in tunnel approaching a station.'

'I thought we were going to look at the train sheds first,' I say.

'I think we need to mind the gap in your digestive system where food ought to be. You can investigate the tog value of a train's duvet on a full stomach.'

'At last, you've recognised my need for sustenance. I've been starving since Collier's Wood.'

Heroically I stagger as far as the nearest café which happens to be Jose's, the local greasy spoon, but it's not greasy at all, it's sparklingly clean. Carole orders double egg and chips which she washes down with a Red Bull, and I have a healthy ham salad with accompanying cappuccino. It's all at a price that is less than two coffees and a slice of cake at Café Nero. It's plain simple fare but well cooked, served with a smile and the bill makes me want to move into the area. Replete we consult the mapette and decide on a visit to a large National Trust Park which boasts a Snuff Mill.

'That's not an opportunity to be sneezed at,' says Carole. The snuff Mill is inside Morden Hall Park.

It's not too far away and soon we are entering a peaceful leafy paradise and we're still walking alongside our old friend the River Wandle.

'Look' says Carole, pointing out the myriad shoals fish.

'They've escaped here to avoid the anglers of Colliers Wood,' she chortles.

'Yea, and the tacky charms of the *Kiss Me Hardy Wacky Warehouse*.' Small, but algae free they dart back and forth in a state piscatorial bliss.

We arrive at the Snuff Mill Heritage Site only to find it closed.

'Well, we'll never know now will we,' says Carole, 'is snuff a harmless pastime, or a perilous precursor to crack cocaine?'

'My Dad used to take it.'

'Crack cocaine?'

'No, snuff you dope. My mum bought him brown handkerchiefs because,' Carole interrupts.

'That's enough. I get the picture, even though I don't want to.'

We wander up to look at the lovely rose garden just beyond the Snuff Mill and then make our way to the National Trust shop to use their facilities. The shop complex displays a potted history of Modern Hall which is not very exciting, neither is the shop but we both manage to buy things to give to our grandchildren. We go and look at the house which has been turned into a restaurant where we are urged to eat, drink and relax, but we've already done that for two-pence-halfpenny at Jose's.

'It's time for the final frontier,' Carole announces.

'I'm glad we left it to the last.' We are about to look upon the final resting places for all the busy trains that end their day's work at Morden. We trudge across a car park.

'Most of these cars wouldn't look out of place in a breakers yard,' Carole says. At the edge of the car park we press our little faces against the chain link fence where we can see the breathtaking majesty of the Morden depot complex.

'We'll get a better view from up there,' Carole says, pointing at a bridge. It's been a long day, but nothing loathe I trail in her wake. We stand on the bridge and she's right, it is better view. The lines spread out in front of us like a river delta, most of them disappearing into train sheds numbered 6 – 25. Most of the sheds are empty.

'I'd like to see the sheds full with all the trains neatly tucked up in rows.' Carole

pats my arm and says gently,

'But then there'd be no trains to get you home. Where are sheds one to five?' Carole asks.

'I imagine that the platforms which are numbered one to five represent the missing numbers.'

For some reason Carole poo poos this idea.

'I really want to know,' she says and I can see that determined look in her face.

It's getting late. The wind is cold and blowing hard on top of the bridge. It's time to go home. Breathing a little satisfied sigh at having completed our southerly journey we head for the station. The train that comes in has been freshly washed and we set off back into the darkness in pristine style. Next time, we'll be going north.

The Tower – *built in the 1960's and now, quite literally, falling apart, this 17 storey building was voted the ugliest in London in a 2006 poll. It even has its own Facebook page:* Lets blow up the Colliers Wood Tower, *started by local residents. Mayor Boris wants to renovate it and turn it into apartments but in the current economic crisis the local residents may well have the final say!*

Merton Abbey Mills – *Describes itself as 'London's alternative market' specializing in arts and crafts. Shops are open daily and there is a busy weekend market as well as live music and activities for both children and families. For more info go to their website: www.mertonabbeymills.org.uk*

Morden Hall Park – *the River Wandle meanders through this National Trust Park of 125 acres in Morden. The estate contains Morden Hall itself, Morden Cottage, an old Snuff Mill and many old farm buildings, some of which are now a garden centre and a city farm. More information is available on the National Trust website: www.nationaltrust.org.uk*

CHAPTER SIX

Bank

Travelling from London Bridge to Bank, Carole and I sit together in silent excitement. This is our first venture in a northerly direction. At last congruence has been achieved, north on the northern line, the God of the Underground must approve. We have also been informed that there are delays going south so we are feeling  seriously smug. Stepping off the train Carole takes a deep breath and says,

'Now this is station to behold.' She runs her hand along the gleaming white tiles affixed to the platform wall. I point to the solemn grey marble which frames the exits and entrances. 'This station screams prosperity,' she says in a tone of wonder, and we admire the way the shiny white marble tiles are adorned by rampant dragons, one each side of the Bank roundel representing the coat of arms of the City of London. Carole grabs my arm as the next train approaches.

'Listen to that, it's like a flock of starlings being tortured in the tunnel.' Well even prosperous stations have their downside I suppose. This is a station for people in a hurry. There's nowhere to linger, the platform is very narrow at one end and is completely devoid of seats. Carole notices this too and appears to be in poetic mood.

'This is a station for people on the move, people going places, ready to hustle and bustle, rush and dash, hurry and scurry, and it must be done with an air of brisk efficiency.'

'Those rampant dragons mean business, I suppose, and that's what the city is about.'

'Yeah, they'll leap off the wall and savage the idle.'

'We better keep an eye on them,' I say nervously but am distracted by the fresh ads that line the tunnel wall all the way along the platform.

'The southbound platform is close,' I say to Carole as we peep through the opening off the platform. 'No more than a hop skip and a jump away even.' It gives me the shivers because if you hopped, skipped and jumped with any gusto, you'd end up on the southbound line.

'This is a very well connected station,' Carole notices, and she's right, it has links to the District and Circle, Central, Waterloo and City Lines as well as the Dockland

Light Railway. Take your pick, you can go practically anywhere from Bank provided you can find your way through the labyrinth of corridors, exits and entrances, turnstiles and escalators.

'It must have been recently refurbished it's so clean,' I say to Carole.

'Clean! It's dazzling white, snow blindness could be a problem if you had to spend too much time down here. My reactolites are definitely confused.' Carole rubs her eyes which seem to be smarting under the glare.

'Your what?' I ask.

'Glasses that react to the light,' she says peering about her. 'Oh look,' she says with some relief, 'poor finishing' pointing out some grotty old switches poking out of the tiling like dishevelled old people behind pristine double glazing.

'It's very windy,' I say to Carole as we battle against a gale of warm stale air on our way to the escalator.

'No ads,' Carole says glumly stepping onto it.

'Messes up our counting system doesn't it,' I say as we ride upwards without the benefit of commercial distractions. The second escalator does have the benefit of ads so we count up to 24 and are impressed by the depth of this two escalator station, but as we later discover, it's not the deepest on our line.

The ticket office is very hot and crowded with people moving in all directions, it's busy even at midday. There are two staff on hand ready to help passengers through the eleven turnstiles, operate the multiple ticket machines, as well as take advantage of cash points and change machines. Carole points out the plethora of funny eyeball security cameras.

'They're peering at me,' she says, 'they're peering at me in a menacing way.' I assure her they're not, but I'm glad she feels that way as it prevents her from opening some silver metal doors with a zigzag pattern carefully etched vertically. These are marked 'Fan' and 'Private', and 'POM'. Without the security camera's 'menace' Carole may well have whipped the 'POM' one open, just to see what was concealed behind.

What Bank station lacks in seats on the platform, it makes up with the number of its exits. Referring to our mapettes it becomes apparent that Bank is situated at the intersection of five main roads and has no less than nine exits. It is Carole's idea that to avoid giving privilege to any one exit/entrance we will sample the lot. We start at exit 6 and go up – don't expect logic. We emerge to a full view of Sainsburys.

'That's posh.' Carole says. I nod in agreement. 'So posh it could be Waitrose,' she says, 'in fact I'm sure it is Waitrose, they've put up the wrong sign.'

I manage to convince Carole that it's posh to fit in with the area, the simplest explanations are usually the best.

We can both hear an alarm which seems to be coming from Pret a Manger.

'It's warning prospective customers of their exorbitant prices and poor quality comestibles.' I get the feeling that Carole doesn't think much of Pret a Manger.

We dive down exit 5 stopping at the bottom of the steps to notice the fine line drawing on an enamel panel depicting the scene above. The drawing is by Doug Patterson and was installed in 1995 when the subway was modernised and there's one at each exit. We approve of this method of informing us about our surroundings as well as exposing us to the work of the artist.

Exit 4 brings us out in the front of the Royal Exchange in a small pedestrian area.

'What do they exchange?' I ask Carole naively. 'Can you exchange crowns and sceptres there, that sort of thing?'

'Perhaps it's possible to exchange the members of our royal household that we'd like to get rid of?' Carole suggests and asks me who I'd nominate.

'No one until I knew who we'd get in exchange.'

The Royal Exchange's pedestrian area provides a little oasis of calm in this buzzing hive of business activity. I can sit on a bench and do up my shoelaces. I'm still wearing my stupid pink boat shoes that are very comfortable and sensible, except for the leather laces that take it in turns to come undone, and do so with monotonous regularity. Carole admires the architecture of The Royal Exchange which is after the Greek style with its eight huge columns;

'Wouldn't be out of place in Athens,' she says. I find that Carole's been looking things up which is not at all what we agreed when we embarked on this journey.

'Did you know,' she begins, as my heart sinks, she knows I don't know, that's why she starts this way, 'this is the third manifestation of this particular building since the first two burned down in 1669 and then 1839?'

'How can a stone building burn down?' I ask.

'Perhaps the architects took their cue from the three little pigs.'

'Eh?' I'm not following.

'The first of straw and the second wood. Throw in a bit of paper money and hey presto, recipe for a jolly good fire.'

She hasn't been looking up what goes on inside the Royal Exchange but it turns out that it's a posh shopping mall, Cartier, De Beers, Tiffanys that sort of thing. It seems you can exchange shed loads of money for jewellery. When we discover this Carole 'goes off on one'.

'How long will it be before Buckingham Palace becomes a giant Tesco and B & Q?' she asks.

'Heaven forfend!' I exclaim. 'Waitrose and Sainsbury's Homebase please!'

There's so much to see, to the left of us is the Mansion House. It's very impressive being tall and is another of those classical buildings, this one with six large columns. It's made all the more imposing because it forms a triangle with the Royal Exchange and the Bank of England, and the three close together present a formidable sight.

Carole and I wander over to look at a statue of a man wearing an Indiana Jones sort of hat. On closer inspection he looks a hearty and a rugged sort of cove. He

turns out to be James Henry Greathead and is portrayed standing holding a piece of paper which he's looking at with some interest. We learn that he was the inventor of the tunnelling device that enabled the tube to be constructed, and that his statue covers one of the air vents from the station which seems appropriate, nice warm air up his jacksey all year round.

We also take a peep at the statue of the Duke of Wellington made from cannon captured from the French at the Battle of Waterloo. He's seated on his horse, all four feet on the ground as appropriate for a man who came out of Waterloo unscathed. It is a myth that the position of the hooves on the horse of a military statue represents the fate of rider. I like myths, so I pass this one on to Carole. It states that if one of the horse's legs is raised the rider was wounded in battle but if both front feet are raised, the man was killed in battle.

'What does it mean if all four feet of the horse are off the ground?' Carole asks.

'Stop drinking and sober up,' is the only advice I can think of.

We also study the short pointy obelisk thing which is in the middle of the pedestrian area. The obelisk thing too has an etching on each of the four sides of its pointy top, of the four views that the visitor can see. It's another aid to identifying the surrounding historic landmarks. We look at the Stock Exchange and Tower 42 and read the claim that Tower 42 is the tallest in the City of London.

'I think that the Stock Exchange looks taller from here,' says Carole

'I think it looks taller too.'

'Why tower 42?' Carole asks. 'Is it related to Douglas Adams' answer to life, the universe and the meaning of everything?' For once I'm sad to know the answer and I tell her it's because the tower has 42 floors, that's all and had to be renamed when the National Westminster Bank sold it off.

'What was it called before that?'

'The Nat West Tower'.

'That's boring' Carole says. 'I prefer Tower 42'.

Going down Exit 3 we are delighted to find toilets.

'How civilised,' Carole says. 'Take note travellers with weak bladders, just follow the Duke of Wellington, you can't go wrong.'

'Oh look,' I exclaim, 'Polly Pocket size shops,' and there they are underground.

'No Tiffany's here,' Carole says.

'Just useful shops, watch repair, key cutting, shoe repair, mobile phone accessorising sort of places.'

'You'd think underground would be a good place for a funeral directors,' Carole suggests but it's not a conversation I feel like pursuing.

We go up Exit 2 which is on the corner of Prince's and Threadneedle Streets next to the Bank of England which is bigger and more impressive than the Royal Exchange. Carole is very interested in the caryatids. They are those statues that look as if they are holding something up, the floor of a building, not a bank, in the sense of a bank robbery if you follow my drift. They're stuck on the side of the wall and seem to be looking to the side in a very odd way. Carole starts giving them names, she thinks they're called Ethel, Doris, Algernon, Horace, Dewberry and Spike. I'm thinking it's highly unlikely but don't say so.

'Everyone has a mobile phone,' Carole says, and as I look about me I realise that she's right, there's hardly anybody who doesn't have one stuck to the side of their head

Back down Exit 2 we come up Exit 1 on the corner of Prince's Street and Poultry. Carole tuts.

'Not a chicken or a duck in sight.' At this point we're tired of the stairs and Carole opts for a destination on the flat so we take a trip to The Worshipful Company of Grocers, perhaps she needs some basmati rice and a jar of pickled eggs.

Wandering down Prince's Street we stop to admire the golden statue of Ariel on top of the Bank of England which is glinting and gleaming in the sunshine. The Worshipful Company of Grocers is not far away tucked inside a courtyard. Bold as brass we step inside a lobby which leads us to a grand interior with a curving staircase, ancient portraits and an imposing desk with two men in attendance. Now I don't want to complain, but as Carole said as we left, the welcoming committee was not alerted to our arrival. Of the two men dressed in very smart livery, one of them is courteous in a curt no nonsense don't bother me sort of way.

'He looked at us as if we were something the cat dragged in,' Carole observed later. During our very brief visit where we get no further than the lobby, Mr. Curt as I'll call him answers my question about membership of the Worshipful Company of Grocers. He says membership is something you have to inherit. He tells me that their function is now purely charitable. He's a tad brusque and I imagine he thinks we're time wasters. He might just have a point. The other uniformed gentleman is of oriental origin and much more congenial and helpful, giving us a brochure, seeing us to the door willing to engage in friendly chat. He shares some information with us about the building, the organisation and its history. He points out the coat of arms with a shield of cloves flanked by two griffins.

'Don't you just love griffins?' I ask Carole, but she's too busy listening to the gentleman's exposition on the coat or arms which is topped off by a camel carrying a pack of spices.

We learn that The Worshipful Company of Grocers began in 1180 as The Guild of Pepperers with twenty-two members with the purpose of stamping out garbling.

'Garbling? What's that?' we ask suspecting that it might be a common practice among tube station employees on tannoy duty. We are told that garbling was a serious problem in 1180 being the impairment of drugs and spices.

'I suppose today it would be useful to have a livery company called The Worshipful Company of Drug Users to prevent the contamination of cannabis, heroin, ecstasy and such like,' Carole suggests, but our informant is not to be drawn into any such diversion. He continues telling us that The Pepperers changed their name to The Grocers in 1443 and they controlled the spice trade until the job was taken over by Customs and Excise following the Great Fire of London in 1666. Since then their function has been the raising of funds for their charitable work.

Thanking our new found friend, who automatically becomes another honourary Dave, we leave and peer rudely through the window into the Piper Hall at the diners enjoying their lunch. There's a magnificent silver representation of a person riding a camel past a couple of figures seated under a palm tree. I wonder who has the job of cleaning it? Whoever it is works hard as it gleams at me through the window.

'We may be a nation of grocers,' Carole says, 'but we're not poor from the look of all that bling in there.'

Later, looking at the glossy brochure I can see that if you've got money you can hire their premises out and the prices don't seem that outrageous to me and the food looks excellent.

Walking back towards the tube Carole says,
'As we're both English through and through we must have a right to inspect our bank and look into the fiscal shenanigans taking place in our name.' I agree wholeheartedly, so we go to the Bank of England and fearlessly walk in the

imposing front door. We are greeted by a very polite doorman dressed in a pink tailcoat and top hat. We like the cut of his jib and say so.

'Nice jacket,' I say. He tells us he's supposed to wear a red waistcoat underneath his jacket, but it's too hot today so he's taken it off. We're not allowed inside the bank, but with good humour and a charming smile he directs us to the Museum round the corner. It's a bit of a trek, this is a very big building, but on entering the spacious mosaic tiled foyer of the museum, we meet another man in a pink coat and top hat as well as the regulation red waistcoat.

'Nice waistcoat,' I remark and shop the other man at the front door who has so carelessly abandoned his full dress. This one snorts disapprovingly implying that his colleague is a *woos* and letting the side down. He thinks he should go on the naughty step for being improperly dressed. We are however unabashed supporters of the guy on the main door who was cheerful and friendly and hot. Isn't a pointless scrap wonderful.

We go through the security check to get into the museum and Carole chats up the plain clothes guard who says he doesn't think men should wear pink.

We admire his manly attitude until he confesses it's because his mum never let him wear pink.

The Bank of England Museum is well worth a visit with lots of things to see and some things to do. It houses the Bank's original charter setting it up in 1649 so it's all that William III's fault. Carole says that he should have done his homework and found out about the perils of sub-prime mortgages. As we peer into cases and read information about the exhibits we learn that fiscal villains have always tried to subvert the system.

'Our current preoccupation with rogues dressed in banker's clothing is nothing new,' Carole says.

I rather like the interactive options and stand in a representation of a hot air balloon and pull a handle which lights a mock flame which shows the balloon rising representing the economy overheating. I deflate the balloon by pulling another handle and so inflation is explained. I bet the Governor of the Bank of England wishes the control of inflation were so simple. In the next room there's a gold ingot to lift. It's inside a box and it's only possible to get one hand inside with no chance of removing it as it's worth £180,098 at the time of viewing. I can't lift it up with one hand. I buy a fake gold bar made out of cardboard and inside there is dark chocolate. That I can lift with one hand.

Carole and I look nostalgically at the old bank notes, in particular the mauve and blue ones with the acanthus design.

'I really liked the ten bob note,' I say.

'It was a lot of money when we were children,' Carole says.

'I remember the first ten bob note I ever had. I kept taking it out of my purse and looking at it.' We look at an exhibition of all the people who have appeared on our currency and that makes me think of some of the notable omissions.

'There's not been a philosopher so far,' I say to Carole.

'Why would you want to nominate a philosopher, they're all bastards?'

'I'm interested in people with ideas.'

'So who would you choose?' Carole asks.

'Jeremy Bentham, not because he's the greatest of British philosophers but he strikes me as being the most posthumously entertaining. I'll take you to see him when we get to Warren Street.'

'Go on, I've heard of him but I don't know much about him.'

'Okay, he was a Utilitarian whose philosophy focussed on political policies that resulted in 'the greatest happiness of the greatest number.' Carole nods.

'Not a bad idea.'

'I'm not nominating him for his philosophy so much as for his association with University College London as one of its founders. He believed that education should be open to all.'

'How come you know so much about him?'

'Went to UCL didn't I.'

'So. I've been to the David Beckham Academy of Football but I wouldn't nominate him!'

'Who would you nominate?' I ask her.

'I'd like to see more women, perhaps Mary Seacoal, Shirley Williams, Mo Mowlam, Glennis Kinnock, Annie Lennox.'

'Why Annie Lennox?'

'For having a wonderful voice and her work for charities.' Carole frequently threatens to provide me with a musical education.

Leaving the Museum we return below to continue our onward journey. I have to confess that we failed to go either up or down exits 8 and 9. 7 was shut off with an iron gate, but no complaints please, we did our bit.

Moorgate

'This is nothing like as grand as Bank station,' I say to Carole as we step off the train. 'Nice class of tiled floor though and great slatted ceiling.' Carole nods. Whilst the ads go all the way along the platform, the place has much more of a grubby air and is nowhere near as glossy as Bank.

'There's seating here for the weary traveller,' Carole notes, 'and it's nothing like as busy.'

'A tranquil station,' I have to agree, 'but I don't like those seats.'

'Why not?' Carole asks.

'I don't like the way the metal seat sticks out from the wall, and there's no arm rest.'

'Picky,' Carole says. 'Listen, I can hear a train coming,', but she's wrong, it's my tummy rumbling, I'm starving. We leave the platform and take the 40 APE escalator and find our mapettes.

We make our way out into the sunshine to the nearest food outlet which is 'Eat'. From our table we can look at people working in an office opposite and wonder about their lives. I have the delicious Gujarati red lentil soup with a splurge of yoghurt on the top.

'What is this modern obsession with rocket?' Carole asks as she picks it out of her salmon sandwich. 'Whatever happened to good old lettuce or cucumber? Why ruin a tasty piece of fish with something that looks and tastes like dandelion leaves?' It's not a question I can answer as I really like rocket and enjoy its peppery flavour, and I like the shape of it.

'When did you last eat a dandelion leaf?' I ask.

'It's a hypothetical dandelion leaf,' she says. I finish my delicious soup. Who's picky now I think.

Consulting the mapette we decide we have to visit Finsbury Circus which is nowhere near the real Finsbury. Coffee finished, we set out in completely the wrong direction and have to strike down a turning which runs beside one of the many London Metropolitan University campuses. This opens out into Finsbury Circus, an oval road running round a very English oval park with a bowling green in the centre. It's a surprising place for both being elliptical and having attractive gardens in the heart of the city. It also has the City of London's Bowling Green at its centre. The bowling club has its own wine bar and restaurant. The park boasts a bandstand and the cutest little rondavel housing an old-fashioned drinking fountain. Various people are sprawled on the grass enjoying their lunch in the sunshine, some are stretched out taking a well earned rest from their frenetic commercial activities, or perhaps sleeping off a worshipful lunch.

The Stock Exchange towers over the skyline and we wonder if the people inside ever have time to look out at the tranquillity that is Finsbury Circus. Another worshipful company is in evidence here as a not so well cropped raised flowerbed announces the celebration of the seven hundredth anniversary of The Worshipful Company of Barbers, the plants depicting their coat of arms, and the dates 1308 – 2008. Ironically the plants need a bit of a clip, as some of them are decidedly straggly. Short back and sides please Edward Scissorhands. The circus is surrounded by beautiful buildings and we tire of telling each other to look at that funny shaped window with the bobbly pillars, or asking, what do you call that funny pointy bit at the top. We decide we are in need of a dictionary of architectural terminology.

'Look,' says Carole clutching my arm. I await another, isn't that a lovely feature moment, but one look at her face puts me right. 'It's there again,' she says in a hollow whisper, pointing at Tower 42 that has just popped up from nowhere hoving into sight. 'I think it's stalking us. It seems to be getting closer.' I tell Carole it's time to move on and she seems very relieved to be retracing our steps back to the safety of the underground.

On the way back to the tube station we stop at a Barbers shop which has both of us squealing with nostalgia. The shop window is strikingly attractive and is obviously old. We look inside and find that the interior is a period piece with marble bowls and mahogany fittings. Proper barbers lurk here adorning men's stubbly faces with hot towels before lathering them up with proper shaving brushes and shaving soap prior to shaving them with cut-throat razors sharpened on a strop.

'I expect they ask the men if they would like something for the weekend,' Carole says and we both get a fit of the giggles.

We talk to the proprietor who tells us he is too busy working to be part of The worshipful Company of Barbers, which seems a shame for such an old established business. We chat to him for a good ten minutes and he doesn't seem that busy to us, as we watch six or seven barbers behind him working their socks off. He tells us of his illustrious clients who travel across continents for a close shave and how his shop has been used in the making of films. We smile admiringly at his business prowess and watch the efficiency of his barbers as they silently get on with the job of cutting the hair of their customers. I buy some proper shaving soap, not for my own use I hasten to explain. We leave, congratulating the boss on the state of this anachronistically pristine emporium. He puffs up like a proud mother hen.

'He didn't offer us anything for the weekend,' says Carole as we walk away.

Royal Exchange: has its own website listing the stores, restaurants and events which it houses, as well as outlining its history: www.theroyalexchange.com

Bank of England: go to: www.bankofengland.co.uk *for more information and look under Education to find out about the Museum opening times.*

Worshipful Company of Grocers: Originally known as the Guild of Pepperers, they rank second in the Twelve Great Livery Companies of the City of London behind the Worshipful Company of Mercers. Guess who's bottom ranked at 106 and 107? Yes it's International Bankers and Tax Advisers. No surprises there! To find out more about Guilds go to: www.gofs.co.uk

Finsbury Circus: You may not be able to see this in all its glory soon as it will be one of the main worksites for the construction of Crossrail in this area but should be fully restored when the construction is finished in 2016 (even the fountains may be working). Incidentally the Worshipful Company of Barbers comes in at number 17 in the Livery Companies ranking list.

Barber's shop: Although a very traditional Barber's established in 1904, F. Flittner has its own website so to find out more go to: www.fflittner.com *or just drop in for a traditional shave with hot towels or a haircut to 86 Moorgate EC2M 6SE*

CHAPTER SEVEN

Old Street

'We'll feel at home here,' Carole says as we step off the train and hobble our ancient way to a seat set in the wall, from which advantage we can admire the brilliantly sparkly non-slip floor. Carole stares at it hard.

'What are you looking for?' I need to know.

'I'm looking for handprints of the stars, it's that sort of place.'

'Who would want to have their paw print on the floor of a tube station on the Northern Line? It would have to be someone seriously self-obsessed.'

'Russell Brand?' Carole offers.

There's no 'Mind the gap' admonition here, perhaps because there isn't one, a gap that is, but, as with so many stations, there's about an eight inch drop between the train and the platform.

'Not so good for the myopic arthritic geriatric,' Carole says.

'Perhaps there should be a notice 'Mind the drop', but then if they were short-sighted they wouldn't see it.'

The ceiling is something we've not seen before, it's corrugated with white stripes and not so white stripes alternately. We speculate on what it's made from and Carole offers up artex always having the edge trotting out terms I've never heard of having been a builder's moll for years. We both jump at the sound of the tannoy which is particularly loud and very clear, we're not used to being able to understand every single word.

'Stand here,' Carole orders, 'next to me,' and she takes a picture of us reflected in the convex mirror on the exit wall. She doesn't flash. We leave and mount the steps admiring the dusky pink wall tiles on the corridor that leads us to the 34 APE escalator, and then to a foyer with red mosaic pillars and deep blue tiles behind the wall of the ticket desk.

'This is decidedly the most colourful station so far.' I say and Carole comments on the silestone flooring.

'What's that?' I ask, silestone being an unfamiliar term and she explains patiently that it's a manufactured quartz used for floorings and kitchen surfaces that looks like granite. Well I ponder, she's a mine of useless information today.

Looking about we see that there are eight exits.

'Right,' says Carole briskly and my heart sinks. I know what she's going to suggest. 'Shall we do them all?' My feet are aching as are my legs, who are not doing what they usually do with the effortless ease that I am accustomed to. I groan. 'That's what happens when you get to Old Street,' Carole says cheerfully as we walk up a sloping passage. But as we emerge and look about us the smile disappears from her face. Any resemblance between this place and Bank stops once you have counted the exits.

'This is just hideous, grotesque, ugly. It's a travesty.' I can only agree as the station lies beneath a seriously unattractive roundabout with constant traffic whistling by. The centre of the roundabout is adorned, for want of a better word, with two curved metal structures arching across some of the saddest shrubbery in London.

'Look,' says Carole pointing, 'it's arboreal depression.'

'Why does that arch support a hanging box?' I ask.

'It's an advertisement for a mobile phone provider,' Carole says patiently, 'offering unlimited access to e-mail on your mobile phone.'

'Why would I want that?' I ask. 'Is there to be no peace in the world?' Carole looks at me affectionately and pats my arm in a reassuring way. I know she thinks I'm out of touch, and what's worse, she's right, but we both agree the box is hideous, as are most of the surrounding buildings.

We go up and down a couple more exits and look at the views of the roundabout with its pointless arching metal decoration and get different perspectives of it, but they are all equally horrible.

'These buildings are very unappealing,' I say.

'They could star in a film called *The Clash of the Architectural Nightmares,* featuring Prince Charles quivering with rage.' Carole wrinkles her nose. 'Poo, what's that smell?' We both sniff and there it is, that unmistakeable scent of fast food halitosis with the nauseating odour of fries, burgers and chicken nuggets cooked in cheap oil filling the air. 'They should rename this station Stinky Street,' Carole says. 'If it were proper Old Street, it would smell of fish and chips and vinegar from the sort of shop where you could buy giant pickled onions and wallies.'

'And pickled eggs,' I add.

'And they'd be wrapped up in newspaper. Did anyone die of newspaper poisoning? Did children suffer from allergies and food intolerance then?'

'Ah, the good old days, eh?' I sigh and decide we've moaned enough, it's time to move on. One exit does sport a very good bookshop and we cheer ourselves up by looking at their amusing collection of postcards.

'There really are only four exits here,' said Carole, 'each one is double sided.'

'We need to leave,' I say. 'We can't be expected to stay in a station that lies about such things.'

Consulting the mapette I can immediately see that I have to visit Shepherdess Walk. Carole mutters something about spending too much time listening to the Archers and what do I expect, flocks of sheep and women with poke bonnets and crooks. Ignoring her jibes, we set off.

'Look, another candidate for UBIL award,' Carole says as we approach Baldwin Street.

'Ugliest Building in London?' She nods. This building is worthy of note so we take a walk round it, our mouths open in amazement at the crumbling apparition in concrete and glass.

'Whoever has to work in there, in that tatty and tasteless place would do better asking for a transfer to Wormwood Scrubs,' Carole says.

'Now there's a name that conjures up a vision of tawdry hideousness.'

'But this one is a good rival for that building that shocked us so profoundly at Colliers Wood.' I ponder on what Carole has just said. She's suggesting that would make it only the second ugliest building in London. I'm not sure, it's a close run thing as I peruse the end of the oblong seven story building's cladding which is concrete panels of dull brown with dark stains on them. I think the stains are supposed to be a pattern, or a design. It could be even more unsightly than Colliers Wood.

'It's uglier than the roundabout,' Carole whispers in an awed voice.

We discover the hideous building has a slightly more attractive younger sister to which it is linked by an elevated walkway. The new building, all dark glass and gleaming expansiveness, looks great in comparison. I stop a random passer-by and ask him what the ugly building is. He's not a local and doesn't have a clue. He' very nice and politely listens to my ranting on about the awfulness of the place.

'Looks quite attractive to me, but then I come from Birmingham,' he says with a wry grin.

We move on and find the Children's Eye Centre which is a newly designed part of Moorefield's Eye Hospital situated down a side street ironically called Peerless Street. It has a large canopied entrance with several floors rising above which can only be described as 'decorated'.

'That's eye catching,' I say.

'Very funny,' Carole says dryly in that not funny at all tone of voice. I hadn't actually meant to be funny, but I don't say anything. There are bits of silver metal that look as if they float out from the front of the building which certainly would be literally eye catching if they were lower down, but they don't start until the first floor.

'That orange box that sticks out at an angle about a third of the way up the building looks like a nasty sty in need of lancing,' Carole says. I wince.

'I think it looks as if a window cleaner's hoist has got jammed at an awkward angle.'

'It would have to be a 70's retro window cleaner to have painted it orange.'

We look at the domino effect stuck to the side of the building.

'It's all right,' Carole sighs, 'but I can't help feeling in twenty years or so when the shiny newness and the novelty has worn off, this could be a contender for a UBIL award.'

We trot on and I get all excited because I've only just noticed that we're in the City Road and naturally, I think of *Pop Goes the Weasel*. I'm just saying this to Carole, when, knock me down with half a pound of tuppenny rice, and there it is, The Eagle in Shepherdess Walk. They've even put the rhyme on the side of the wall of the pub in case we're in any doubt whether it's the real one. We don't go in, we've nothing to pop today. We do go into the Shepherdess Café which is heaving and I surmise that busy means good. The service is super efficient with the waitress there to take my order before I've got to the bottom of the sandwich menu. I order a liver sausage sandwich, something I haven't had in years, and it comes in a flash. Everything comes with chips, including my sandwich, which is made with white bread. I sort of expected a salad garnish, but I got chips. The food is unadventurous but cheap and cheerful, as is the atmosphere with loads of people talking. This place is full of life. It's great for those in a hurry who like white bread and chips. As for the liver sausage, well I won't be returning to it in a hurry.

Replete, we wander off back down City Road and look across at the front of Moorefield's Eye Hospital. We admire the old entrance and despise the new one. Carole pours scorn on the stainless steel covering of the modern entrance as completely out of keeping with the existing building. I notice the cutest clock above the old entrance which is shaped like an eye.

Carole's attention is caught by a shop that sells chandeliers, old radiators and old fireplaces. Entering its portals is like passing through the back of the wardrobe into a magical land of glittering crystal and ornate marble. We walk about and admire all around us. We engage the proprietor in conversation. She knows we're not serious customers but she doesn't seem to mind. Her customers don't arrive in jeans and faded tee-shirts with the dust of the Northern Line upon them, but our delight and gasps of horror at the price tags seem to entertain rather than to annoy her. One chandelier in the doorway catches my attention. It's constructed from a mass of banana shaped pieces of glass and the effect is modern and striking. Unashamedly I ask the price. She tells us the chandelier is called a Josephine Baker after the singer and dancer who performed wearing only a skirt of bananas and it costs twelve thousand pounds. We leave, quickly.

Angel

It's windy as we step off the train noticing that there is a 'Mind the gap' warning here. The ceiling comprises white panels which we've seen at other stations and there are grey metal seats at intervals along the platform.

'Why isn't there a standard issue for doing up the tube?' Carole's not listening.

'Eh?' she says.

'They must have immense purchasing power, so why not buy a job lot of tiles, roof cladding, seats and stuff at a knock down price?'

'Think how boring if would be with every station being exactly the same,' Carole says.

'But think of the savings my dear, just think of the savings.'

We leave the platform. The 21 APE escalator leads to a bendy corridor with excellent acoustics which flatter the voice and musical skills of a busker who is situated at the bottom of another very long escalator. He is singing for all his worth about a would-be singer who went to Nashville to seek fame and fortune leaving his lover behind. By the time we have reached the top of the next 60 APE escalator we have learnt that he has found fame and fortune but what he really wanted was his lost love.

'That's sad,' I say.

'What a twit,' Carole says unsympathetically

We surface at the top of the escalator into a small foyer where we are confronted by an eight foot metal sculpture. It's one long thick piece of metal, like a wide ribbon, twisted to look like a figure. Carole points out it's supposed to be an angel. I point out it needs dusting. It sort of sums up the difference between us.

'It looks more like a superhero. Man of steel – stainless,' Carole says. She steps back looking at it intently. 'No, it's an outsize untarnishable kitchen utensil. I could

put it in my kitchen.'

'You wouldn't have room for anything else,' I say.

'That's all right, I don't like cooking much anyway.' I can hear her humming. I know what it is, it's Annie Lennox's number, 'Must be talking to an angel.'

We emerge from the station onto a single road which comes as something of a relief after the terrible bustle of the Old Street roundabout.

'It's obvious where we have to go,' I say to Carole scrutinising my mapette and she nods in an understanding way.

'Pentonville Road,' I sigh in awe and of course aficionados of Monopoly will understand why.

'It's blue,' Carole says.

'Not dark blue, that's Mayfair and Park Lane.' Carole grins and I continue, 'and it can be bought for £120 and will form a set together with Euston Road and The Angel Islington.'

'And it also houses the Crafts Council Gallery which we might be worth a visit.' So, we set off.

The real Pentonville Road turns out to be a pleasant long street with regency houses on one side and a few quality shops on the other. Walking along we find the Craft Council Gallery. Much to my relief a supercilious receptionist informs us there's no exhibition on. I don't like Carole to know this and feign disappointment, she's already decided that I'm a philistine.

'We no longer have exhibitions here, only travelling ones,' the receptionist informs us coldly. Carole is about to open her mouth and I know she's going to ask where is it travelling to, when I call her over to look at some of the crafty things on display in the entrance hall. The receptionist keeps a close eye on us in case we put dirty fingerprints on anything.

I point out a bracelet which is square and made from copper and has sticking out bits that would take the eye out of any companion sitting within conversational distance of the wearer.

'Perhaps the designer works in conjunction with Moorefield's Eye Hospital,' I whisper to Carole and now the receptionist gets really suspicious and looks at us through narrowed eyes as we giggle together conspiratorially. I like Rod Kelly's

'Blackthorn and Sloe Vase,' and make Carole look at it because it's made out of metal and is shiny. She reads the little label alongside the exhibit.

'He's a freeman of the Goldsmiths Company,' she says.

'What could the Grocer's Company put in an exhibition?' I ask.

'They could run the café and make bacon sandwiches perhaps?'

There's a weird clock that's square and looks half finished, and the door handles on the double doors that go into some inner sanctum we won't be allowed into, are wavy metal jobs all coppery blue that look as if they have inset eyeballs. Moorefield's definitely does have an influence here.

Back outside it's spitting with rain so we head for the bustle and liveliness of Chapel Market. It's getting late and the stalls are just beginning to pack up. I buy some skate for tea. (It was lovely.) I produce an umbrella.

'Judy super-hero with her rain repellent device,' says Carole cheerfully as we huddle together to avoid the drizzle. Turning left into Liverpool Road we encounter our second stainless steel angel straddling what appears to be a circular plinth in front of the North Islington shopping centre. It's huge.

'It looks more like a giant mayfly,' Carole says.

'That one wouldn't fit in your kitchen,' I say.

Our next stop is Camden Passage antique market, except that this too is closing down. It's raining quite heavily now and we wish we had got here earlier as it is a charming pedestrian street of small shops. Having said that I have second thoughts. I'm at that point in life where less is more. I've spent a lifetime of *getting and spending* and as I look around at the lovely old things I think about my house full of old toot and how all that accumulated stuff is cluttering up my living space.

'It's just a glorified car boot sale for rich people,' is Carole's take on it.

Dripping and shivering we make for the refuge of the Design Centre which is on the opposite side of the road. Walking in the foyer we are greeted by a door person. Now there are people who we've met on our journey whose job it is to act as a barrier between the likes of us, the vagrant pointless timewasters, and the likes of them, those that have an invitation, belong to the club, have a right to go in. This doorkeeper is the best so far. He looks so far down his nose at us that we are reduced to a piece of shit on the floor. We are definitely not invited to the New Designers Awards Exhibition but we could, as mere members of the public, come back tomorrow and pay £9 for the privilege of viewing the exhibition.

Clutching a leaflet and nursing our bruised self-esteem we leave and go next door to Ask for a cup of something sustaining. We discuss other door people, always returning to Dave at the Oval, still our top man for friendliness, humour and the best smile going. We order coffee. We look at the leaflet that advertises the event we can't go to which is an exhibition of graduate designers' work. On the front of the leaflet there are three similarly shaped objects all made from different materials, one wood, one metal and one looking as if it was made from pipe-cleaners.

'What do you think these objects are for,' I ask in my somewhat prosaic way. Carole turns the leaflet upside-down and ponders.

'The metal object might be used as parallel bars for toddlers?'

'I don't think there's much call for that,' I say.

'We didn't want to go to their silly old exhibition anyway,' says Carole and the coffee arrives a good fifteen minutes after we ordered it. There are two other people in the huge restaurant. The service is terrible, maybe the doorman at the Design Centre has warned them about us.

We wait so long to pay our bill that the weather has cheered up so we decide to venture to the outer reaches of our mapette, to the one place left that beckons us on, and we can't ignore that metaphorical finger. According to the map it looks as if the Regents Canal comes to a stop in Colebrook Row so we have to go and see.

What we determine from our visit is that it doesn't stop, the water carries on to somewhere else through rather a dank and uninviting tunnel. Peering down over the bridge at the murky stretch of purple and green water we see several barges moored so we walk down leafy steps to the tow path. Chatting to a friendly barge owner, with an even friendlier Staffordshire bull terrier, we learn that the tunnel is half a mile long. He says it's very narrow and that there's no towpath so the bargees used to push the boat through with their feet, whilst the horses were taken overground to the place where the canal emerges again. He bandies about names like Little Venice, Limehouse and Battlebridge Basin. I smile politely and nod and turn my head as he points as if I can see these places, but inwardly I'm bemused knowing that my sense of direction is nonexistent.

'Do you think underground passengers would have to do the same if the train broke down in a tunnel?' Carole asks as we move on. I shake my head and clear it by peering into the bargey bedrooms and living rooms.

'Doesn't it look romantic,' I enthuse.

'Yea,' Carole says, and I know that dismissive 'yea' of hers. 'I bet it's cold in winter and very cramped.'

'I've never been on a barge,' I say and look wistfully at the row of moored boats just waiting to take off to tranquil places.

'I went on a barge holiday once,' Carole says. 'It rained for five of the seven days holiday and then we had to pay a fine for breaking the flippin' barge pole which was bent when we got it anyway.'

We walk on to look at the lock and the place where the canal divides, our bit carrying on, another bit going all the way to somewhere else and the third bit going nowhere for any distance, but providing a picturesque view for the very expensive looking flats that overlook this area. From the dividing point of the waters we can see the gherkin. London continues to surprise. One minute we're in the middle of rushing traffic and the next we're in a haven of peace and tranquillity. Carole and I decide to take a ride on the Regents Canal when we get to Camden, but for now, it's back to the Northern Line.

Moorfields: Founded in 1805 it is the oldest eye hospital in the world and together with the UCL Institute of Ophthalmology, which is adjacent to the Hospital, it forms the world's largest site for eye care and research. www.moorfields.nhs.uk

The Eagle: Now a listed building and a popular, trendy, Hoxton pub, it was immortalized in the Nursery rhyme 'Pop goes the Weasel'. In 1855 this was a music hall song and at that time the building was a music hall (The London Music Hall) and only rebuilt as a public house in 1901. It is now renowned for its range of beers and excellent food. www.theeaglehoxton.co.uk

Crafts Council Gallery: The national development agency for contemporary crafts in the UK. To find out more about what they do, exhibitions, fairs and courses go to their website: www.craftscouncil.org.uk

Camden Passage Antiques Market: In the nineteenth century Islington was a very trendy place to live but its fortunes faded. The early 1960's saw the opening of the first antique shop and subsequently markets were created from bomb sites and small shops built. The area attracted antiques dealers and the present antiques 'village' has around 350 dealers. Well worth a visit for the ambience even if you're not interested in antiques and you can drop into the **Camden Head** for a pint. Main market trading days are Wednesday and Saturday but many shops are open all week.

Business Design Centre: primarily for businesses and designers wishing to present their products/ talents. A pretty impressive building, formerly the Royal Agricultural Hall, it is the venue for the London Art Fair and Country Living Fair, as well as many more specialist events. www.businessdesigncentre.co.uk

CHAPTER EIGHT

Kings Cross & St Pancras

Blimey, it's busy when we get off the train. I steer Carole towards the shelter of a seat, or does she steer me? Either way, we are anxious to free ourselves from the sheer weight of people heading for the exit, and to our surprise, there's only one, so they all have to queue to get off the platform and we watch as they shuffle along slowly.

'Do you think that those people trying to squeeze themselves through the exit ever suffer from rucksack rage or suitcase wrath?' she asks. I doubt it but comment on the danger if someone were to trip.

'Health and safety,' Carole and I say in chorus and wonder who's done the risk assessment for our trip.

Once they've all gone we've a brief time to look about us.

'No mind the gap,' Carole points out.

'No ceiling cladding,' I say as if this is a competition where we both state the obvious in turn.

'This is the Castor and Pollux of the Northern Line,' Carole observes, anxious to spice up the conversation. 'Two railway stations so close together they have to share an underground station.'

'No wonder it's so crowded,' I say.

Carole points out what we think is a first and that's the 'No smoking' sign above the station's name on the wall opposite the platform. She also comments on the dinginess of the digital display so we take our sunglasses off. The tannoy comes on and neither of us can understand a word of what is being said. There are grubby ads all the way along the platform but the station is remarkably free from litter given the numbers using it.

'Nice floor tiles,' Carole says, 'I like that shade of blue.'

'They're not blue, they're green,' I say.

'We really must bring a colour card with us,' Carole sighs.

'Let's say they're greeny-blue,' I suggest and so we compromise.

'But I don't know if finding that something is like *raspberry diva* or *mineral haze 1* or *rum caramel* is likely to mean anything to anyone, unless they happen to be in B & Q looking a colour card.' She's got a point, but it might stop us arguing.

Carole is staring at the station sign.

'It's lop-sided, probably put up by a fitter with a dyslexic spirit level.' I can see she's thinking. There's more to come. 'This station reminds me of St Peter's in

Rome,' she says. 'These are two of London's most famous railway stations; the glitz and glamour is all above ground, but below escalator, it's cheap and cheerful.'

'What's that got to do with St Peter's in Rome?' I'm bemused.

'I climbed up into the dome at St Peter's years ago and was shocked to find that that the grand statues that face out onto the square were all unfinished at the back. They were just rough stone, terrible, it's the sculptural equivalent of sweeping the dust under the mat.'

'I can't see anything wrong with that,' I mutter under my breath.

'Do you think that travellers will be so overwhelmed with the grandeur of the mainline stations that they'll forget about the tawdry underground dungeon they've just come up from? Assuming they come out unscathed, without third degree luggage injuries,' Carole continues, but I'm still bemused.

'What grandeur would that be?' I ask.

'Wait till you see St.Pancras.'

A short 21 APE escalator takes us up to a depressing lobby where every bit of wiring is exposed and the yellow tiles show signs of age and considerable wear. This leads us to the next escalator area. There are three of them and only one is working, fortunately it's ours and it's going up. Our attention is drawn to the roof above us which is concrete with gaping holes at regular intervals.

'I presume this is the consequence of the fire that took place in this station,' I say. We try to remember the date but can only come up with the decade, the 1980s.

'They've had time to build another tube station since then,' Carole says.

At the top of the escalator we walk across the foyer to the brass clock that commemorates those lost in the Kings Cross fire. We read that thirty-one people were killed on 18th November, 1987. It doesn't mention the bravery of the firemen who went down this escalator in order to save lives. Sadly one of the fire crew, Station Officer Colin Townsley died. He stopped to help a woman in difficulty and as a direct consequence of his heroism perished in this tragedy. The subsequent investigation showed the fire was caused by a match dropped by a passenger as he or she stood travelling down to the platform and that there had been several fires before underneath the wooden escalator but they had gone out without causing any problems. All wooden escalators on the underground have now been replaced by metal ones and no smoking is strictly enforced so here's hoping it won't ever happen ever again.

We are in an area not unlike an amphitheatre with an open space that leads to a semicircle with steps up to a raised area. The raised part of the foyer houses the ticket office and there's a very long queue shuffling along the tapes that make it snake about in order to leave a place clear for the people on the move. It's very busy, in fact Carole tells me that it's the biggest and busiest interchange station on the underground, linking with five other tube lines as well as two mainline stations.

Now coming along on the train, Carole and I have been having a conversation about doing Shakespeare on the underground. She was suggesting acting a scene then moving on to the next station.

'The perfect place for the opening or final act,' she says indication the semi-circular area. People are constantly on the move crossing and crisscrossing all at speed, so I point out the station would have to be shut which might make a production of something like *Macbeth* very appropriate. Carole is very taken with this idea.

'I don't know what time the tube shuts down, but I bet it's late and I also bet it's dead quiet and spooky when it's empty,' she enthuses.

'You couldn't do the move on bit then, if the tube was shut,' I point out.

'Well if it were the final act it wouldn't matter, long as they didn't lock you in. If they were doing *King Lear* that would take most of the night anyway!'

I can't find a mapette anywhere, and I'm desperate to locate one, as I'm at a loss without it – how will I know where to go? Carole and I look at the one on the wall and decide to go to the British Library. We try to determine which exit will lead us to Euston Road, and the right side of Euston Road as well. The wall map numbers the exits, but there are no numbers on the exit signs. Oops! Carole works it out and we emerge into persistent drizzle.

We admire the facade of St Pancras and dodge inside in order to stay dry. We come across the St Pancras bit of the tube station which is squeaky clean and has

 plenty of windows open in the ticket office so I queue up and come out victorious clutching a mapette. Hoorah! This tube area is nothing like as busy as the Kings Cross bit. We look at the plaque which is a memorial to those who were killed on the underground on 7th July. The flowers that have been placed there are still fresh. I think of that terrible day and of the pointless suffering inflicted on its hapless victims.

'Look at this,' Carole says in a tone of exasperation so I know she's going into grumpy old woman mode. I look at her mapette and see she's pointing to the Royal National Nose, Throat and Ear Hospital.

'Well excuse me,' she says, 'but in my day it was always Ear, Nose and Throat. Since when did noses take precedence?' She looks at me accusingly as if it's all my fault, but in a Stan Laurel gesture I shrug my shoulders and mess up the top of my hair. 'Ear, nose and throat is alphabetical and doesn't imply any seniority. Oh look, here it calls itself the RNTNEH,' pointing at a sign. 'Royal National Throat, Nose and Ear Hospital.'

'Whatever way you look at it, ears are definitely out of favour,' I say.

'Well that's why young people never listen to a thing you tell them.' I nod in agreement.

'Did you know?' (here we go, she knows I don't) 'that an Otolarygolist is doctor who specialises in ears, noses and throats?'

'What do you call a doctor who specialises in throats, noses and ears?' She gives me a dirty look and we move on.

'Oh, Cartwright Gardens,' Carole says looking at the mapette in her hand. 'Do you think that any of the cast of Bonanza are buried there?' I don't reply because I'm too excited about visiting the British Library, a place I've long wanted to see. Carole's been here before and had a reader's ticket for a while. She would. We move from the shelter of the station crossing the road gaining sight of the British Library which is right next door to the station.

There's a large forecourt with an impressive statue of a seated figure of a man leaning forwards, well bent double really. I brave the rain, which is by now quite heavy, to identify the figure.

'It's Newton, after William Blake,' I tell Carole as I scuttle back under the shelter of the canopy.

'Newton came before William Blake,' she says, but I know she's only joking, she understands all right.

'Paolozzi based the design on a picture of Newton by William Blake,' I explain patiently.

'It's very striking and powerful, but why's he in the nude?' Carole asks. 'I don't think he would have slaved over his complex equations in the altogether. What is it with sculptors? What's he supposed to be doing anyway?'

'He's bending forwards to measure the world with his dividers.'

'Well I think he's sitting very badly and if he'd just had his tea he'd end up with indigestion,' Carole says.

'Why not have a sculpture of a poet, playwright or author?' Carole asks. 'Why have a scientist outside the British Library, it doesn't seem right.'

'It should be Shakespeare,' I say and for once Carole agrees with me in spite of not being a big fan.

'Yea, what about Shakespeare in the nude scribbling away with his quill at a jaunty angle.' We laugh.

There are turd look-alike rocks on top of pillars and on closer inspection I can see that there are people's outlines etched on the rock. These are works by Anthony Gormley. I like the space outside the library and would like it even more if it weren't pissing with rain.

The British Library is an impressive shrine to the accumulated wisdom of the world as defined by the British. On entering the foyer I am delighted to see the bust of Sandy Wilson the architect whose energy and enthusiasm for the project enabled it to be completed in spite of the terrible political wrangling and the difficulties inherent in the site.

'The project costing £500 million pounds was three times over budget,' I tell Carole, having always taken a keen interest in its progress.

'Who's surprised about that?' she says scathingly, 'anyone who's tried to put up a garage or a garden shed knows how quickly the cost escalates, and you can't wait for the January sales when you're constructing a major public building.'

The entrance lobby is impressive with wide steps and plenty of space for visitors to wander about. I'm reminded quite forcibly of Dr. Who's tardis because looking at the building on the outside, it's hard to see how it can be so large inside. The effect of the entrance hall is one of simplicity and space. There's a striking tapestry

that hangs on the wall called 'If not, not.' It depicts figures in a landscape and has beautiful colours but I've no idea what it means. There's a metal sculpture of an open book with a ball and chain attached which is a seat so I sit on it. It's cold on the bum so I don't linger. We gaze about a bit taking it all in.

'Coffee?'

'Yea,' says Carole and we make our way to the café and with our comestibles sit around a lift shaft sort of arrangement, but it's not a lift shaft at all, but a very large glass box which is packed with books. Old ones.

'I'm glad they're all locked up in there,' Carole says, jabbing her finger towards the glass clad pillar of books.

'Why?' I'm curious to know.

'I always think that old books smell like wet dog, but you seem to get off on it. I've noticed that when we go into bookshops, you're a bit like a teenager sniffing glue.' Now I can't help thinking that this comparison is going a bit too far, I'm no more a fan of wet dog than she is so I ignore her as I admire the walls and soaring pillars to my left which are clean and smooth and gleaming white. They contrast with the red brick wall on my right and the effect is harmonious. In the café area people sit along the brick wall at tables specially designed to accommodate laptop internet connection. These people don't look up, don't look around, and don't look as if they're eating much. There is serious work going on here.

Coffees consumed we move on to the Sir John Riblat exhibition. It is apparent that Sir John was an exceedingly rich man who donated shed loads of money towards the cost of display cases. Good for him. His gallery is just fabulous because of the selection of artefacts exhibited in them. We make for the Magna Carta display which is housed in its own little recessed slim lobby. It's a bit of a squash and a squeeze and there are school children dressed in green sweatshirts with clipboards in their hands all pressing in to tick off having seen the version that was damaged by fire. The school children are incredibly well behaved and friendly.

'It's good to see them so actively engaged in learning,' Carole says. We peer at the versions of Magna Carta. Carole points at the most damaged fragment. 'It looks as if it's been scraped off the wall at Borough Station,' she whispers.

'It's 800 years old,' I whisper back, shocked at her irreverence.

'The seal looks like a mummified, deflated balloon.' We snigger, very quietly.

Carole and I split up, she wants to look at the original handwritten Lennon and McCartney lyrics and I want to see the handwriting of the dead great and the good. I have to limit myself to what I see as I'm in danger of getting over-excited.

There are significant historical documents such as Cook's journal, a letter from Florence Nightingale, an entry from Victory's log book, Lenin's application for a reading ticket at the British Library, an entry from Captain Scott's diary and Haig's order for the day on 11th April, 1918. Phew! I don't know what it is about seeing the real writing that excites me, but it does, perhaps because it gives a small insight into the identity of the writer. Now that hardly anyone writes by hand I suppose future exhibitions will show the font choices, e-mail addresses and text habits of the future great and good.

In the cabinet hugging the wall I look at a first edition of Sir Phillip Sidney's *Arcadia*, at Milton's commonplace book written in his own hand with jottings he thought would be useful to him. His writing was very easy to read and I was quite touched. I read a bit of Dr. Johnson's account of his journey to Wales. I've seen his handwriting before and it's strong and upright. I try to read one of Jane Austen's letters to her sister Cassandra but can't make much out. The writing slopes forward and is neat and even, with every bit of paper written on. There's a poem by Worsdworth, but more exciting is Charlotte Bronte's manuscript book in which she wrote *Jane Eyre*. The page is open at, 'Reader, I married him.' It's clear and easy to read and has prominence on the page. Quite right for such a strong bold statement. There's a copy of Hardy's manuscript for *Tess of the d'Urbevilles* with loads of crossings out. I want to turn the pages and see if such emendations continue or if, once he got into his flow, he changed less.

'You all Riblatted out?' Carole asks as we bump into each other, and I admit I am. I feel quite overcome by what I've seen already, a bit like a child at a party having too many sweet things to eat. It's only when I get outside that I realise that either I've missed the Folio edition of *Hamlet* which should have been there, or, it's gone on tour. Well you have to if you're a priceless manuscript; you have to consider the needs of your public. I will have to return, just for him, just for Shakespeare and his Prince of Denmark. It's a promise.

'We've got to look round St Pancras station,' Carole says

She's been there before and is of the opinion that they've retained the best of the

old station and it's not been spoilt by the addition of stainless steel and glass. On entering I see she's right, the roof is very impressive, breath-taking really. We walk around the acres of space admiring the original architecture and happen across a larger-than-life, bronze Sir John Betjeman in his baggy trousers clutching a shopping bag and holding on to his hat as he looks up to the roof. Carole stands beside him and slips her hand in his as I take a picture.

We look at the very large statue called *Meeting Place*. A man and a woman embrace, whether in greeting or parting is not clear. I think the statue is in the wrong place but Carole doesn't agree with me. It's very big, set between the front of the original building and the barriers which keep the Euro Star in, and riffraff out. I can't get far enough away from it to enjoy its proportions.

In the middle of our aesthetic disagreement Carole spots the champagne bar. 'This isn't a bad place,' she says. 'I wouldn't mind being delayed here for an hour or two, I mean it's not like the usual station 'caff' with surly staff and gruel-like beverages.'

'With so many places to eat and shopping opportunities,' I add. Carole looks at me sternly and says we've got to go to Kings Cross Station as it's only fair, and if we don't it might throw a tantrum and scream and scream until it's sick, so we do.

'I don't think that stations suffer from jealousy,' I say.

'Why not? Why should St. Pancras get all the attention, just because it's had its roof renewed and is all stainless steel, glass and Eurostar?' Well, there's no answer to that.

Kings Cross is not a patch on St. Pancras but then it hasn't been subjected to a staggeringly expensive face-lift. Kings Cross has 11 platforms, and there's no third rail – shock horror. The trains are powered either by electricity using an overhead pantograph, or by diesel. Now I don't really know what I'm talking about here, but I'm anxious to include the word pantograph which I rather like. We admire the overhead digital display which not only gives the train's destination, time of departure and platform, but has a smaller illuminated script running underneath listing all the stations that train is going to stop at. It's really easy to follow.

'Where's platform 9¾?' Carole asks. Well, one of us had to give it a mention.

'Between platforms 9 and 10, I think,' I reply, but unable to access it we give up all thought of visiting Hogwarts and head back down into the underground instead.

Euston

You might think by now we're all main-line stationed out, but no, it's on to the next stop and it's Euston. On the tube platform we are well served with two very bright digital display units at opposite ends of the platform, but again, there's only one exit. The wooden seats are set back in the wall and I like this, it's just a bit cosy. Ads stretch from end to end of the platform and we stare at the ad opposite us inviting us to an exhibition at the Tate Gallery by the late Francis Bacon.

'That picture is really disturbing,' Carole says. It's of a seated man who looks as if his head is dissolving in an upwardly direction.

'I think you're supposed to be disturbed by it,' I say and Carole and I agree that it's an exhibition we're going to have to miss. The tiles on the walls are grey and have a red design that is a representation of the British Museum.

'This is an *only* station,' Carole says.

'A what?' I say.

'An *only* station, not like Kings Cross and St. Pancras,' she explains, and that's why we are able to leave the platform without feeling as if we've been hit by a tidal wave. We head up the first escalator looking at computer generated pictures of fish which I'm not that keen on, it makes counting a bore. The second and third escalators take us into a terrible foyer area. The ceiling comprises chicken wire so all the bits and pieces of wiring and pipes and such like can been seen in all their glorious dirt.

'That's another first, a triple escalator experience' Carole says, '39, 20 and 10 APE respectively.' She beams with enthusiasm and tells me about her first 'triple lock' experience during a holiday on the Llangollen Canal. 'It took us so long to negotiate the three locks that my friend Beryl was able to finish cooking, cool and ice a gateau. We had a slice when we were unlocked.'

'Gateau on a bateau eh, that's posh,' well she's like that. 'This station must be deep underground to require three escalators'.

'Yea, all put in to prevent us getting the bends. The links allow us time to decompress as we rise to the surface.'

We go up into the main concourse of Euston Station. It's 4 p.m. and early bird migrating commuters are jostling for position as they study the huge digital departure board to find the platform which will take them to their respective nests.

'Eighteen platforms to choose from,' Carole says, 'puts Kings Cross and St. P in the shade doesn't it?'

'I suppose so, but the tube only links to one other line – the Victoria.'

'Where are the facilities?' Carole asks, and we look about for the toilets. We locate a sign which points us to 'temporary toilets, next to platform 18'. Carole is incandescent. 'Look,' she splutters, steam coming out of her ears, pointing at the sign. I look at the sign, it's just the bog standard, (sorry for the pun) notice printed in traditional type that is metal and sturdy and designed to last.

'It's very clear,' I offer.

'It's a proper sign,' Carole shouts. 'Can you imagine how long it takes to order such a sign, have it designed and manufactured and then erected? If the speed of the service of Network rail is anything to go by it would take best part of a year. Temporary toilets, my arse!' People are starting to give us curious looks so I steer her away from the offending sign and we look around the station concourse.

I can't imagine anyone fighting to preserve this station, as John Betjeman did to save St. Pancras. Built in the 60s, it's like an aircraft hanger with retail outlets hugging the walls and inside three large octagons on the station concourse. The three octagons take up valuable standing space, and it's very crowded and desperately uncomfortable because of the press of incoming people having to push past those standing. I can't help thinking that most travellers could dispense with *Paper Chase*, the *Body Shop* and *Impulse* in exchange for more room. British Rail litter their stations with these retail outlets for commercial gain rather than passenger convenience. Don't get me wrong, I've nothing against any of these shops, but they aren't necessary, and space is. I can see the point of the array of food outlets, the necessity of Smiths and Boots but who needs eight different shades of wrapping paper on a long train journey? There are about three seats to sit on making this a station not only uncomfortable but also unsuitable for the elderly or infirm.

We make our way to the door and stand outside looking at the rain.

'I'm not getting wet,' Carole says, so that limits our view of the environs of Euston. I'd rather hoped we'd visit the London Canal Museum which is on the Kings Cross mapette as there's nothing else that interests us here. No point in arguing, I know Carole's views on the rain.

We peer rather wistfully outside and see a fully clothed statue of Robert Stephenson.

'He's very upright, and he looks rather self-satisfied,' Carole says.

'He's probably pleased that he wasn't sculpted by Paolozzi, half-naked crouching over a steam engine. Guess what he and I have got in common.'

'You invented the steam iron?'

'Don't be silly, no, it's not that. He always used to get his birthday date wrong. He was born on 16th October and always thought it was 16th November. I always used to get my birthday date wrong too.' Carole's unimpressed.

To our right of the square in front of the station there are poles fixed together at awkward angles with bright coloured decorations.

'They look like outsize windsurfing sails,' Carole says and she's right. I've noticed the plethora of fag ends littering the floor. At the opposite side of the square office buildings are conveniently raised on stilts providing ample shelter for those waiting for buses which regularly circle the square dropping off the migratory passengers in the forecourt. Carole starts singing:

Commuters in the rain, exchanging glances,
Wonderin' in the rain, what were the chances,
That their bus might come,
Before they get wet through.

It's very funny, but I've had enough. We're retired. We don't have to tolerate the purgatory of eternal commuterdom.

'Come on you,' I say and taking her by the hand we disappear back down the escalator...........*music*.........*picture fades.*

British Library: *The British Library, the national library of Great Britain, was created in 1973 and moved to its current location in 1997. The building was designed by the architect Colin St.John Wilson around a central glass tower containing the* **Kings Library** *– 65,000 books, pamphlets, manuscripts and maps collected by King George III. Anyone with a permanent address wishing to carry out research can apply for a readers pass to use the collection. The Exhibition galleries and shop are open to everyone. For opening times and more information go to:* www.bl.uk

St Pancras Station: *A Grade 1 listed building, it was opened in 1868 by the Midland Railway and escaped demolition in the 1960's to be renovated and expanded in the 2000's at a cost of £800 million. Now known as St Pancras International it has a security-sealed terminal for Eurostar services to Europe along with 15 platforms, a shopping centre, a bus station and access to the underground,a s well as the longest champagne bar in Europe.* www.stpancras.com

Euston: *The original station was the first inter-city station to be built in London, Euston opened in 1837. It was designed by a classically trained architect, Philip Hardwick, who erected an impressive 'Doric propylaeum' as a portico at the entrance and became renowned as the 'Euston Arch'. This was demolished in 1961 and the current 'functional' terminal was completed in 1968.*

London Canal Museum: *Housed in Gatti's Ice House in New Wharf Rd beside the Battlebridge Basin it's only a few hundred yards from Kings Cross Station and well signposted. A medium sized museum on two floors, the exhibitions tell two linked stories of London's canals and the ice trade for which the building was erected. It is open six days a week (not Mondays except Bank Holidays).* www.canalmuseum.org.uk

CHAPTER NINE

Waterloo

I am very taken with the overall ambience of streamlined modernity and cleanliness as we step off the train. The walls are tiled in cream and I'm especially impressed with the platform flooring so I tell Carole.

'It reminds me of the shiny speckly granite tiles in your kitchen that you're always complaining about,' she says.

'Oh but mine are only grey,' I reply. 'Whereas these are black, white and grey and laid out in a pleasing symmetrical pattern. Anyway my kitchen is having a makeover and I'm getting new tiles laid.'

'And what colour will they be?' she enquires.

'Grey but…'

'That's the trouble with getting older,' she cuts in before I can explain why the *new* grey tiles will be vastly superior to the old ones. 'You lose your sense of adventure.' At that moment our conversation is fortuitously interrupted by a totally incomprehensible announcement which we *think* is about the current state of the tube service but it could just as well have been the shipping forecast for all the sense it made.

'Nice platform, shame about the announcer,' says Carole as we make towards the exit. Halfway along the platform a man in a suit with an expensive looking camera is taking photographs of the platform, the walls and the rails.

'That's our job,' protests Carole embarrassingly loudly as we approach. I distract her by pointing out the two overhead projectors which are beaming Health and Safety messages on to the opposite wall warning drunks away from the edge of the platform and politely requesting passengers not to drop fast food and packaging on to the floor.

'I wonder what he's up to,' I muse, but quietly. By the time I've plucked up the courage to accost him and ask him he has disappeared without a trace and we decide he is either a spy from the Metropolitan line or a member of the secret *Mind the Gap Police*. Either way he looked very official and had studiously avoided flashing and alerting the station *dazzle watch*.

Now Waterloo overground is a BIG station. It has nineteen platforms, not even counting the ones that were specially constructed for Eurostar and the five in its annexe – Waterloo East. Consequently the underground connection is constantly busy and, during the rush hour the process of catching a train is a little like shooting the rapids. In order to cope with the volume of commuters there are many entrances and exits to platforms, some of which are locked up during non-peak times giving it the appearance of a subterranean jail. There are no less than twenty five turnstile exits/entrances and one group of seven is closed with locked concertina type gates barring further ingress. We stand and stare and then Carole pulls out her camera and takes a picture. She flashes. The station staff are as vigilant as prison guards although fortunately, more susceptible to flattery, so I am able to side track a stern TfL man who is highly suspicious when he catches us in mid dazzle. I tell him how wonderfully clean and neat his station is and he puffs up with pride and proceeds to explain how the barriers are locked or opened depending on the volume of passengers.

'You'd think he was personally responsible for polished platforms and gleaming rails,' I remark as we walk away.

'Yeh and I bet the cleaners are female since most men seem to suffer from *dirt blindness*', says Carole.

'Is that a recognised medical condition, or just something housework-shy husbands feign?' I enquire. No answer is forthcoming since she is now in full flow.

'…whereas being a female stickler for cleanliness carries the stigma of being labelled houseproud, neurotic or being diagnosed with OCD.'

'But if you want a clean station a platoon of OCD cleaners would ensure that careless drunks could eat their fast-food takeaways off the floor thus killing two Health and Safety hazards with one mop!' I add triumphantly

The foyer is a maze of entrances and exits and Carole makes it her duty to explore them all, so she drags me down a short staircase with a *No Entry* sign which we soon discover leads straight to a platform. As we realise this a train arrives and we beat a hasty retreat before we are washed away by a tidal wave of commuters travelling up the stairs as we travel down. Fortunately it is not the rush hour, and the expected tidal wave is merely a trickle but another hawkeyed employee has noticed our forbidden exploration and bars our escape with her ample frame. We smile ingenuously and show our tickets to prove we are not attempting to gain a free ride but just investigators. Her features soften as she warns us, like a parent cautioning naughty children, that to attempt this in the rush hour would be highly dangerous. Looking suitably admonished we scamper up the steps to the exit on Waterloo mainline station concourse.

Perusing our mapettes we decide upon a brief detour to the Old Vic just along

Waterloo Road not far from the station. On arrival we are struck by the inset plaque on the wall announcing the serenity of his Highness the Prince of Saxe Coburg and his wife the Princess Charlotte of Wales the original royal patrons of the theatre. Such was the intensity of their tranquillity that they didn't even bother to turn up to lay the first stone, and had an Alderman called Goodbehere do it by proxy. Carole suggests their indolence was wacky baccy induced serenity that rendered them too *laid back* to throw a bit of cement on a stone that had already been put in place by some poor stonemason. I guess if you have royal blood you are allowed excesses of serenity which, in other lesser mortals would be regarded as bone idle laziness. His Bone Idleness the Prince of Saxe Coburg and her Couldn't Care Lessness Princess Charlotte of Wales. At least the current royals put themselves about a bit (in the *line of duty* sense) but your average subject was probably more forgiving two hundred years ago.

Tutting disapprovingly we make our way across the road to Lower Marsh with a short stop off at the little green open space where a smilingly serene Jamaican gentleman and his industrious but equally happy partner are serving rice and peas and jerk chicken. Even Carole has to admit that it smells very appetising. Rice and peas are misleadingly named, the truth is the dish is made from rice and beans. The chicken is of course, still and with those lazy royals in mind we rename it *serene chicken*. We share a portion of beany rice and peas but I am drooling and sniffing the air like a starving hyena smelling blood. I cannot resist the aroma of the cooking chicken and I'm soon tucking in to some spicy legs and wings with much appreciative lip smacking and finger licking.

We make our way to Greensmiths café where I manage to resist the siren smells of the carrot and artichoke soup but my resolve caves in completely when we sit down at a long table to order our coffee. In front of us, seductively displayed on large plates under plastic domes is a tantalising selection of home made cake. I plump for the cherry cake while Carole prefers the carrot.

'I really am going to have to get you a bib – all this drooling is most unseemly!' she says as we exit, me wiping cake crumbs from my chops.

We set off at a smart pace in the hope of walking off the cake calories and turn right at the end of Long Marsh into Westminster Bridge Road which takes us under the railway arches. Somewhere around here, according to Carole, is a dead end street which is frequented by skate boarders and graffiti artists which she suggests we should see. All we can find are dank corners smelling of urine, and the very narrow pavements and thundering traffic make this a risky pursuit, so we give up after a near death experience with a speeding taxi and head for St Thomas' Hospital and the Florence Nightingale Museum.

We emerge from the railway bridges to be confronted by a building site in the middle of a busy roundabout. A huge hotel complex is under construction and there are cranes, cement lorries and men in hard hats all over the place. As we cross the road a large sign informs us that it will be a hotel. The upper rooms on the west side will have beautiful views of the river but those on the east side could only appeal to train spotters as all they'll be able to see are railway lines.

The Florence Nightingale Museum is no longer located in the position marked on the map and we follow various signs into the bowels of St Thomas' where another near death experience with an ambulance almost leaves us needing A&E. Still, if you have to get run over in London where better than the grounds of a hospital **and** by an ambulance. It appears all very chaotic because there is building

going on. I estimate there are two men in hard hats to every patient.

Looking up we can see an amazing sculpture silhouetted against the skyline. It's of two giant stainless steel humanoids seemingly jiving and/or attempting to pull each other off their plinths. We decide that, after Florence, we will go and investigate further. This doesn't take very long since Florence is in the process of being refurbished and her museum is still under construction but none of the signs bother to tell you this. Bring back matrons that's what I say. A matron would have made sure that places were properly signposted. When we reach the statues at least they have erected a plaque offering some information. The work is titled *Cross the Divide* created by Rick Kirby and was unveiled by Her Royal Highness The Princess Margaret, Countess of Snowdon on 25th September 2000. We like it. It's big, bold and eye catching, conveying a message and the sculptor is British. What more could you ask for in a piece of public art? What's more Princess Margaret must have liked it too – enough to leave the serenity of Mustique to come and unveil it. In front of the statue between the hospital and the river is a beautifully laid out garden with a stainless steel fountain in the centre spraying water in various arching patterns through which we can see the Houses of Parliament; the view is perfect.

We move closer to reach the Embankment pathway only to find our way blocked by miscellaneous wrought iron locked gates. Why they are locked we cannot fathom and we end up having to walk halfway around the hospital to find our way back to the road. Someone in Waterloo is obsessively security conscious.

Crossing the road we come face to face with the entrance to the building formerly known as County Hall in the good old days of the LCC and GLC. Now it is home to many things including the Marriott Hotel which is one place where you can see some of the original splendour of the architecture of this grade II listed building. We decide to go in for coffee and are greeted by a commissionaire in a smart uniform and a smartly suited manager who asks if he can help us. We notice that a pillar in the foyer bears the inscription *Noes Lobby* and ask him where the *Ayes Lobby* is. He points to the other side of a rather plush sitting area. When we express an interest in the building's former incarnation as County Hall he takes us to the reception area which has photographs of halcyon London County Council and Greater London Council days on the walls. He is very knowledgeable even though his accent suggests he is a relatively recent arrival in the UK. Finally we run out of questions and he politely directs us to the bar/restaurant where we are seated on comfortable armchairs overlooking the river and order coffee. This proves to be no more expensive than Costa or Starbucks even though the ambience is vastly superior. It is quiet, comfortable, the surroundings are luxurious and we are served by a dishy young waiter with a twinkle in his eye. (Well maybe we imagined the twinkle but there's no harm in a bit of wishful thinking). On our way out we visit the Ladies Cloakroom for a decadent toilet experience. Cleaner than the kitchens in most restaurants, subtly lit, with classy brand of hand wash and individual hand towels this is indeed the bees knees of *facilitie*s.

Elated and feeling quite privileged by our Marriot hotel experience we walk around the corner to the *seemier* side of the building. Frequented by tourists because it runs along the embankment from the London Eye, this houses the Movieum, Dali Universe, Sea Life Aquarium, an evil smelling fast-food outlet, and a horror maze called *Death Trap* from which pre-recorded screams and tortured groans emanate. We enter a noisy amusement arcade and descend an escalator into a garish neon basement housing a *corporate event venue* called *Namoco Station.* Video games abound and there are also bumper cars, a bowling alley, pool tables, enormous TV screens and a long high tech cocktail bar. We decide that, should we ever have occasion to hold a corporate event, it would be in the Marriot Hotel rather than this subterranean equivalent of a seaside pier.

Once past County Hall the South Bank becomes more civilized. We decide that we like street theatre and stop to watch a very agile young man limboing under a pole which is less than a foot from the ground. Why are we impressed by this? Well because we can't do it and that, generally, is our definition of *clever*. Something we can't do. It need not be something that we particularly want to do, but the fact that we couldn't even if we did want to, makes it clever, like swallowing balloons, which is what the next street entertainer is busily engaged in. I suppose it's the total pointlessness of it too which is quite remarkable. But then travelling the Northern line just for the sake of it seems pretty daft and we're spending a lot longer doing that than it takes to limbo under a pole or swallow a balloon. Each to his/her own pointless activities eh?

A short visit to the Festival Hall has us reminiscing about the joys of the Festival of Britain. The RFH is quiet and there are many places to sit and contemplate the river in warmth and comfort. The Poetry Library is closed but Foyles is open so we browse and buy books before heading off. As we make for the next station we look back down the river. It's a magnificent sight which we'll explore from its opposite shores.

Embankment

North of the Thames, we alight on to a *cool curvy* platform.

'This is the curviest platform we've been on so far,' I proclaim trying not to sound like an excited train spotter.

'Yes,' agrees Carole, 'If we were in the front carriage we wouldn't be able to see the back one. Must play havoc with the driver's rear view mirror.' As we leave the train an announcement in perfectly enunciated BBC English warns us to *Mind the Gap*. Now where we alighted from the train this was a step rather than a gap and Carole insists that only dyspraxic dwarf stick people would be in danger.

'Ah, but since the platform is curved and carriages straight, very distinct fissures are apparent at the front and rear of the train,' I observe haughtily.

Carole gives me a withering *smarty pants* look as I move towards the metal bench wearing a benignly supercilious smile. We sit, as is our custom, better to appreciate the technological and artistic features of the platform and are almost deafened by the metallic screeching sound of the train leaving the station. This spoils an initially good impression and we wonder whether the train or the rails are responsible. The next train, which is driven by a woman, arrives and departs almost silently by comparison. Question answered – men drivers! If we ever get to visit the depot we must ask about driver training and whether they are discouraged from doing *wheelies* when accelerating away from a station.

The floor has grey marble tiles and the walls are clad in white enamel with red, black and blue lines seemingly randomly decorating them. I expect Robyn Denny, who produced the *design* in 1985, spent years at Art school honing his talents in preparation for said design, but I can't help wondering whether my six year old granddaughter could have drawn them.

We travel up two escalators animatedly discussing our options for the day and forget to count the ads, so sorry, we've no APE for this station. The foyer is busy and grubby with two wide exits/entrances, opening on one side into Villiers Street and on the other to Victoria embankment. Not much of a station but gateway to many parts of London since you can catch District, Circle and Bakerloo line trains from here as well as crossing the road to Embankment pier and taking a boat down the Thames to Greenwich or up to Putney.

We have already decided on the boat option so, battling our way across the flow of incoming passengers we cross the road and join the queue to purchase our ticket. A sympathetic ticket vendor allows me to go half price, despite the lack of a Travel Pass since she argues that all pensioners should get some benefits. Sometimes it's not so bad being an OAP, although reduced rates of travel cannot fully compensate for the general grouchy attitude and wrinkles. We join a line of other OAP's only to discover that they are booked on to the luxurious restaurant boat whereas we have only paid for a circular cruise on a smaller, rather more basic craft.

The coffee on board HMS Cheapskate is pretty awful but the toilets are clean and the top deck offers great views of London. This service is especially useful for tourists who can use the ticket all day and hop on and off at any of the fourteen stops. Our leisurely chunter down the river gives us time to appreciate the full glory of buildings such as Sea Container House.

'Bet it doesn't have many friends with a name like that,' says Carole.

'Accurately descriptive no doubt, but completely lacking in imagination.'

'They might as well have called it Henry.'

When we reach Tower Bridge the boat turns around giving us a close up view of the white plastic wrapping covering the supporting structure.

'Have the Saudi's bought it to erect in Dubai and want it gift wrapped?' Carole asks. I assure her that they are only cleaning it but this doesn't seem to satisfy her. 'Why do they need to cover it to clean it? I don't draw the curtains when I'm doing my housework.'

The boat now proceeds upstream and a cheeky young boatman – not sure what to call him, he can't be a seaman because we are on a river – asks if we would like a commentary on the return journey. You bet we do so Carole and I cheer loud and long and he treats us to a rather amusing, if historically questionable commentary about the sights of London which more than makes up for the execrable coffee.

We learn lots. Tower Bridge's bascules have failed to open only once in 1894 at the opening ceremony he recounts, much to everyone's amusement. Further research fails to substantiate this claim but who cares, truth may well be beauty but it isn't as amusing as fiction. The Tower of London is a Norman keep – a place where people called Norman are kept we are told. HMS Belfast last saw service in Korea; London Bridge was sinking into the mud which is why it was sold to the Americans who took it down brick by brick and reassembled it on Lake Havasue in Arizona. We are told the names of all the bridges we pass under and brief details of their histories and then our boat trip comes to an end. We give our commentary man a round of applause and Carole drops 50p into his hat.

We alight at Westminster Pier and head east along the Embankment, past the City loos.

'Look at that,' cries Carole indignantly. 'I thought 20p at Charing Cross was bad enough but it costs 50p for a wee in there.'

'Expect it's because of the proximity to the Houses of Parliament,' I suggest lamely. 'You could have afforded it if you hadn't given it to the river man.' She ignores me and carries on

'I consider this to be outrageous and a clear case of discrimination against the elderly and incontinent, not to mention women since men can wee anywhere.'

'And often do,' I add, thankful that I had the foresight to use the facilities on the boat. To take her mind off urinary matters I point to Cleopatra's needle.

'Did you know that was a gift from the Egyptians for defeating Napoleon at the battle of the Nile,' I ask, but since it, like Tower Bridge, is now covered in plastic, far from being impressed by my general knowledge she respond with:

'Then it's about time we unwrapped it.'

I am wearing my pink shoes today and I had almost forgotten about the recalcitrant laces when Carole points to my feet and we make an unscheduled shoe fastening stop. This gives her the opportunity to take another picture of me retying my laces and to clamber up on to one of the bronze Sphinxes flanking the needle, and sit between its huge black paws.

The Embankment is littered with miscellaneous statues, sculptures and obelisks but the one which gains our approval is a memorial to Sir Joseph Bazalgette. This Victorian civil engineer is responsible for the construction of the Embankment and the sewage system which helped to transform the Thames from an open sewer into a well used tourist attraction.

'There was one hot summer when they actually had to close Parliament due to the stink,' I say.

'So they had expenses scandals in Victorian times too?' Carole says.

'No, well yes, they probably did, but on this particular occasion it was because of the build-up of raw sewage swilling around under the windows of the Palace of Westminster,' I continue. 'People like Bazalgette deserve to be feted for their vision, determination and commitment to improving society.'

'He certainly saved more lives than most of the self important dignitaries whose statues grace our capital, especially those sabre rattling military types,' adds Carole. Contemplating a life without sewers – which is a bit like reflecting on knickers without elastic – we walk briskly to Somerset House. All this musing on things lavatorial has stimulated our desire to empty our bladders. Having been *caught short* outside Somerset House once before, I guide Carole to the sneaky rear entrance, which once we later discover, enabled small boats direct access to the building. (This would have been pre-Balzalgette, which in my opinion should be a phrase as much used as pre-Raphaelite, I mean what would you rather have? A William Morris print or a flushing toilet and drains? No contest really).

Bladders assuaged, stomachs begin to rumble as we give the exhibits produced by local schools on ecology and the environment a cursory glance. It is a sad fact of human life that bodily functions will take precedence over art or intellect which is another reason why Bazalgette is more important than Raphael. Carole says she never did like his fat ladies and much prefers Beryl Cook.

Time to concentrate on ingestion.....well *I* am. Carole, a strange abstemious creature without a hunger pang to her name, is more interested in the staircase we are using which is called the *Stamp Stairs*.

'No point in stamping up these stairs,' she observes. 'They're made of stone and would just make your knees ache.' Fortunately the contemplation of stair stamping does stimulate the semblance of an appetite in her and we make our way to the cafeteria. We take our sandwiches out on to the terrace to enjoy the view of the river and we sit gazing upstream towards the London Eye with the sun glinting on the water, the architecture stately and a feeling of great pride in our wonderful capital city.

Passing through the Seamen's Hall after lunch we discover that a tour of the building is imminent and approach the two aged (well older than us!), conscientious but somewhat vague ladies behind the counter. They provide us with tickets and visitor stickers and we await the arrival of our guide, watching the antics of a group of children who are having great fun playing in the fountains in the courtyard. The guide is a rather nervous gentleman called Ken who proves to be very knowledgeable, gathers us, his charges, around him like a mother hen.

First stop, Nelson's Stairs named, not after Admiral Lord Horatio, but his little known brother Maurice, a quill pusher at the admiralty. The spiral staircase changes at each floor, becoming more ornate at each level because only important people were allowed on the upper floors.

Moving to a different staircase we descend into a subterranean world of arches and passageways running along three sides of the courtyard above. The most surprising thing we are taken to see are the tombstones set in the wall under the main courtyard. Pigeons fly in as we stand looking at what is a bizarre collection all taken from the chapel demolished to make way for the new Somerset House as designed by Sir William Chambers. Why these were preserved while others were destroyed is a matter of speculation.

Back inside the main building we discover that the *Stamp Stairs* were so named because people had to ascend them to reach the office where they had their documents stamped. Now this tour is well worth taking, particularly for the visit to the underground tunnels and the insights into the history of Somerset House. Down in the basement we see where the pre-Bazalgette boats would have docked and a fascinating video recreates the development of the building from its beginnings in the 16th century to the present day. The biggest difference is the Thames which is now far narrower, deeper and faster flowing which is why we will never again have frost fairs on the Thames. It will no longer ice over, not because of global warming, but because it doesn't stand still for long enough.

Too much serious inquiry and no play make Carole and Judy dull girls so we

collect a cup of tea and sit watching the fountains – all fifty five of them – which seem randomly to spout, die down and then stop completely.

'What do you think are the chances of walking through the fountains and not getting wet?' I ask.

'Dunno,' Carole responds unhelpfully, but it was a rhetorical question anyway.

Within minutes, following Carole's intrepid lead, we are both wandering playfully in and out of the water spouts with only slightly damp shoes. A fun end to a perfect station.

Millenium Green: a small park on the corner of Baylis Road and Waterloo Road opened to celebrate the millennium. You can get the best Jamaican take-away at the stall here at a very reasonable price. They always have barbecued jerk chicken and rice and peas with an alternative of goat curry or beef stew depending upon the day.

Greensmiths: A small local supermarket in Lower Marsh incorporating a butcher, baker, greengrocer, coffee specialist and wine merchant as well as a café where they prepare a range of cakes, snacks and main courses from the fresh shop ingredients, to eat in or take away. For more information on their menu and produce go to their website: www.greensmithsfood.co.uk

Florence Nightingale Museum: situated in the grounds of St Thomas Hospital the new museum is now open to the public from 9 – 5pm on weekdays with an entrance fee of £5.80 for adults. Conducted tours can be arranged for groups and for school children. www.florence-nightingale.co.uk

Joseph Bazalgette: knighted in 1875 and elected president of the Institution of Civil Engineers, he was the creator of the sewer network for central London which transformed the Thames and streets of London resulting in a dramatic improvement in the health of Londoners. He oversaw the construction of over 1,100 miles of underground sewers having the foresight to make them of sufficient diameter to cope with the present demand. More information about him on Wikipedia – he even has a Facebook page!

Somerset House: a stunning building oozing with history and running a year round programme of visual and live arts. It incorporates the Courtauld Gallery with its collection of iconic Impressionist and Post Impressionist paintings. The Fountain Court is used as a venue for open air films and concerts in the summer and becomes an ice rink in Winter. www.somersethouse.org.uk

CHAPTER TEN

Charing Cross

Just in case you don't know why
Charing Cross is called Charing
Cross, a gentleman called David,
David Gentleman to be precise,
has created a medieval style mural
which runs the length of the
platform, telling the story of the
funeral journey of Eleanor of
Castille from Lincoln to London,
and the erection of the twelve
crosses which mark the resting

places of her body on the way. The pictures that cover all the walls of the platform
side of the tunnel are the distinguishing feature of this station. They depict
medieval craftsmen at work using a cartoon style of representation and are drawn
in thick black lines against a white background, or not so white at the bottom. I
watch as Carole wipes her finger on the white of the wall behind us.

'This is filthy,' she says showing me a blackened finger. She gets all experimental
and using the remaining clean fingers, explores the extent of the dirt working her
way up the wall, finding that it's much dirtier at the bottom than it is at the top. I
watch her as she writes the word 'DIRTY' in the dirt in capital letters and stand
back to admire her handiwork.

'I bet the cleaner's a man,' she says, 'look, he's only cleaned the bit within the
narrow parameters of his tunnel, dirt excluding vision.'

'Not many women depicted are there,' I say looking at the medieval pictures, 'and
they're either sweeping or cooking.'

'It's not like the Bayeux Tapestry,' Carole says, 'there aren't any rude bits.'

'I should think not,' I say dreadfully shocked. 'Did you know that the cross
outside isn't in its original position and it's a Victorian construction erected to
publicise the opening of Charing Cross Hotel?' Well she didn't and she's impressed
by my knowledge and so am I.

'I doubt if many commuters really look at the pictures,' Carole says, and in some
ways that's the point of our journey, we look at things that regular tube users only
see.

'They've all got pointy hoods,' Carole says.

'They needed them I suppose, it must have been terribly cold. It's quite a good design don't you think like a big scarf that goes over your shoulders and can be pulled over the head.'

'Yea, it's a handy bit of kit but it would get you thrown out of Bluewater.' Carole remarks.

We're too absorbed by the pictures to notice too much else about the station, except that the white background to the pictures appears dazzlingly pristine in comparison with the grubby cracked magnolia of the opposite wall and half the ceiling. Once we finish admiring the artistic work of David Gentleman we peruse a huge advertisement for Liverpool where it claims 'It's all happening.'

'It may well be all happening in Liverpool with their excess of cathedrals but they want to get that wall cleaned up unless they're trying to advertise their grubby scouse habits.' I open my mouth to protest that the grubbiness is that of London rather than Liverpool but Carole's off muttering to herself. 'Isn't cleanliness supposed to be next to Godliness?' she asks as we leave the platform. It occurs to me that in her case it should be silliness, but she's no Goddess.

In the tunnel a busker is playing a Beatles song and we like it so we give him some money and ask for another. He obliges and we skip off to the escalator gaily singing along to *Norwegian Wood*. It's a 33 APE escalator with digital ads which makes counting very boring. The ads which are identical in every panel and change simultaneously depict an air brushed to perfection woman supposedly wearing perfume. Carole can't contain herself and having slagged off Liverpool, she abandons the count to air her views on perfume ads.

'Pointless! Now at least if they were scratch and sniff I could see the reasoning and it would help the consumer to decide if they liked the fragrance. They could squirt different perfumes from each side of the escalator shaft so the traveler could experience one on the left going up, and another on the right going down.'

'Could be dangerous for the passenger, I mean imagine all those women travelling half the way up the escalator facing forwards and then turning to travel backwards to get a squirt of perfume behind the other ear. And, if you were very tall, the perfume might hit your armpit, and if you were very small it'd go over your head. And women of a certain height might get a squirt in the eye which would be very painful.'

'They could install sensors and adjust according to height.'

'What if you can't stand the smell of the perfume being sprayed?' Carole doesn't currently have an answer for this but seems to be working on it, however, she is convinced that one day someone will receive a Queens' Award to Industry for such a necessary, life enhancing improvement. I think the idea's pants.

We reach the well known foyer; well, well known to us that is. What strikes us about this foyer is the predominance of luminous green which is very much in evidence as cladding for the various offices, such as the three ticket offices and three shops, a sweetie kiosk, a jewelers and a photo shop.

'Why's it so green?' Carole asks as we search around for a clue and then reading the certificates posted in the window of the glass-fronted office we understand.

'It's a top station for saving energy,' Carole says.

'An underground eco-warrior,' I exclaim excitedly.

'How do they do that?' Carole asks, I mean how do they measure it?'

'Look at their electricity bill?' I suggest.

'And how would they save energy?' Carole wonders. 'Turn the lights off at closing time or only have one escalator working?' I shrug. I don't know the answer.

'They could start saving even more energy by turning off those digital ads,' Carole suggests.

'This is very well lit and clean in comparison with grimy old Embankment,' I say looking around me.

'It's not so open to the elements, Carole says and of course the foyer is underground with either a short escalator ride to the mainline station or steps up to the great outside. I'm looking at Carole as she notices the number of exits. I've got my fingers crossed that she doesn't suggest trying them all.

'I've never been up exit 6 so let's try that one,' she says. Phew! The passageway is wide and takes us to steps which lead up to the east side of Trafalgar Square. We're heading for St. Martin-in-the-Fields which incidentally doesn't have a blade of grass to its name. We've promised ourselves a visit to the newly opened refurbished and renovated crypt. On the way we stop to look at Maggi Hambling's sculpture of Oscar Wilde in the pedestrian precinct of Adelaide Street.

'It's very coffin like, don't you think?' Carole nods. 'And corpse like too,' I say. Carole thinks for a bit.

'The hair looks like snakes, sort of pre-Raphelite even though it's post-Bazalgette,' Carole says, head on one side. 'I'm not sure that I'd like to be remembered in black marble with my head sticking out of my coffin looking like I'm having a bad hair day.'

'It's artistic licence,' I add.

'Oh,' Carole exclaims, 'do you have to go to art school for that? Is it something Tracey Emin's got?'

'Of course.'

'Even though she can't make her own bed? Look, it's called *a conversation with Oscar Wilde*. I suppose the idea is that people can sit on it and chat with him.'

I shudder.

'It's a bit scary, I don't think people sit on it unless they're very drunk.'

'Oscar wouldn't mind that,' Carole says. We turn the corner and our destination comes into view.

'It's only just been unpacked from its scaffolding and plastic wrapping,' Carole says as she takes pictures of the new entrance to the crypt of St. Martin's which is circular with white stone at the base and top and is all glass in between.

'Who was St. Martin, and when did he hang out?' I ask.

'He was decidedly pre-Bazlegette, a fourth century Roman soldier.'

'And what was his claim to fame? What makes him deserve his St. status?'

'He saw a shivering beggar sheltering in a doorway one freezing wintery night and he tore his cloak in half and gave it away.'

'Is that it? I mean if he'd given all his cloak I'd be more impressed.'

'It's the act that set him on the path to becoming the Bishop of Tours and he devoted himself to helping the poor.'

'It's appropriate then that St. Martin's has become such a centre for helping and caring for the homeless,' I say.

'Like the Romans,' Carole says.

'What did the Romans ever do for us?' I say quoting the well known phrase from *The Life of Brian*.

'Gave us plumbing from what I can remember from my primary school visit to Lullingstone Roman Villa, and from *The Life of Brian*.'

'Yea, but they didn't have flush toilets then did they? Some poor old slave had to tip buckets of water down the pan to flush the poo away.' Carole frowns at me.

'Back to St. Martin,' she says sternly despising my infantile preoccupation with things lavatorial. 'Generally speaking I don't have much time for Bishops, but if half of what is written about Martin is true - he was a conscientious objector, rejected torture and execution in favour of mercy and forgiveness, stood up for what he believed in and led a simple life – then he has to go on my list of heroes together with Terry the drain man.'

'Okay, St. Martin and Sir Joseph Bazlegette. Perhaps Terry the storm drain man should become a saint.'

We enter into the new round glass entrance to the Crypt and in Willy Wonka fashion I step into the new circular glass life and glide downstairs. Carole takes the stairs. Why she rejects the lift is a mystery to me but I'm a sucker for new experiences and I've never been in a circular glass lift before. Downstairs in the basement we come upon the London Brass rubbing centre. It is possible to create a *do-it-yourself* rubbing, for anything from £6-£30 depending on the size of the brass.

'William Shakespeare's cheap,' I point out to Carole.

'That's because he's only got a head,' she says looking at his brass portrait. 'He should get together with Oscar Wilde as they both have decapitation axes to grind.'

'Time for lunch,' I say and we move into the delightful setting of the crypt where everyone who serves us smiles and we can look up and admire the vaulted ceiling.

Next we explore an exhibition titled Chaos + Cosmos, a solo show of work by Sungfeel Yun. The works are all made from iron filings with patterns and shapes relating to the cosmos created using a magnet. I like them but they're huge and expensive.

'Who has walls large enough for the size of these canvases?' Carole asks.

'Looking at the prices, rich people. I'd rather have a picture from the Hubble Space Telescope,' I say. We move on. We are impressed with the exhibition of artwork from the St. John's Bible, a completely handwritten and illuminated version produced at a scriptorium in Wales under the direction of David Jackson. It's a new commission costing $4 million and the artwork is just stunning. The use of colour is wonderful and we wander round mouths open at the beauty of it. My only criticism is that in places the calligraphers have used the modern fashion for putting capital letters on top of other capital letters as if they're standing on each other's heads. I find this very difficult to read, but it's small beer beside the artwork.

'I think that St. Martin would prefer the money to be spent on helping the poor and needy,' Carole says.

Before heading up to visit the church we look round the shop. I tut over the Christmas decorations hanging up for sale.

'Far too soon,' I say to Carole and then buy two because I like them and I might not see them anywhere else and the profit goes to a good cause.

We go into the church and slip into a pew as musicians are rehearsing for a concert. There's fourteen of them and their sound reverberates magnificently around the space. When they stop we leave and sit outside on the step in the sunshine overlooking Trafalgar Square watching the crowds pass by.

'St. Martin's really does embody all the things a church should be,' Carole says.

'Such as?' I ask.

'It's an integral and vibrant part of the community providing support for the homeless and needy as well as a place for people to meet, eat, talk and enjoy art and music.' We sit musing over both church and saint as Lord Horatio gazes superciliously down on the tourists wandering around the fountains and climbing on the lions to have their photos taken.

'Let's go and look at the plinth,' Carole suggests. In case you are not aware of what I refer to I'll explain. Trafalgar Square in London has four plinths for statues. Three are occupied by permanent statues, the fourth is empty. There have been various temporary exhibits, the most notable the statue of Alison Lapper Pregnant. This statue of a naked pregnant disabled woman attracted much attention from the media. During our visit to Charing Cross it was the turn of Antony Gormley, the sculptor of the Angel of the North who had come up with the idea of allowing people an hour each on the plinth to do what they please, this event lasting for one hundred days and so involving 2,400 people if my maths is right. As we approach the plinth we can see a man with his bottom sticking up in the air, then we see the torso of a blow up doll. It's all very weird until we work out that the contortions of his body as he moves himself into bizarre poses are explained because he's playing a game of twister with two blow up dolls. The dolls are clothed as is he in case your imagination is running away with itself.

'Whatever turns you on,' Carole says.

There's a limited view from below the plinth and a limited amount of time we're prepared to watch a man play twister with blow up dollies. On the way to our next adventure we stop to admire a man covered entirely in silver who is pretending to be a statue. For the paltry sum of 20p he gets up close and personal with Carole. (She usually pays more.)

'I'm glad you're not on Facebook,' she says as I take an incriminating picture and smile my secret smile. I'm not going to tell her that I am on Facebook. Rejecting more glamorous and popular attractions such as the National Gallery and the Admiralty Arch we head for Craven Street to seek out the delights of the British Optical Association Museum. Sandwiched between Boots and Next this narrow, now insignificant little road once housed Benjamin Franklin and guided tours are advertised as being available during the week.

'What do you know about him?' Carole asks. 'He's described as 'the founding father of the United States' so he's got a lot to answer for.' I can't tell her much. My only impression comes from a play about Thomas Paine where he was represented as being the voice of balance and reason, a man of intelligence and humanity. We carry on examining our scant knowledge and find ourselves at the bottom of the road where several stage hands are smoking and talking outside the stage door of *La Cage au Folles*.

'Have you seen it?' Carole asks and I shake my head. 'Have you seen *Chicago* or *Les Mis?*' I shake my head again.

'I've read the novel *Les Miserables*,' I say, 'and I do go to the theatre,' trying to make myself sound just a tad more hip.

'Yea, but only to see Shakespeare,' Carole says disparagingly. 'You'd go to *Hamlet on Ice* or *Othello the Musical*. How about Robin Cousins and Barry White as leads? Have you seen *West Side Story?*' I admit to having seen the film.

'Well it's got to be the best interpretation of *Romeo and Juliet*,' she says. I don't think there's any 'got to be' but I'm not going to argue so I remind her of our fond memories of the production we saw together of *Macbeth* on a bouncy castle at the Edinburgh Festival. I suggest I'm open to interesting interpretations. She raises her eyebrows indicating that she doesn't really believe me.

We find we've walked past the British Optical Association Museum and whilst this is somewhere neither of us have ever thought of visiting, let alone heard of, the difficulty of locating it increases our resolve.

It turns out to be our lucky day. The museum is only open by appointment but the museum's curator might be available the receptionist tells us. He is, and we're in. We are escorted downstairs to two rooms that comprise the museum, though we are assured that this is just a fraction of what the British Optical Association owns. It's a spectacular sight. A museum that looks at you as you look at it. You really won't believe your eyes. Corny remarks? Oh yes, but they started it in the leaflet they gave us.

We are shown artifacts that take us through the history of aids to vision that have been created over the centuries. Some are very ancient carved from bone and originating in Egypt. We see a hollow bone with narrow slits which were used to protect Eskimos eyes from the sun. We see lorgnettes, pince nez, NHS plastic rimmed glasses and a pair of specs that are reputed to have belonged to Dr. Johnson. The attribution is not fully confirmed but they fit his death mask which is kept in a museum in Gough Square. I'm happy to believe that they belonged to the great man. There are other fascinating exhibits including an 18th century flea viewer.

'You had to catch a flea, impale it on a spike and then place the lens over the top,' our extremely knowledgeable and obliging curator informs us. He also points out jealousy glasses which resemble ordinary opera glasses, but enable the user to look sideways and keep an eye on the antics of others.

'I suppose that glasses were only for the rich,' I say. Not at all we are told. Shipwrecks are revealing that spectacles were not as rare as had previously been thought. They are being found by the ship-load. We learn that early glasses had no arms to fit over the ears, they were just glasses that hung over the nose. It must have been very awkward when leaning forward. We learn that glasses were most commonly found in monasteries which is where of course all the learned people were. The monks also owned herds of cattle and as the early frames were made of bone they had a ready made source of material at hand. We also find out that St. Odilie is the patron saint of opticians and optometrist. She was supposedly born blind and regained her sight when her mother had her baptized.

'Probably at St Specsavers in contact lens fluid,' Carole whispers in my ear. I have a bit of fun trying on various glasses available in a drawer as Carole looks on. When I've finished she tells me I've gone from Dame Edna, through Buddy Holly to Harry Worth. Our curator is a qualified optician himself and we discuss the Worshipful Company of Spectacle Makers that includes all aspects of the professions to do with eyesight. They have a charitable function and support various hospitals, including Moorfields. We enjoy our visit and learn a lot. I can't take the contact lens exhibition very seriously, mainly because I can't see them, they're too small and I can't come to terms with the idea of poking things in my eyes.

'Time to move on I think,' I say

'Eye eye cap'n,' responds Carole with a mock salute.

Leicester Square

'I expected it to be grander than this,' I say to Carole as I step off the train. Despite the pleasing patterns of red and black that create a border suggesting film tape, our impression is that the station is rather tatty. Not only is it tatty, it's very busy and narrow so we head straight for the nearest set of metal seats. As we park ourselves we find we're tilted at a curious angle.

'These seats have been used by crash test dummies checking the efficiency of air bags,' Carole says and she's right. During a lull in passengers, between one train disgorging and the briefest of gaps when the platform is as clear as it gets, we change to another set of seats and find ourselves very low down. 'These were made for baby bear,' Carole says and we move again, third time lucky.

I look down at the freckly cream tiles on the floor that start off looking dirty before anyone even walks on them; I look up at the unclad ceiling and look along the slightly curving platform which appears to be short and whilst I know that the platforms are pretty much the same length I have a slight feeling of claustrophobia, perhaps due to the crush of people becoming a positive maelstrom every two or three minutes.

'Lets go,' Carole says and we exit amongst the press of jostling humanity unable to stop to admire the vertical film strip pattern which borders the exit. We take some steps which lead us to a 41 APE escalator, and that delivers us to a hobbit style foyer which is round with low ceilings and has a circular room around which passengers flow.

'Oh look, shopettes!' Carole exclaims pointing towards some very small retail outlets, comprising Timpson's shoe repair shop, a sandwich bar and booth for buying theatre tickets. We pick up our mapettes and find that this area has the most places marked to visit. Most of them are cinemas and theatres, there are around thirty within spitting distance (I suppose it depends if you're an Olympic trained spitter, but you get the picture).

'Four exits,' Carole says looking at the mapette and heads off in the direction of exit 2 with me trailing along behind. We emerge into the sunshine.

'I can't sit in the cinema on a day like this,' I say to Carole as we look around the  square at the many advertising billboards trying to entice us into the dark, she agrees so we decide to explore the garden which is at the centre of Leicester Square.

'Do you know I've been here dozens of times but never really looked at it,' I say.

'Well now's your chance,' Carole says as we pass through the first portal and stop to read something of the history of the area. Carole's looking at the statue of Hogarth, artist and satirist and reading information about him. I've gravitated to a board that explains that the square was named after a great house, Leicester House that was occupied by the princes of Hanover prior to their accession to the throne. The most shocking fact was that George II's son who was George III's father, was killed by being hit in the throat by a cricket ball. I'm so surprised I have to tell Carole who swaps her more mundane information about Hogarth having lived and worked in the area from 1726 until his death in 1764.

'He was only 44 when he died,' I tell Carole, still shocked by the unlikely manner of Prince Frederick's demise. We move on into the garden. We'd like to sit down but all the seats are occupied by tourists eating ice creams and crisps and young people sending text messages on their mobiles.

'Even the crash test dummy seats would be welcome,' Carole says looking around.

There are four statues that occupy each corner of Leicester Square gardens standing as disembodied sentries, each depicting a prominent resident from the past. We've seen Hogarth on one corner. In the middle there's a fountain with my mate, William Shakespeare in the centre of it all. He seems to be watching some starlings that are splishing and splashing, tweeting and twittering and generally having a great time in the water.

'Why aren't the pigeons using the fountain?' I ask Carole, as if she'd know.

'They're too busy waiting for dropped sandwich crusts and ice cream cones,' she says. 'Perhaps that's why they're referred to as vermin. They're the great ornithological unwashed.'

'Perhaps they're modest and don't like bathing in front of an audience. Perhaps they sneak back at night and take a splash when the crowds have disappeared,' I offer. We stop to read the inscription to Albert Grant MP who left the garden 'for the free use and enjoyment of the public.'

'What a good egg,' I say.

'Yea, and he doesn't need a statue of himself to celebrate his philanthropy.'

'A noted absence of megalomania,' I say. We admire the bronze statue of Charlie Chaplin and make our way to the second corner displaying the bust of Joshua Reynolds who lived in Leicester Fields when there were fewer buildings, more greenery and considerably fewer people.

'He was quite prolific,' I tell Carole.

'Oh yea, worked his socks off painting did he?'

'It paid off, it made him lots of money painting the great and the good.' This gives me the idea to visit the National Portrait Gallery. Passing through the thronging crowds once more we look at Newton on the third corner whose bust has not worn well. Carole puts it down to too much gravity. He's placed in a lovely bed of red flowers but as Carole points out he looks as if he's suffering from some form of rocky leprosy. We wander down the road looking for Newton's house which we find just around the corner, the site now being Westminster Library. Returning to the square we pay scant attention to the fourth statue of John Hunter, the founder of scientific surgery. The square is fringed by cinemas all advertising their films. There are restaurants galore and a queue snakes its way towards the window of the half price ticket booth. It teems with people and pigeons and I crave some quiet. I shoo a pigeon away that wants to peck at my feet. Carole looks thoughtful.

'They've just as much right to be here as we do,' she says looking at the pigeon that has fluttered a few feet away and struts about aimlessly looking for any old crap to peck at.

'But they poo everywhere,' I say. Carole sighs and nods.

'True, and it's very potent poo too. I bet if Bazalgette were alive he'd think of a way of detoxifying pigeon poo, or at least create a drainage system for it.'

'Potty training?' I suggest.

'That could be a bit of a problem,' Carole says and gives me a sideways look.

'Let's go to the Portrait Gallery,' I suggest, and so we do.

Inside it's calm and in the interests of sanity we decide to limit our visit to the modern section. I easily get overpowered when there's too much to see. My first port of call is the portrait of Judi Dench by Alessandro Raho. She is shown standing against a stark white background wearing trousers and a raincoat with her hands in her pocket. She looks very alone but also seems to look out of her picture as if to challenge our observation of her. Carole thinks she looks regal. On the opposite wall I look at the picture of the late Harold Pinter painted by Justin Morimer. This is not a full length portrait like Judie Dench, it depicts his head and shoulders set against a sea of books that provides a horizontal line passing behind his head at the level of his ears. The books threaten to overwhelm him. A large expanse of the portrait is occupied by an intense orange wall that rather dwarfs Pinter. He looks reflective and serious as would I if I had that weight of writing behind me.

We take a passing glimpse of that lovely picture of Darcy Bussell by Allen Jones. It's not just the wonderful figure which is shown in profile en pointe, but the colours, the blues, yellows, greens, and oranges that shade the parts of the body and how they are set against a pinky red background. It's gorgeous.

'I'd get arthritic toes posing like that,' Carole comments pointing at her feet. I wander into a room and walk round a glass cupboard that contains a skull which is glowing red and seems a remarkably accurate human representation, except for the colour. I read the blurb and have to call Carole.

'It's Marc Quinn,' I say gesturing towards the head, 'it's a transparent mould of his own head filled up with his own blood and kept frozen.' Carole looks at it with her head on one side.

'Yuk!' she mutters. 'Wonder what his real head looks like with all the blood drained out of it?'

I like the Maggi Hambling portrait of George Melly so we go and stand in front of that for a bit admiring her use of vivid brush strokes.

'There's a vitality in this painting,' I say. Carole nods in agreement, but we're lacking in vitality and somewhat weary so it's time to move on again.

Tottenham Court Road – and the British Museum

'Now this is a busy bustling station,' I say, stating the obvious as we alight from the train with a battalion of tourists, shoppers and miscellaneous business persons, identifiable by their suits and palpable sense of purpose. This is not surprising given its location at the intersection of New Oxford Street and (Old) Oxford

Street, Charing Cross Road and the eponymous Tottenham Court Road. Many of the stations we have visited have periods when the platforms are either empty, or there are so few people on them that there is a temporary, but very real sense of tranquility about them. That is not the case here.

'It's not just busy with people,' remarks Carole pointing at the floor and walls. 'Take a look at those tiles. It's enough to give you a migraine'. Refurbished in 1984, the floor is tiled in small oblong shapes with very pronounced black grouting which demands attention. But not as much as the walls which are decorated, not just on the platform, but also in the foyers and stair wells, with the tessellated mural mosaics of Eduardo Paolozzi. Unsure whether it is just an abstract pattern or meant to represent something, we spend a while gazing at parts of it from different angles to see if it reveals a recognizable shape. Carole thinks she can see a butterfly, but I think it's a fish. No consensus there then.

'Ultimately it's a bit like gazing at clouds and seeing pictures in them – there is no *right* answer,' I muse

'Which is good,' says Carole. 'Life is too full of *right answers* and smart arses who know them.'

Does she mean me?

To the booming cacophony of an indecipherable announcement we leave the platform against an incoming tide of people and go up a 21 APE then a 32er. We have already decided on our destination since the weather has turned cold and wet. We are going to the British Museum, an odd name for a place which is stuffed full of things from abroad. Having been there before we both know the way, but dutifully collect our mapettes at the turnstile and our visit is briefly delayed while Carole points out that the station has five exits. Two are situated on either side of Centre point, that notorious symbol of 70's property speculation.

'Did you know it's now a Grade II listed building?' Carole asks

'Surely not. It's a *concrete carbuncle* as Prince Charles would say,' I reply indignantly. Carole shrugs.

'I guess you can get planning permission for anything if you're rich enough.' Having never experienced a Centre Point exit, Carole is keen to try one of them but I already have and dismiss her request to sample its delights since it is in the wrong direction and would involve us in unnecessary road crossing – always a fraught occupation in this part of town. We emerge opposite the Dominion Theatre which is surrounded by scaffolding and hole diggery.

'Wonder what they're up to?' I say, nodding towards the noisy workmen.

'Maybe they are exhuming a hairy mammoth or undermining Centre Point so that it will disappear into the earth to make way for a more modest and attractive edifice,' suggests Carole.

'They'd probably replace it with a huge Tesco, or worse a giant McDonalds – Grade II listed of course!' I say.

Research reveals that they are refurbishing the station's entrances and exits because it is an area of Grade I listed congestion and they sometimes have to be closed because of Health and Safety considerations.

We enter Great Russell Street passing many crocodiles of small children clutching clip boards who are obviously on their way to the same destination. Delighted to be out of prison for the day despite the cold and rain, they chatter excitedly, not looking where they are going and bouncing off passers-by like pinballs. One is being severely reprimanded by a teacher who looks as if she could do with a stiff gin and tonic or 5mg of Valium. At least the youngsters are enthusiastic and too young to be disappearing into local pubs like the Museum Tavern. Formerly known as The Dog and Duck, this place is full of architectural interest, not to mention good food and drink, but doesn't qualify for a Grading. There is no justice in the world!

The British Museum is mighty impressive – both inside and out – with its imposing neo-classical façade and Norman Foster's Great Court. As we mount the steps I regale Carole with tales of my youth when I was seventeen and working for the Ministry of Aviation.

'I came here one lunchtimewith two of my friends and a man in his fifties who was a keen photographer asked us to pose on these steps,' I tell her.

'Sounds like a pervert to me. If it happened now he'd probably get arrested, or your pictures would appear on Facebook the next day cut and pasted on to naked bodies in seductive poses with the Elgin Marbles,' snorts Carole. In the Great Hall we are very taken with a weird looking structure which resembles a large lump of very shiny silvery rock. It is about ten feet high and we walk around it noticing how the light falls on the uneven surface creating dark areas contrasting with the luminous shining surface and the distorted reflections of its surroundings.

'It's got to be a sculpture because it's standing on a plinth,' I observe.

'Yes it's a giant Terminator 2 in the throes of metamrphosing into Arnold Schwarznegger,' says Carole,tilting her head this way and that to appreciate its full effects.

'Have you noticed how, when the colours change it looks almost fluid?'

We stand and stare fascinated by the multifarious distorted reflections and wanting to poke, stroke and push its glistening surface.

'That's the trouble with sculpture, it invariably invites you, entices you, almost dares you to touch it but that is always strictly forbidden,' I say gesturing towards the hawk-eyed museum security guards with their *don't even think about it* expressions.

Fortunately, on this occasion, Carole does not rise to the challenge so we wander about a bit admiring the symetry and wonderful roof of the Great Court created from glass and steel with each piece of glass different from all others. We circumnavigate the reading room whilst discussing what we have seen here in past visits. At the ticket counter we discover that there are two exhibitions and plump for £8 worth of Babylon which is much older (well over 4000 years) and more interesting than we had suspected. The only things we know about it are from the Boney M song and a vague notion of a lost exotic power which created the Hanging Gardens of 'seven wonders of the world' fame.

'Of course I've heard of it,' says Carole, 'But I don't have a clue where it was'.

'According to this map it was situated in what is now Iraq, near to Baghdad on the river Euphrates,' I reply, scrutinising the first exhibit. 'Its most famous king was Nebuchadnezzar'.

'Now I recognise that name,' says Carole. 'I wonder what his mates called him? Neb? Chad/ Nezzie?'

'I doubt he had many mates. Says here he went a bit mad'.

'Was that the official diagnosis?'

'Well historians believe he suffered from porphyria, the disease that afflicted George III,' I say.

'That's not *a bit mad*. That's stark raving mad. What is it with kings and their mental health? You never get queens going *a bit mad*. They're far more stable give or take a bit of PMT', Carole observes

'I think William Blake would have agreed judging by this,' I declare indicating a copy of his painting showing Nebuchadnezzar on all fours, naked and wild eyed with long matted hair and beard.

'I don't think he ever recovered from the sight of Shadrac, Meshac and Abednego emerging from that fiery furnace. It must have been a bit of a shock,' she grins. The exhibition shows that Nebuchadnezzar was supposedly responsible for the hanging gardens. There are many artists' impressions of these in the exhibition, but nobody seems to be quite sure what they looked like or precisely where they were. In fact some historians think they may have been confused with other gardens in Nineveh. Easily done!

It seems that Babylon was, for hundreds of years, a great centre of learning and commerce and, judging by some of the exhibits, very small writing. When someone talks about tablets of stone, I imagine great slabs of stone which you would hardly carry about with you for a quick read while travelling home in your chariot. But in Babylon they were writing on these tiny slivers of stone – larger than your average paracetamol, but no bigger than computer memory stick.

'They must have had very good eyesight!' says Carole squinting at the tiny symbols.

'Look at this one,' I enthuse. 'It's a list of plants growing in the garden including things like cucumber and mangel worzel.'

The reconstruction of the Ishtar Gate shows it to be a grand imposing structure approached by a long walkway decorated with a tiled mosaic of white lions – it would be a pretty impressive entrance to a modern city, but in 600BC it must have been breathtaking and awe inspiring. Didn't do them much good though, because despite the city's amazing fortifications the Persians re-routed the River Euphrates and walked in through the gates during a feast when all the Babylonians were drunk.

'See, all that accumulated wisdom and the wine gets the better of them,' muses Carole.

'Just about sums up the human condition really, speaking of which I could do with a cup of coffee.' All Babyloned out, we make our way to the 'caff'. Our final stop, via several mummies, is the gift shop, then it's back down the steps and out into the cold.

We decide that we *hold with* the British Museum since it belongs to us, even if the ownership of some of its contents is a source of dispute. Quite spontaneously we burst into song….. 'Land of hope and glory….etc' Well, you've got to do something to keep your spirits up!

St Martin in the Fields: has its own websie: www.stmartin-in-the-fields.org

British Optical Association Museum: founded in 1901 and taken over by the new College of Optometrists in 1981. Members of the public can visit by prior appointment tel: 0207 766 4353 or go to the College's website: www.college-optometrists.org and look under MusEYEum.

Benjamin Franklin House: built around 1730 the house is further down Craven Street and is also open to the public as a museum and educational facility. Born to an American mother and British father in Boston Massachusetts in 1706, Franklin was a key founder of the United States as well as a contributor to philosophy, science and printing. www.benjaminfranklinhouse.org

Leicester Square: In the early 17th century this area was common land and despite the efforts of subsequent owners, including the 2nd Earl of Leicester from whom it gets its name, the garden area was purchased in 1874 by the flamboyant Albert Grant who laid out the original garden and donated to the Metropolitan Board of Works. Now an entertainment centre, Leicester Square is home to many cinemas and restaurants and is in the heart of London's theatreland.

British Museum: museum of human history and culture with a collection of over 7million objects. Established in 1753 it is largely based on the collections of Sir Hans Sloane and opened to the public in 1759. Entry is free although there is a charge for special exhibitions. For details of these, opening hours and collections go to: www.britishmuseum.org

CHAPTER ELEVEN

Goodge Street

The platform side wall has a covering of cream tiles with the standard green and black borders and I once again comment on the sparkly black floor which I find so attractive. Unusually the facing wall is painted black and completely devoid of advertisement, its pitchy length broken only by the patriotic red white and blue of the Goodge Street roundels. I like the effect but Carole finds it rather sinister.

'If they're gonna keep it that colour they'll have to rename it 'Ghoul Street'', she remarks.

'They could claim it's haunted and open it up as an alternative to the London dungeon,' I suggest,

'Perhaps they could run a *ghost train* between here and Warren Street with holograms of Dracula and vampires which leap out at you in the tunnel,' continues Carole, warming to her subject, but at that moment a strong, authoritative voice commands travellers to *mind the gap*. 'Could it be Vincent Price – now that would be a nice little eerie touch.'

'I think the black wall is stylish and restful, better than the migraine inducing Tottenham Court Road,' says I. '*and* of course, black doesn't show the dirt!'

It's a fairly quiet station with few passengers in evidence, according to Carole because they find it too spooky and avoid it. Having minded the gap we are exhorted to *mind the doors* as we enter the lift to travel to the surface. No escalators here and we notice that the emergency exit is via a spiral staircase like those in the early stations we visited south of the river. The exterior too is built to the familiar brown glaze tiled, arch windowed Leslie Green design. Before we can get there we are accosted by a helpful TfL employee called Vasili who, having seen us studying our mapettes, wants to help direct us somewhere. After several abortive attempts to assure him that we are not searching for anything in particular, just looking for places that interest us, he shrugs resignedly and suggests that we try the Eisenhower Centre.

Intrigued by Vasili's suggestion since it is not marked on the map, we make our way across the road half expecting to find a memorial to JFK if this recommendation is as accurate as that given to us by the well meaning gent at Tufnell Park. There are some very interesting buildings in Chenies Street, both old and new, but the Eisenhower Centre, at first sight, isn't one of them. Poor old Dwight would turn in his grave if he saw the place which carries his name – well some of his name since the sign now reads: THE EI ENhO\ER CENTRE. At least they spelled '*centre*' correctly! It looks like a refuge for the homeless - all tightly locked up. I spot an intercom on the door and speak to a helpful woman inside who informs me that it *was* General Eisenhower's wartime headquarters but it is now a storage facility. Doesn't look big enough, but she reveals that it is actually the entrance to a large deep tunnel built in the early 1940's – one of a series that were designed to be used as air raid shelters. The idea was to link them up after the war when they would become a new high-speed London underground railway. The building we see is a pill box entrance to this tunnel.

We wander on down the road past the Drill Hall and RADA. I get all excited because I've never known where the Royal Society of Dramatic Arts was located and here it is in front of my eyes. It's a large red brick building, unremarkable apart from the fact that all the windows seem to be blacked out or to have their curtains firmly drawn. The trainee *luvvies* are unaccountably shy. We turn left into Gower Street which is flanked by terraces of imposing regency houses which have now been largely converted to cheap hotels and B&B's or student accommodation. There is also another RADA building with transparent windows for the more advanced and extraverted students.

'Inhospitable railings,' remarks Carole pointing to the frequent notices warning cyclists that bikes chained to them would be *removed*. 'Damned if you do, damned if you don't – 'cos if they don't lock up their bikes there is a good chance someone will remove 'em by stealing 'em. What harm are they doing?' Carole asks.

'I suppose it's not as pretty to look at as the railings, but most of these houses have seen better days,' I respond.

'Typical of the snobby attitude of people in Bloomsbury!' Carole proceeds to regale me with her wonderful vision of the Tour de France passing through London and all the competitors stopping for a wee in Gower Street.

'A couple of hundred men in lycra all chaining their machines to the railings and peeing in the gutter. Eat your heart out George Dance Junior. I don't care if the pre-Raphaelite movement was formed here – even artists have bladders.'

'Yeh but they probably didn't have bikes.'

We walk up Gower Street and come to a blue plaque on Bonham-Carter House announcing that the first anaesthetic was administered here in 1846. I am about to comment on the horrors of life before anaesthesia but Carole wades in with:

'Even the bloody houses around here have double barrelled names.' She is better disposed towards the Darwin Building but unfortunately the Grant Museum housed therein is not open until 1.00pm, which is a great pity since it looks very interesting. No matter, I am taking Carole to see the auto-icon of Jeremy Bentham in the cloisters of University College.

'What's an auto-icon?' demands Carole. 'A Rolls Royce? A Cadillac?'

'No, it's an icon of himself made from Jeremy Betham's actual remains,' I say. Undeterred by Carole's puzzled grimace and comment of *Weirdo* I continue. 'He left his body to his friend, a Dr Southwood Smith, who dissected him in a series of lectures for the benefit of medical students. Following this procedure his skeleton was articulated to create a frame for the auto icon.'

'Was he a goth?' she enquires. I ignore her comment.

'The skeleton is padded with straw and encased in stockinet.' I'm well into tour guide mode now.

'Did he posthumously star in *The Wizard of Oz*?'

'They were going to preserve his head as well but it was damaged in the embalming process so Southwood had one made of wax.'

'What did they do with his real head? Bury it without a body?' muses Carole.

'They kept it in a box for quite a while but students kept stealing it. The auto icon is wearing Bentham's clothes though.'

'So how come you know so much about this weirdo?'

'I did my degree here,' I answer proudly. 'And Bentham's ideas strongly influenced the founders of UCL.'

'Oh don't tell me they're all stuffed as well,' she retorts

'Some should have been,' I say.

Arriving in the South Cloisters of UCL we look at Bentham in his box, and read about his life and ideas. His views were liberal and egalitarian. He thought that law should be understood and accessed by all, advocated the decriminalisation of homosexuality and believed in the equal rights and enfranchisement of women.

'He was so progressive he was almost subversive,' I remark. 'It says here that the ban on teaching his work was only lifted in 2002 at Rosario University in Colombia!'

'It would be great if some contemporary Frankenstein could wake him up so we could get his views on the current state of society. I wonder what he'd make of our politicians and the media?' muses Carole. 'I think I hold with JB.'

'*And* he has the same initials as your other hero.'

'I'm not *that* keen on James Bond, well not since Sean Connery left,' she protests. 'Not the secret agent, the sewer man, Joseph Bazalgette!'

Enjoying my walk down memory lane I insist we eat with the students and we make our way down to what is reassuringly still referred to as the *Refectory*. It's good to know that traditions are being upheld in some esteemed seats of learning.

'It's far more impressive than the North East London Polytechnic where I did my degree,' admits Carole as we wander downstairs to the basement. 'The Psychology department was on the top floor of a Victorian Primary School in Plaistow and the car park was part of the playground. No refectory for us, just a squalid little cafeteria where the hot meals consisted almost solely of cheese on toast or sausage and chips.'

This refectory has been refurbished; it wasn't this luxurious in my day. It must be subsidized, however, since a huge brie and cranberry baguette and a sizeable berry muffin, both of which we share, and two cups of coffee only come to just over £6. As we get up to leave a fire alarm sounds.

'It's Jeremy,' Carole says. 'He's so incensed by the policies of the coalition and the financial shenanigans in the city that he has spontaneously combusted.' Given the lack of urgency in the students' departure to the assembly point we assume it's only a fire drill and as we leave by the main gate firemen are languidly alighting from two fire engines. They've probably come for a cheap cuppa and sandwich.

Passing University College Hospital, a magnificent red building resembling a palace or cathedral despite being shrouded in scaffolding, we make our way back to Goodge Street heading for Pollock's Toy museum. We pay £4 to go into a series of small, shabby rooms – I don't think anyone has cleaned any of the floors or carpets since the place was built in the 1880's. We peer into cabinets and find things that we both remember. I am particularly nostalgic about the Pollocks miniature toy theatres that are on display.

'My father bought me one like that. It had footlights and overhead lights and a wooden drop-down curtain as well as scenery and characters,' I sigh. 'I loved it but never really put on a play because the little cardboard figures were dressed in eighteenth century period costume and they looked ridiculous to me.'

'They've got some more up-to-date outfits now,' remarks Carole. 'Look, those must be at least 1930's.'

'Now if I'd had that as a child I might have turned into Peter Hall!'

We do not much like the dolls, at best they look grubby, at worst downright sinister. We like the teddies (there's something quite charming and comforting about tatty teddies) and the dolls houses. I am captivated by the 1950's dolls house display. It's all so authentic from the low coffee table, the standard lamp with its

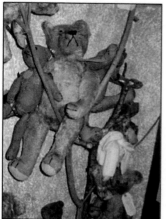

modern 50s shade, the television set that now looks so dated, and best of all the flight of miniature ducks stuck on the wall. Like everything else in the museum it's dirty and dusty. What this display needs is a teensy weensy Kim and Aggie to spruce it up.

We spend almost as much time browsing in the shop as we spent in the museum – it's certainly a bit cleaner and full of stuff that has us squealing with delight – 'I had one of those,' 'Oooh look at these!' We buy some jacks, claiming they are for our grandchildren, and are disappointed by the lack of five stones.

It's too late for the Grant Museum, so promising ourselves a trip another day, we take the lift back down into the bowels of the Northern Line.

Warren Street

Warren Street and Goodge Street are so close together the train takes no time to travel between the two and come to a stop. We alight and look about us.

'Fine old mess of a station this is,' Carole says looking up at the paneling above the name strip that has been removed exposing a plethora of wires and tubes. 'It's not what you want to see is it?' and not waiting for an answer she carries on, 'unless you're an electrician that is, but honestly, how do they make sense of it all?'

'They have diagrams don't they?' I venture.

'Yes, but they look like plates of spaghetti to me.'

'It could be viewed as artistic,' I suggest, 'you know like the Pompidou Centre where all the services are on the outside of the building.' Carole snorts in derision.

'It's like putting a glass panel in your stomach so you can see your digestive system at work. Not nice at all,' she says shaking her head. 'Such things are better covered up and taken for granted if you ask me.' Well I didn't and I like an argument.

'You could say that it reveals the complexity of the system and so should make us all more tolerant when things go wrong,' I offer, but there's another train leaving Goodge Street and it gets louder as it approaches our platform bringing a rush of warm air in its wake. I think I hear Carole mutter 'bloody miracle that anything works,' as the train screeches to a halt.

The platform is dead straight and half-empty with only two sets of metal chairs, so it's not a place to linger and we leave stopping only to admire an old-fashioned sign on the tiles set inside a fancy box pointing the way out.

'What use is Warren Street?' Carole asks. 'Given the time to take the lift from Goodge Street, walk to the platform, wait for a train, disembark, go up to ground level by the escalator, it's probably quicker to walk between the two stations,' Carole says as we step onto the moving stairs. I'm too shocked by her heresy to reply – tube stations are currently meat and drink to me.

'What's Warren Street got that Goodge Street lacks?' she asks.

'Its location, on the corner of Euston Road?' I offer.

'Now that's another thing, this station was originally called Euston Road when it was first opened in 1907 and that's when Goodge Street was called Tottenham Court Road. A year later they were both renamed.'

'That's very confusing,' I say as we step onto the second escalator.

'Warren Street, formerly known as Euston Road – doesn't that sound like some pretentious rock star? So I ask you again, what does Warren have that Goodge doesn't?' Right we're down to first name terms I see and search my brain for an answer.

'Visible wiring and piping?' I suggest.

'And an escalator called Hugh,' Carole says. I look around the circular foyer for clues as to the naming of the escalator. 'I've just made that up,' she says.

'And a connection to the Victoria Line,' I offer and that's it, mapettes in hand, we're off outside.

'Let's explore Fitzrovia,' I suggest.

'What's that then?' she asks.

'An area that currently has lots of well known advertising agencies, television companies and media related offices in general, but in the past was a bohemian centre for famous artists.'

'Such as?' Carole asks as she sets her eyes steadfastly towards the tower block of the New University College Hospital. I know she wants to drag me up to the top to look at the vistas over London, but I don't want to do that so I've done my homework in an attempt to distract her.

'Dylan Thomas, George Orwell and Quentin Crisp, to name a few. Ian McEwan lives here and he set his novel *Saturday* around here.'

'All right,' Carole concedes as we walk towards the sedate charms of Fitzroy Square which is only a stone's throw away from the noisy, bustling race track that is the Euston Road. We come into an elegant pedestrianised area which reeks of affluence and the numerous blue plaques on the well kept large terraced houses attest to the eminence of the former inhabitants of this elite square.

'Look, a plaque to Robert Adams,' I say. 'He designed two sides of the square.' Carole nods and we admire the elegant façade of the row of terraced houses. I am particularly taken by no. 29 which was formerly the home of George Bernard Shaw and Virginia Woolf. It strikes me as remarkable that two such eminent literary figures should at different times occupy the same house. The square now houses embassies of countries such as Liberia, Croatia and Mozambique, and firms of accountants and investment companies. We come across St. Luke's Hospital for the clergy which looks very inviting inside.

'I bet they specialize in knee operations,' Carole says, 'all that genuflecting must take its toll.'

'What about surgical removal of dog collars as part of their retirement plan?' I add.

At the centre of the square there's an imprisoned garden. It's enclosed by railings and the gate is firmly locked, entry the privilege of residents only. It's a nice day and various people are seated on the pavement their backs propped up against the railings. I can't help thinking it wouldn't hurt to allow them in to enjoy the cool of the garden.

'Keeps out the riff-raff,' Carole says as she peers in at the mini-park through the railings, 'but in its favour there are no signs forbidding the chaining of bicycles.'

Another remarkable fact about Fitzroy Square is its proximity to the concrete phallic symbol, the Post Office Tower which looms over it like a cross between an alien invader and a Victorian folly.

'I bet that GBS would have had something to say about that erection,' Carole says as we amble towards it.

'It just pops up all over the place,' I say and then hastily qualify my remark. 'The Post Office Tower that is.'

'The building formerly known as the Post Office Tower, now the Telecom Tower,' Carole says correcting me as we move towards its base. It's strange to be standing right at the foot of the building seeing where it's firmly anchored to the ground, not floating about as it seems to be doing from so many vantage points. Situated in Cleveland Mews, apart from its size, it now has little of interest to offer.

'I always wanted to go to the revolving restaurant at the top,' I say. 'The views would be spectacular.'

'Yea,' Carole agrees, 'since the IRA planted a bomb it's been a no go area for the public, so what about the University College Hospital Tower?' My heart sinks as Carole turns around and we begin to retrace our steps, this time heading in a northerly direction. On our way we continue our wanderings around Fitzrovia passing a stream of sweaty men in ill assorted sports gear and find an attractive children's playground adjacent to which, in a specially designed cage several captive footballers are having their turn at playing the beautiful game during their lunch break. The fencing is about 20ft high but it doesn't stop a football from soaring over the top, bouncing in the road, and knocking the condiments off the table outside Olive Caff. We watch as a hitherto disinterested passer-by is galvanized into full footie fitness as he enthusiastically returns the ball with one well aimed kick. Even Fitzrovia has its would-be Beckhams.

Further on we come to Whitfield Street and the Marie Stopes Clinic, located here since 1952.

'Her first marriage was annulled for non-consumation,' I tell Carole.

'The ultimate form of birth control,' she replies.

'She's another hero, on the scale of Bazlegette in my book,' I say. Carole agrees and we discuss the tremendous contribution she made to the equality of women and we contemplate what our lives would have been like without the availability of birth control and thinking about the past and the dangers of illegal abortions.

'We should give her a standing ovation,' I say.

'We're too old to even give her a sitting ovation,' Carole says, 'but I salute her courage and her achievement.'

Time's up. I can't keep Carole amused or diverted for any longer, and we come into sight of the UCH tower.

'What if we're not allowed up there?' I ask in my scardy-cat way. I'm not that comfortable in blagging my way in to places and assuming I've a right to wander about at will. Taking no notice of my nerves we walk in and Carole spots the loos which she visits coming out grinning from ear to ear reporting the use of another Dyson Airblade hand dryer.

'We haven't seen one of those since the Oval,' Carole reminds me cheerfully.

'Oh look, the lifts,' she says. I'm about to say we're probably not allowed in the lift

but Carole has already told me that if there are wards then there are patients, and patients have visitors, so of course we're allowed. Before I know it we're through a door and into a high-tec stainless steel lift. It's a bit stuffy and I've broken out into a gentle sweat at the prospect of irate matrons armed with bedpans and loud hailers proclaiming my imposter status and ordering me out of the hospital. As it happens we exit at the top on floor sixteen to a deserted corridor with a huge picture window at one end. The views are great and yes, we can see the building formerly known as the Post Office Tower from up here.

'I wonder if the Post Office Tower will become a museum of communications,' Carole speculates as she stands transfixed by the view. She's right up at the window and I'm hovering by the lift taking a cursory look at the panorama of London spread way below me.

'Look Jude, I can see the London Eye,' Carole exclaims excitedly. I nod wishing she'd be very quiet and agree to leave, as I'd like to get down to the ground without incident.

'It's very swish isn't it,' Carole says as she finally agrees to leave and I can breathe once more. 'It's probably got more machines that go *ping* per patient than any other in London – that's not counting the private ones – and what with that stunning view and a Dyson Airblade in the Ladies, what more could any patient want?' Carole asks. 'That was great,' she says enthusiastically. I don't answer, I thought it purgatory, but we're off on our next adventure. Next stop please.

The Grant Museum: *founded in 1828 as a teaching collection, this is the only remaining university zoological museum in London. It houses numerous skeletons, mounted animals and specimens preserved in fluid and many of the species are now endangered or extinct. There's even a box of Dodo bones! To find out more about this and other UCL collections go to:* www.ucl.ac.uk/museums

UCL: *University College London, founded in 1826, was the first in England to be secular, admitting students regardless of their religion and women on equal terms with men. The main campus is in Bloomsbury and the whole of the main building, called the Octagon, was designed by the architect William Wilkins, who also designed the National Gallery. The Cloisters are one of the main thoroughfares of the college and house a series of exhibitions and events throughout the year, as well as the auto-icon of Jeremy Bentham.*

Polloks Toy Museum: *Located in Scala Street, behind Goodge Street Station, it is open from 10am-5pm Monday to Saturday. It began in 1956 in an attic room near Covent Garden where Pollok's Toy Theatres were also sold. It moved to its present location in 1969 and is run by the grandson of the founder, Marguerite Fawdry.* www.pollokstoymuseum.com

Fitzrovia: *Probably named after the* Fitzroy Tavern, *and lying partly in Camden and partly in the City of Westminster, the name of this area was adopted in recognition of the artistic and bohemian community habitually found at the public house. It was once the home to such writers as Virginia Wolf, George Bernard Shaw and Arthur Rimbaud, more recently known as a media and advertising hub. Polloks Toy museum is actually in Fitzrovia. Nick Bailey's 1981 book,* Fitzrovia, *examines the history of the area.*

CHAPTER TWELVE

Camden Town

'You know, the further we go north, the longer it takes us to get there,' I say as we speed down the tunnel towards Camden Town. Carole looks at me.

'Well that's hardly rocket science now is it?'

'I just mean we're spending a lot of our time joy riding on the Northern Line, so when we arrive we'll need *a little something* as Winnie the Pooh would say.'

So we arrive at Camden Town on the High Barnett branch platform, and yes this station has two lines, the other going to Edgware; excitement abounds. We are greeted by a blast of warm wind as we step off the train. The train leaves and the platform is revealed in all its barren glory with an absence of ads as they've all been scraped off, but this bareness is mitigated by its pleasing gentle curve. The only thing to catch the eye is a sign in a fancy box on the tiled wall signalling the direction to Highgate, the letters tastefully picked out in pale blue on white. It's an original and has been preserved for our delectation.

Behind us as we sit on the platform we admire the pale cream tiles their uniformity broken by a blue horizontal pattern that joins up at regular intervals with lines of darker blue tiles that span the roof. These dark strips of tiles are set against the pale cream of the ceiling and the effect is felicitous. One side of the station has been done up, and presumably the other side is waiting its turn.

'This platform would be heaving if it was the weekend,' Carole tells me. She's been here before but I haven't. 'You're a Camden virgin?' she says incredulously, when I admit I've never been to the market or the shops. 'It's alternative,' Carole explains, 'and attracts the really alternative and the would-be- alternative people from far and wide. Oh, and watch out for your change, it's also quite notorious for circulating forged banknotes.' I can't wait.

In the spirit of underground enquiry we go to visit the Edgware platform and find it identical to the one we've just left. The 34 APE escalator takes us up to the station concourse which is grubby, tiled in green, black and cream and has exits on two sides. We hunt for our mapettes and fail to find them. Carole approaches a man in uniform who grudgingly finds them for us.

'He seems to be having a bad day,' I say.

'He smelt,' Carole says dismissively as we leave, but we've scored a small victory, we got him to twitch his mouth into a smile with our profuse thanks.

Walking down Camden High Street I feel quite overwhelmed by the sheer number, colour, noise and diversity of the shops and stalls. We dive into the recesses of one of the group of stalls, one particularly catches my eye, and find T-shirts with amusing slogans, such as 'hard work pays off tomorrow, laziness pays off today.' All the stalls seem to be piled high with small trendy clothes that require a size 12 figure and an age not in excess of 20. We have neither – well, I have neither, and Carole doesn't fit the age requirement.

Crossing over the canal we remember our intention to take a boat trip. We don't know where to go to book a trip and an obliging man called Sean, who overhears our debate, points out the booking office to us, leaving his trendy hairdressing salon and risking his coiffure in the light drizzle that has begun to fall. He's tall and dark haired.

'Not bad,' I say.

'He's a bit porky,' Carole says. I don't think so, but then I suppose it depends from which side of porky one is judging.

The canal boat office displays a notice informing us that there are no boats running today, but we soon happen upon the water taxi terminus and find we can get a boat to Regents Park Zoo, Little Venice and disembark at Paddington, but first we must eat. I'm seduced by the smell of the multi-cultural range of comestibles on offer. We enter the market proper and are assailed by offers of free food, enticing tasters from mainly Chinese outlets, but the choice is wide, we could have Mexican, Caribbean, Moroccan and Doughnuts or Crepes as well. I order some Chinese food and two coffees, whilst Carole opts for a crepe. Carole enjoys her food and mine is all right but the coffee is made out of dish water.

'Well they might have mastered all things sweet and sour and in oyster sauce with cashew nuts, but they have yet to master cappuccino,' Carole says stirring the muddy concoction which is masquerading as coffee. She brightens at the prospect of taking me into Cyber Dog and as we eat, perched on high stalls in a very cramped corner, she describes its delights.

'It's a MUST,' she says, and I know not to argue with her when she talks in capital letters.

So to Cyber Dog which is located in underground railway arches and emits the deafening thump of trance beat which fills my ears. On entering my already overstretched senses are assailed by the clothes, white or luminescent yellow, orange, green or pink glowing eerily in the semi darkness from the ultra violet lighting.

'These clothes are outrageous,' I say admiring a pair of 70s flares. 'When do people wear them?'

'When they go clubbing,' Carole says casually. Now the only clubbing I've ever done was inflicted on a wasp that had stung me so I gaze around in shock and awe. The clothes are garishly attractive, here are some of the things I could have bought for my clubbing night out, had I been so inclined: small shorts with a hooped skirt attachment making it stick out; fluorescent leggings with a variety of tops to match, or to contrast, my favourite comedy item was the fluorescent orange mesh top with a hood with hoops in it so it could be pulled up like the hood on a child's pram. Rest assured dear reader I resisted the desire to purchase any of these items knowing that persons of discernment would pay money to avoid seeing me thus attired. Carole admires some stretchy white fluorescent things (I can't bring myself to call them trousers) that are smooth until the knee when they burst into shaggy strips of material; they remind me of heavy horses' legs. Note to self; could buy them for Carole's next birthday.

My heart sinks when Carole spots a sign strictly forbidding photography. She finds two ridiculous hats which we don, and forces me to creep to a corner where she surreptitiously clicks away at our reflection in a mirror. We are rumbled when the camera flashes and a young assistant comes to admonish us.

'We're only taking silly pictures,' Carole assures the young sales girl, 'we're not stealing your designs, I mean do we look like fashion espionage grannies?' The

assistant remains unimpressed, so tails between our legs, we leave the shop.

Next we make our way to the Horse Tunnel Market. This area is a part of the original Victorian horse tunnels which housed the animals that pulled the barges and worked in the railway goods yards. At the entrance there are huge bronze horses.

'I admire the artistry, but what would you do with such a thing?' Here many of the stalls are inside the original stables and are locked and shut.

'This market is buzzing at the weekend, that's the time to come,' Carole says. Now she tells me.

I remain overwhelmed by the choice and variety of goods on offer and promising to return I stagger back to the canal boat area with the help of a much less stimulated Carole. We watch our barge arrive and as it does, a very slight and slim young woman springs off and starts tugging the canal boat so that it docks neatly. She leans back straining pulling the rope and another woman who is waiting exchanges sympathetic looks with me.

'This is no work for an eight stone girl,' I say to Carole.

'No, it's a big hefty muscly man's work,' Carole says.

'Call me sexist if you like, but men are just a tad stronger and better adapted to making canal barges tow the line – nice metaphor eh?' Carole gives me a dismissive look.

Having purchased our OAP tickets, Carole and I board the boat and sit right up the front on a bare wooden seat. Spotting cushions on an adjacent empty seat we take two to make our journey more comfortable. We will have a great view and we can both pretend we're driving (even though we know the boat is driven from the other end.)

'Why is that?' I ask Carole. 'Wouldn't it be better to drive from the front, not the back end? Imagine driving your car from the boot?' Before she can answer the poor little girl who struggled with dragging the boat to be tied up comes round and asks for her cushions back. She tells us we are not allowed to move them.

'There are three other passengers on the boat,' Carole points out politely. 'If there's an influx of passengers and we are depriving anyone of their comfort we will return them, what's more, we will return them to their rightful place at the end of the journey.' The girl becomes quite agitated, insisting that, 'the owner won't like it.' Carole's hardly warmed up yet. 'Now is that because there's a danger of upsetting the equilibrium of the boat by the wanton relocation of two pretty thin and not particularly comfortable cushions? Does the plimsoll line of the barge have to remain exactly parallel to the surface of the water when on the canal or would it be in danger of capsizing?'

'The cushions have to be put back in their proper place,' she repeats.

'What if two very large people get on and sit together on one side?' Carole asks. I look at the layout of the barge, there are two seats on each side of the pointy front bit where Carole and I are ensconced and then pairs of seats laid out in neat rows on each side with an aisle dissecting the middle. I chime in.

'Why do the cushions need to be returned to a seat that is not being used?' I ask, but it's getting too much. She's being pedantic and punctilious, but we don't want to be the precipitators of a nervous breakdown, and I see the fear in her eyes, and it's not fear of us.

'My manager's driving the boat,' she whispers and we understand her predicament and conform, returning the cushions to their rightful place where they remain unused throughout our journey.

'It's the mentality of those *dressed in a little brief authority*. It's from *King Lear*,' I say apologetically to Carole as I know of her aversion to Shakespeare.

This incident, and the hard seats without benefit of artificial padding in no way detracts from our enjoyment of the canal journey. The pace of travel is slow and there's time to look about as we speculate on the lives of those who live in some of the des. res. houses whose gardens abut the canal. There are some truly amazing pieces of real estate, not to mention a few examples of 'unreal' estate like the structure which resembles a Greek temple, and a large red pagoda which seems to be built half on land and half on a barge on the water.

Our first stop is London Zoo and we enjoy an excellent view of Lord Snowdon's aviary. We pass through various tunnels. Deep in the middle of one Carole says thoughtfully,

'Do you know, fifty years ago, when I was uninhibited and unaware of the delicate balance of the boat, I would have stuck my head out of the window and whooped with joy, just to enjoy the echo.'

'Just as well you haven't done that today,' I say primly as we emerge back into the light, 'or you would be forced to walk the plank by the fearsome owner-driver. She wouldn't tolerate any drunken sailor shenanigans on her watch!'

'There's loads of gates on the towpath,' Carole points out.

'And no cycling notices,' I say. They're not going to be choosing this as a possible stage in the Tour de France next year.'

'Of course not, neither do the snobby rich people want ordinary people walking along the canal path, it might obscure their view.' Carole pauses deep in thought, then a mischievous grin spreads across her face. 'Global warming will deliver their comeuppance when the canal overflows!'

Little Venice is home to a positive flotilla of barges, there is even one called Jude, the name my family have called me by for many a year.

'No gondolas,' Carole says.

'Ever the pragmatist,' Carole says. 'Stick to your semi then.'

Our poor put-upon conductress is rushing around desperately shutting the windows, the energy she expends is disproportionate to the slight drizzle that is falling. On docking at Paddington we watch the bossy fussy manager stride up and down the canal boat in an orgy of self-importance and irritation. As we disembark we hear the harridan, hereinafter referred to as Captain Bligh, berating the conductress for failing to close the windows properly.

'Good job we gave in over the cushions,' I whisper.

'Yea, she'd probably be keel hauled if they'd been found out of place.'

'Funny she's making such a fuss about nothing, I mean her docking was terrible, worthy of Leslie Phillips in HMS Troutbridge.'

Camden Lock: *There has been a small local food market in Inverness Road since the beginning of the 20th century but the current diverse markets only started in 1974 with the opening of a weekly Sunday crafts market. Situated on the Regents Canal between Camden and Chalk Farm stations the group of smaller markets, collectively known as Camden Lock now open seven days a week and are the fourth most popular visitor attraction in London.* www.camdenlock.net

Cyberdog: *is a trance music and cyber clothing/ accessory shop situated in the Stables Market at Camden specialising in way-out fluorescent dance clothing. It's worth a visit even if you don't like the music or clothing to explore its cavernous depths and experience the futuristic design of the items on sale (often modelled by the shop assistants) and the sci-fi fitting rooms.* www.cyberdog.net

CHAPTER THIRTEEN

The line divides at Camden, one going in the direction of High Barnet, the other to Edgeware so we discuss which line we should take first, but having no real knowledge of either destination it is a conversation entirely lacking in substance.

'I visited a friend in High Barnet once,' Carole says. 'I always wondered where Low and Middle Barnet were.' That is no help at all. We consider tossing a coin, but then a train comes in and I suggest we get on it and see where it takes us. As a result we end up in Kentish Town and we're on our way to High Barnet.

Kentish Town

We emit squeals of delight as we arrive at the station. What excites us is the writing of Kentish Town in huge capital letters using an old-fashioned script on the wall tiles.

'Pale cream tiles,' Carole murmurs as we step off the train, 'set against the name of the station picked out in burnt sienna.'

'Sounds so much more classy than off white and brown,' I say. 'Don't you think it announces the place in a bold way that captures something of the old romance of the tube. Imagine being one of the early travellers thrilling to the speed and the ease of the journey.'

'Yes and almost choking to death from the smoke of the steam engine. Very romantic!' snorts Carole giving me her *get real and smell the excrement look.*

'Even better, imagine being Bumper Harris.' I continue. 'Do you remember him?'

'How could I forget a one legged man on an escalator?' she mutters dismissively. 'Perhaps TfL should have a Bumper Harris day when everyone has to pretend to be a unidexter. It would bring a whole new meaning to 'hop on the tube.' I've been very taken with Bumper since we learned at Clapham Common that he was the one-legged man employed to ride the escalators and reassure the public of their safety when they first opened in 1911, but Carole insists that it was all a stunt, that they probably had to ply him with alcohol to get him on there and that he wasn't called 'Bumper' for nothing.

Carole is taken with the name of this station and *goes off on one* as people say.

'I think it was named after a bloke called Ken who sneezed a lot and he had a cat called Townie, and they came to London because they believed the that the streets were paved with Kleenex.' She's being very silly so I ignore her and look about me.

'There's an historical, almost decadent feel to the station, don't you think?' Carole asks and I agree, in spite of the modern metal seating and florescent lighting. These effects are countered not only by the colouring of the tiles, but also by the large antique brass clock with roman numerals.

'Oh, look,' I enthuse, 'it's got hands with those heart shaped holes just before you get to the pointy, this is the time bit.' Now one of the things I like about Carole is she understands what I'm talking about.

'It's exactly the same clock as they have at Tooting Bec Station,' she says.

'Yea, it's a self-winding clock, now isn't that clever. They were made in New York in the 1920s. Now why, in a time of financial crisis, was the London underground ordering clocks from America?'

'Search me but however much they cost they're pretty good value for money if they're still going and keeping good time,' she observes. 'Bet there aren't any digital clocks that will still be working in the 22nd century.'

The lady who announces the trains also enunciates her words perfectly and has a voice that is very easy to listen to because it has a natural warmth to it. Carole and I could stay all day, but duty calls. As we are about to leave the platform we notice the doors of a train shut on a man's suitcase and one of the wheels falls outside as the train pulls away. Carole picks it up and waves it at the departing train in a pointless gesture of sympathy.

'I wonder how he'll get on without it?' I say.

'He'll just have to call his case Bumper Harris,' she grins. 'He'll have fun on the escalator with it'.

'I wonder what else gets caught in the doors and is parted from its owner.' Carole and I leave the platform giggling in a very unseemly way for matrons of our years.

We ride up the 70 APE escalator.

'The ads are very close together,' Carole says.

'True, our means of measuring the length and height of an escalator is extraordinarily inaccurate,' I say as if I care, but neither of us are bothered. There's only one exit so we know that we are out of town and in the sticks. We go through the barrier and look for a mapette. There are none so Carole queues up at the ticket office to ask for one, but I see where they are and nip back through the barrier to retrieve them, but then I can't get out. I've only just come through this barrier and that machine knows it. I discover, the hard way, that London Transport won't let me through a second time. I have to ask a man nicely and when he does let me through, look suitably apologetic.

We wander outside and stare at our mapettes; this announces to passers-by, *we are visitors here and don't have a clue about where we're going next,* which inevitably draws attention to ourselves. We have been very lucky so far in that the attention we have drawn has been of the, *Can I help you?* variety, not the, *you don't know where you are so I'll steal your handbag* sort. This time is no exception. There's a man selling the

Evening Standard in the old days before they gave it away free. He sits outside the station and he watches us so I catch his eye; we fall into conversation, learn his name is Mike, and then we're all the best of friends.

It turns out to be Mike's birthday today so he tells us something of his life story. He used to be a sandblaster working on historic buildings such as The Tate Gallery, Westminster Abbey and The Houses of Parliament until his career and his left arm were cut short in an accident. He's an interesting raconteur and we spend some twenty minutes happily chatting. His stories focus on his time working at the Houses of Parliament and the famous people he came into contact with. He tells us about Maggie Thatcher's insistence that all the Portland stone for the repair of the Houses of Parliament should come from Britain rather than the cheaper French Portland stone.

'The Houses of Parliament were made by British men using British stone and that's how it should be,' he alleges she said in his hearing.

'How can Portland stone come from France?' Carole asks, and Mike tells us but this bit of information is now lost in the mists of time, geology never having been either of our strong points. We don't know why it would be cheaper in France, and we don't ask, he might just tell us.

We remark on the tidiness of his papers which, despite his disability, are arranged with the utmost precision. He dislikes his obsession with order and neatness which he blames on his birthday sign, he's a Virgo. This reminds us that it is his birthday today, so we offer to sing him 'Happy Birthday' which we would have done, loudly, with gusto, unashamedly, and got innocent and less extrovert passers-by to join in. He declines our offer.

'Wise man,' Carole says.

Coffee calls and we go where Mike directs us. Crossing the road we come to two alternative venues and we're not sure which one he's recommended. One looks like a café and is called Mamma Mia, the other looks very much more upmarket, perhaps it's a wine bar.

'Definitely the sort of place where you'd get Balsamic Vinegar whereas the café is the place where you'd get Sarsons,' Carole says. Sarsons wins the day and we are not at all disappointed. I order a ham salad which has loads of ham and yes, I am offered oil and Sarson's vinegar. The service is good, coffee very pleasant, bill probably half the price of the place next door.

'There are four churches in this area,' Carole says examining the mapette, 'and two have the same name.'

'Which is?' I ask.

'Luther Tyndale.'

'Why not have one called Martin Luther and the other William Tyndale?' I ask, but this is a question we can't answer.

'These churches believe that when you die your soul goes to sleep,' Carole says. 'That would do me, I don't like the idea of my soul wandering around and frightening people and causing trouble when I'm dead.'

'Your soul would be pink, in the shape of a flamingo, so a little strange, but not too scary,' I say reassuringly.

We leave the café and having found nothing on the mapette of interest, we wander round the local streets. There's a mixture of housing here, though most prevalent are large Victorian houses that have been converted in flats. Some look run down and neglected, but then as we turn a corner we come upon a row of houses with neat gardens containing interesting plants adorning the space they occupy, as opposed to those that have just landed there by chance and flourished in the Darwinian competition against all the other weeds. The curtains in the respective houses are a bit of a give-away. Clean and matching, the house is cared for: dirty and hanging at odd angles, the owners are not coping too well. I'm glad I'm not making these judgements about my own house.

'The dogs must be literate round here,' Carole says pointing at a special paving stone which contains a canine poo prohibition warning.

'Well I haven't seen any dog faeces so it must work,' I say.

Back at the station I buy a newspaper from Mike which comes with a free magazine called ES. I hadn't seen anyone else pick it up and as soon as I open it the reason becomes apparent. It is devoted to *fashion* and I sit on the train contemplating a picture of several stick thin, unhappy looking young women in long evening dresses dragging a deflating hot air balloon across a muddy field. I point to a caption which identifies one of the dresses as a design by Erdem and priced at £4,577.

'That would be a stupid thing to do even if she'd only paid a tenner in Primark, think of the mud sticking to the hem of her dress,' comments Carole.

'And who on earth is Erdem?' I ask superciliously.

'Some French designer I expect,' she replies. 'After all erdem is an anagram for 'merde' which is French for…..' Fortunately the train has stopped and her final words are drowned out by the sound of the doors sliding open and the *mind the gap* announcement.

Tufnell Park

We no longer squeal at the sight of the name of the station announcing itself just as it did in Kentish Town, only this time, on close inspection, the colour of the letters is different from the previous station.

'What shade would you call that?' Carole asks.

'Maroon? Carole shakes her head. 'Magenta?' is rejected out of hand. 'Puce?' is offered in desperation and when that too is dismissed a coolness begins between us. I think of offering her mauve but I'm blowed if I will just so she can turn her nose up at it.

'Claret,' Carole says in a voice that brooks no argument. 'It's somewhere between Rich chestnut and Redcurrant glory according to the Dulux colour chart.' I soften and offer her terracotta. 'No,' Carole says in an unnecessarily strident tone of voice.

'Why not? What's wrong with terracotta?' I ask.

'It's like baby's dirty nappies after eating mixed vegetable puree.'

'Wouldn't that depend somewhat on the baby and the mix of vegetables?'

She doesn't answer me so I admire the platform which is concave, (curving inwards,) and so we can see each end wherever we sit. I like it, until we listen to the announcer's voice which is masculine and lacks the quality of the Kentish Town announcer. Not only does he lack warmth but he continually reminds us about not smoking which we're not doing anyway. There's the same clock as the last station on this platform, but it's not in such good nick and so fails to impress, it's time to move on.

We find the mapette at the small unimpressive station concourse and open it. A close perusal again reveals absolutely nothing of interest at all, the only place marked being Holloway Bus Garage. In desperation Carole asks the man on the barrier if there's anywhere of interest to go in the locality.

'Yes,' he assures us. 'You can go and see Stalin's tomb.'

Now this is where the comedy element of our visit begins. We believe him. On reflection, with the benefit of hindsight, I can't understand why we didn't laugh out loud instead of following his directions, entering into a long discussion about Stalin's life, and whether we could remember his first name. We set off up the road to catch the number four bus. We had been assured it would take us to Stalin's tomb, just get off by the hospital. This leads to an altercation.

'We can't catch a bus,' I say to Carole.

'Why not?'

'It's against the rules,' I say. 'We're tube travelling, not bus travelling.'

'Rules are made to be broken,' she says in her anarchist fashion which would have Stalin turning in his tomb and undoubtedly have seen her dispatched to Siberia.

'It will take us out of the area,' I say, but as fate would have it, we arrive at the bus stop just as a number four pulls up, and, without hesitation she gets on. Like a faithful unquestioning lackey I follow and we speed off to goodness knows where. 'We'll be off the map,' I say. I'm almost panicking. Now I know how those poor souls who were the first to sail beyond the horizon felt in the days when everyone thought the earth was flat. Carole has a very cheeky grin and I know that she's enjoying my conformist discomfort. We don't even know where to get off the bus except for *by the hospital* and I am reminded that my mother warned about people like Carole. When the bus turns right and I can see a large municipal building, I call a halt. We've gone far enough. We've gone too far in my estimation and I mutter under my breath about how difficult this will be to write up. I really think Carole should tell me to shut up at this point, but she's far too kind.

'Where now?' I say looking to Carole; she's got me into this mess.

'We could go into the hospital and ask for Stalin,' she suggests.

'Probably not,' I say and point at the sign that says 'Highgate Mental Health Trust.' 'If we go in there asking for Stalin they'll probably admit us.'

For want of a better option, we set off up the hill.

'I'm a bit surprised that Stalin's buried in London, aren't you?' I say to Carole.

'Perhaps it's a sort monument to him rather than his tomb,' Carole offers.

'But the man at the tube said, Stalin's tomb.' It never occurs to us to question the wisdom of a London Transport employee.

'What was Stalin's first name,' Carole asks and a long pause ensues whilst we search the recesses of our brains, and continue to pant our way up the hill.

'Joseph,' it's just come to me. 'I remember because the Russian people used to refer to him as Uncle Joe.'

'That's right,' Carole says, 'they looked on him as the father of the people, didn't they.'

'Yes, and many wept at his death, I heard it on a recent radio programme.'

'Amazing considering that he was responsible for the deaths of millions of Russians through his ruthless five year plans, purges and wholesale persecutions of those he thought opposed him.'

'I expect his mum was proud of him'. We pause at the top of the hill.

'Why do we even want to look at his tomb?' I ask, and then we both have an epiphany.

'It's not Stalin's tomb that's around here, it's Karl Marx,' Carole says. I've just realised it too and we laugh long and loud at our own foolishness. It's an embarrassed, aren't we silly sort of laugh, a we should have known better laugh.

'He's sent us to Highgate Cemetery hasn't he?' Carole nods.

'Yup,' but we still don't know where it is.

'Should we challenge him when we get back?' I ask.

'Nah,' Carole says. 'He'll probably say, seen one Russian, you've seen 'em all.'

A little further on we come across Waterlow Park. We read the information board telling us about the history of the place and spot a café on the map which we head for. I get all excited because part of Waterlow Park is formed from Andrew Marvell's garden.

Never heard of him,' Carole says dismissively.

'He's a poet and author of a poem entitled 'To His Coy Mistress,' written to urge a young woman to enjoy love and how he would spend an eternity praising her beauties, but there just wasn't the time. I recite a bit:

> The grave's a fine and private place,
> But none I think do there embrace.

He talks about worms trying her virginity and what a terrible waste that would be, in an effort I say to Carole, to get her to *come across*, using a vulgar modern phrase so that she gets the message. Being something of a poet herself she recites her own version. It's a bit shorter and not so lyrical as Marvell's, but I leave you to judge for yourself.

> No time to dally, for time's a drag,
> Off with you knickers, let's have a shag.

Hm.

The ghost of Marvell does not rise up in horror so we continue to weave our way around the park looking for the café because I think it's time for a cup of tea. We are directed by various people, all in the wrong direction, and no one thinks to tell us that the café is inside Lauderdale House which we don't see anyway. We give up and leave this lovely park which was donated to be a *garden for the gardenless* by Sydney Waterlow, a generous gesture that still stands as his memorial. We award him posthumous Dave status.

Continuing up the hill, my SEFPS locks on. This is what Carole has named my Starvation Enhanced Food Perception System. It enables me to focus on locating a suitable eating establishment when I'm peckish. I point out to Carole that it didn't work in Waterlow Park by which time we gain the top of the hill and we're in Highgate. There are charming shops and best of all High Teas of Highgate.

'This will do nicely,' Carole says so we enter into a very pretty pink painted room full of people taking tea and have to squash ourselves into a back room that is already occupied by two young women with large pushchairs and a child apiece. We are given a menu and in the way of research, using my best Queen's English accent, I order a slice of chocolate cake. The things I do in your interest dear reader! The tea comes and we sip elegantly, fingers cocked in a self-congratulatory gesture. Having ordered the cake, I give you the report. Well, it was moist and had just the right density, it was clearly made with the finest chocolate as it was not too sweet and yet the chocolate taste filled the mouth. It had chocolate icing on top, not too much, not too sickly and chocolate icing in the middle. I persuade Carole to help me out with it, and generously, she does, but equally generously, she doesn't have much.

'I never know when I might need to squeeze into an evening dress so I can pull a deflated hot air balloon through the mud,' she says with a wry grin.

We fall into conversation with the two young women who are the owners of the pushchairs and mothers of the children that sit in them. We learn that they have been to Lauderdale House to a baby Mozart session. One child is called Dylan, the other Bryn, almost a Magic Roundabout duo. Dylan's Mum is very friendly and she tells us that he will be one in two days time. As she leaves to go into a slightly chilly autumn afternoon we watch sympathetically as she tries to make him keep his hat on. She puts it on, he takes it off.

'I'm going to win this battle,' she says smiling. We smile too and keep quiet thinking that the smart money is on Dylan. I'm ill advised to ask if he's got to go home to compose his first symphony. Bryn's Mum gives us directions to Highgate Cemetery where we won't see the grave of Stalin as he is buried in Moscow, but we will see that of Karl Marx. We've got to walk through Waterlow Park again and we already feel that we've spent half a lifetime there. Perhaps Carole will compose another of her charming poems.

Fortunately our way through the park is downhill and by now it's busy with small children enjoying the fresh air and facilities after a day at school. We find the way by ignoring my instincts and going with Carole's. We look at the London Cemetery which has daily guided tours during the season – the season for being dead I wonder, but no, it's the season, as in summer time.

'Isn't winter time an appropriate time for indulging in one's taphophilic tendencies?' Carole suggests.

'What's that mean?' I ask resentfully thinking she's being patronising.

'You don't know what taphophilic means?' Carole asks. She's definitely being patronising.

'No,' I say in a bored voice. 'Do tell me, please.'

'It's an unhealthy interest in graves. Not something I have. I mean what sorts of people have huge mausoleums?

'Dead ones?' I offer.

'All right, but why? They take up so much space for a start – just imagine if everyone who had ever died had a monument, or even a large gravestone, the whole country would be covered in mausolea.' Carole has to stop to pause for breath.

'Is that a real plural, mausolea? It sounds like something you'd get treatment for at the Royal National Nose, Throat and Ear Hospital.' She ignores me. I don't think it's a real plural, I think she's just made it up but I've already been intimidated by taphophilia.

'If everyone had a large gravestone,' she says giving me a severe look, 'engineers would have to construct a Great Britain shaped mezzanine floor for us to live on. What's wrong with putting bodies out for the vultures to eat, and then the bones could be made into xylophones? I bet you could play some interesting tunes on Karl Marx.'

'The Parsis do that. They take their dead bodies to The Towers of Silence and leave them on slats so that when the sun and the vultures have disposed of the flesh, the bones fall to the bottom of the tower.'

'A xylophone factory,' Carole says lightening our conversation.

We pay £3 to go into Highgate cemetery and are given a map to assist us in locating what Carole calls 'the dead famous'. The minute we enter we are overwhelmed by the sheer number of graves. We orientate ourselves and set of in the direction of Stalin, oh no, I mean Karl Marx's tomb.

'George Eliot's grave is near Marx,' I observe, scrutinising the map. 'I'd like to find that too'.

'Wasn't he a woman?' asks Carole. 'Not that it makes any difference when you're dead. Incidentally,' she adds studying the map again, 'I see neither William Tyndale nor Martin Luther are buried here.'

'Just as well. Their souls wouldn't get much sleep in a place as busy as this.'

'Yeh, if it's not the taphophile tourists it's the Parsis playing their xylophones all night.'

We continue our discussion about the need we witness all around us to erect huge tombs and write epitaphs for the deceased.

'It's all very unhealthy,' Carole says 'I prefer the practice carried out in Varanasi in India where the bodies of Hindus are cremated and their ashes are committed to the Ganges. There's a humility to it.' It's a quality which is very much lacking in Highgate Cemetery with its competition for the biggest statues and mausoleums. It's not raining, but it is very damp and dull, and the proximity of the graves one with another, and the variety of statuary, slab and inscription, together with the lushness of the surrounding vegetation inculcates a feeling of overweening depression.

We arrive at the place where Karl Marx is buried. There is a marble plinth and on top a huge head of Marx.

'My goodness,' Carole exclaims, 'his head is the cranial equivalent of a 40DD bust.'

'No wonder he was so gifted, a philosopher, a political thinker, a man who wrote about economics and social history,' I say.

'I know that his influence on the twentieth century has been profound, but do you really think he'd have wanted such a bloody great monument?' Carole asks. 'I thought the same about Jesus when I went to St. Peter's in Rome.'

Call me prosaic, but I can't get over the magnificence of his head of hair, even his facial hair has a thickness to it seldom seen. Well, not in dead people.

'WORKERS OF ALL LANDS UNITE,' Carole reads from his monument. 'Hah! That's ironic in the light of the current recession induced xenophobia.'

We walk about a bit looking at various graves.

'I find this too depressing,' Carole says. 'I don't approve of turning this cemetery into a museum and charging people to go in and stare at the gravestones of famous people. I can't help thinking about their various states of decay. At least when you go on a conducted bus tour of Hollywood there's a chance you might see one of the stars whose houses you stop to ogle.' She wanders off to sit on a bench leaving me to find George Eliot on my own.

I consult my map and make little sense of it. I meet up with some women from Birmingham and we fall into conversation about how crowded the cemetery is and how difficult it is to find the notables. Finally, depressed and fed up, I give up and go off to join Carole. I'm some distance away when one of the Birmingham ladies calls me back. She's found it and I turn round and go and stare at a marble slab and obelisk which marks the grave of George Eliot. I'd like to be moved, but I'm not.

Carole's sitting on a bench watching squirrels eating berries. I look at the leaflet and start telling Carole about the people whose graves I'd like to see. I pick out Radcliffe-Hall who wrote *The Well of Loneliness* an early book about lesbian love, and also Mrs. Henry Wood another novelist whose name is the antithesis of lesbian love. She was diminutive woman who wrote some rather sensational novels, my favourite being *East Lynne*, a novel about marital infidelity, infant death, redemption and forgiveness and contains some really sensational twists and turns. I would like to pay my respects to Stella Webb who was better known as Stella Gibbons, author of *Cold Comfort Farm*. If you haven't read it, do so now.

Immediately, drop this and go and immerse yourself in that comic masterpiece. I would also have liked to see the grave of Christina Rossetti but it needs a degree of determination, time and patience to root out the inmates and my liking for the task is not sufficient to the effort required.

'Squirrels don't bother with tombs and gravestones. They're blissfully unaware of their surroundings,' she says as we watch one tuck in to a cheery red berry.

'They just get eaten by foxes.'

'I wonder if foxes can play the xylophone?'

Waterlow Park: Bequeathed by Sir Sidney Waterlow in 1889, the 20-acre park is bordered on two sides by Highgate Cemetery (as we eventually discovered). Historic Lauderdale House is situated within its grounds as well as three ponds, six tennis courts and an infant playground. It has friends, but not a page on Facebook.
www.waterlowpark.org.uk

Highgate Cemetery: This Grade I listed cemetery is in two parts, East and West, situated on either side of Swains Lane N6 6PJ. It was opened in 1839, one the first of seven large modern cemeteries built around the outside of London. The nearest tube station is actually Archway.
www.highgate_cemetery.org

CHAPTER FOURTEEN

Archway

'Sparkly floor, my favourite,' I say to Carole as we alight from the train at Archway Station. Sitting down on the metal regulation tube seat my initial excitement is replaced by disgust as I glance at the ceiling. It's had nothing done to it for years and is a dingy white which is just waiting for a makeover.

'That clock looks as if it's been lobbed up there,' Carole says.

'I don't like modern clocks that have marks instead of numbers,' I say. Carole looks at me kindly as she would at an idiot. She attempts to distract me.

'Hey, there's no Mind the Gap here,' Carole says.

'That's terrible,' I'm deeply shocked. Carole pats my hand consolingly.

'There's no mind the gap, because there's no gap, somebody's actually hit on the idea of making the train fit the platform,' she says.

'I knew a woman who was blown off the platform between the carriages of a stationary train in the gales of 1987, not on the tube of course.'

'No room to squeeze a cat between the carriages of a tube,' Carole says.

'And there's no bobbly bit to tell the short of sight or blind drunk that they're at the edge of the platform.'

'A dangerous station,' Carole says.

'That digital display could do with a wipe,' I add, however, the Way Out sign is brightly illuminated so we take its advice and leave.

We travel up a 35 APE escalator. We locate the mapettes in the small, rather nondescript foyer.

'Look,' I say accusingly. 'This is where we should have visited Highgate Cemetery.' I stare at Carole. She takes the wind from my sails.

'That's the modern cemetery shown on the map, the famous one is behind Waterlow Park.' I'm deflated.

'What about visiting Lauderdale House?' I suggest, anxious to make amends for my angry outburst.

'I can't face another trip to Waterlow Park,' Carole says. 'There's a lot of places named Whittington around here.'

'Do you think there's any association with Dick?' I ask but we're unable to answer the question. There's a large hospital which we subsequently learn was originally the site of a leper colony, but we're not in hospital visiting mode and Carole needs the loo.

Outside the station a very busy junction which is overshadowed by the hideous building Archway Tower confronts us. We cross the road to a pub called The

Archway Tavern. I stand outside and wait whilst Carole disappears inside and I get into conversation with an Irish man who tells me that Archway Tower used to be owned by the DHS and is now commercial offices. He tells me there were plans to pull the thing down (good) but it was decided that it would cause too much disruption at a very busy junction and so it still stands (bad). He also says that

there's usually a terrible wind pattern created around the station due to the location of the tower in relation to the prevailing wind – another reason to knock the ugly thing down. On the railings opposite Archway Tower there are lovely flower baskets that cascade nearly to the ground and brighten the place up no end. Well done local parks and railings flower authorities. There is oddly a disconnected abandoned lavatory on the pavement which I point out to Carole as she emerges from the pub.

'It was quite deserted inside which made sneaking past the bar to the ladies difficult. I was trying to be unobtrusive and nonchalant.'

'A hard act to pull off successfully,' I say.

'Isn't it odd how God works in mysterious ways,' Carole says and I wait. I know there's more to come. She studies her mapette.

'There's the Salvation Army Citadel and eight other bastions of Christianity in this location and I have to go into one of the Devil's Houses for relief.'

'What about going here?' I suggest to Carole, pointing at an area with interesting road names in a small location not far from the station. 'Lysander Grove and Mews, Miranda, Prospero, Parolles and Cressida Roads are all named after characters in Shakespeare's plays.'

'Let's visit them,' Carole says and so we do. In the process our pronouncements sound like a cross between estate agents and those two women who have become television celebrities by cleaning the houses of hygienically challenged members of the public. We comment on the state of the house and garden, the colour of the paintwork, the condition of the front gate and walls and in particular, the nasty nets.

We start off in Lysander Grove.

'Lysander belongs in *A Midsummer Night's Dream*,' I tell Carole, 'he's one of the lovers who spends the night running around the woods outside Athens whilst fairies mix things up for him.'

'Happens all the time,' Carole says. The road is neat, its houses well kept and regular so we pass into Miranda Road.

'Miranda is the daughter of Prospero in *The Tempest*, all innocent of the world having been brought up on an island by her father and never seen civilisation.' Carole nods humouring me, she's not really interested. 'Some of these houses in Miranda Road look barely civilised with their unkempt front gardens and dirty nets badly pinned up in the windows.'

'Hey, that's good,' Carole says, and for one foolish moment I think it's my analogy that she's referring to, but no, she's pointing to an upstairs window where a young woman is seated looking out of the window. I'm just thinking it's rude to point when I realise I'm looking at a model. We look at the motionless unnerving presence of the manikin staring unblinkingly down at us.

'Weird,' I say and we are busy discussing the stylish clothes it is dressed in when we are politely asked to move aside so a lady can access her house. She tells us that when it first appeared she thought it was the young lady who occupied the upstairs flat and thought it very rude of her not to return her wave.

We turn into Parolles Road, and I'm at a loss. He's a character from that very odd play, *All's Well that Ends Well*. Where to start in explaining the plot? I won't, even I think Shakespeare was having an off day when he wrote that one. What might interest Carole?..........hmmm

'In this play, the main character Betram is tricked into having sex with one woman who he doesn't fancy, whilst he thinks he's having it off with someone else who he does fancy.' Carole stares at me as if I'm mad.

'Was he drunk?'

'No. He has to creep into the bed in the dark and not say anything,' I explain.

'And then creep out again before she has a chance to say anything?' Carole snorts in derision. 'The plot with the fairies mixing things up is more plausible.' I'll never get Carole to see the point of the bard's plays.

By the time we reach Prospero Road we've become inarticulate in our architectural admiration saying things like: 'Ooh, look at those lovely thingies over the door,' and, 'I do like those sticky up bits on the roof.' It's not a very enlightening conversation.

'If I lived in London this is the sort of road I'd like to live in,' Carole says and I nod in agreement, I like the names. We pass by a builder who is standing back admiring his handiwork. 'Nice houses,' Carole says gesturing in the general direction of the surrounding area. He's a proper builder, sucks saliva through his teeth, shakes his head and tells us that many of the properties need underpinning. He points out a nasty crack in a house opposite and we see what he means.

'Gosh, this house expert stuff isn't as easy as it seems,' I say to Carole and we press on down the road to Cressida (don't worry, I'm not even going to try to tell you,) past Meadows Organic Hairdresser.

'What other types of hairdresser are there?' Carole asks. I don't know so I don't answer.

'Cressida Road goes downhill as it goes uphill,' I observe. 'The state of the houses deteriorate as the gradient rises,' I explain.

'So does my tolerance of this becoming a presenter on *Relocation, Relocation,*' Carole says. 'Let's find somewhere to eat.' Now that's unexpected, it's usually me who suggests a little snackeroony first.

We turn into Flowers Mews and come to a place called La Voute. We enter. Carole's in a hurry and asks for something that is quick. She is pointed in the direction of goats cheese quiche and salad. It turns out to be no ordinary quiche and no ordinary salad. Carole tucks in and is soon, very strangely, waxing lyrical about the grub.

'This meal is a delicate, flavoursome combination of ingredients, the quiche is light but oh so tasty, and there are four different salads incorporating asparagus, broccoli and mixed beans in a yummy minty dressing.' I'm amazed that she's recognised the quality of the food, but I know that she's right because my soup is delicious and the texture and flavour of the bread divine.

'It's a tragedy that we don't have time for pud,' I say eyeing the cakes and tarts seductively displayed on platters behind the counter.

'They're luring diners to a premature cholesterol induced death,' Carole says.

'Be worth it, the food here is just wonderful,' I say.

'It's undoubtedly the best fast food I've ever had.' I can't quite get over Carole's enthusiasm, it's the first time she's understood that food can be terrific. I say so.

'I think the problem is that my food isn't terrific and so I seldom think about it.'

'I think about food most of the time,' I confess.

'I wonder if you think about food as often as young men are supposed to think about sex,' Carole says.

'Eh?'

'But come to think of it, how do those that bandy such observations about know how often young men think about sex? Do they attach a sexometer to their brains?'

'Do you know what the word bistro means in its original language?' I ask anxious not to pursue the former topic of conversation for fear of descending into hopeless vulgarity.

'No,' Carole says.

'It's derived from the Russian for 'quickly' I say. 'It came up in a quiz last week.'

'I suppose Cossacks in a hurry en route to the next pogrom would shout 'bistro' at the waiter,' Carole says, but there's no pogrom waiting for us, just Carole's pressing need to get on. We would have liked to spend longer in this lip smacking lunch location but needs must, so on our way out we compliment the chef.

'If there's any justice in the culinary world that young man will go far,' Carole says.

'Yea, he'd look good on tele,' I say.

'Trouble is he hasn't written a book yet and that seems to be the prerequisite of stardom,' Carole says.

'When he does I'll buy it for you. You can add it to your other cookery book,' I say sniggering. I know exactly what it is, she's shown me, it's called *Cookery in Colour* by Marguerite Patten and it was a wedding present. Nothing wrong in that I agree, but most of us who began with Marguerite Patten have progressed and I own a couple of shelves of cookery books. Carole currently has the one.

'Oh my goodness,' Carole exclaims, pointing at Archway Tower, 'how come I didn't notice that when we left the station.'

'Well I saw it,' I say. 'I had a conversation with an Irishman about it. I think you were too preoccupied with the state of your bladder and your mapette.' We both stare upwards at the great grey slab of a building. 'It's newer than the Colliers Wood monstrosity.'

'Mmm, and being inhabited it lacks the ghoulish desolate quality of its younger sibling,' Carole says. She's decided they are related though. 'But it towers over the surroundings like Darth Vader in the land of the Ewoks.'

Back at the station we scurry underground like a pair of frightened Ewoks. We have to use the spiral staircase which is encased in a giant metal tube. The notice at the top of the stairs says there are 113 steps so we don't bother to count them. At the bottom the sign says there are 96 steps.

'So where are the missing 17 steps?' I ask Carole.

'Ah,' she says sagely, 'if you walked back to the top would that then say 96?'

'I don't think I'd walk up that many steps even if Darth Vader was coming to get me,' I say as our onward journey continues.

Highgate

We step off from the tube train onto a very brightly lit station with a long straight platform.

'Hey, the train doesn't fill the platform,' Carole says and we stare in wonder at the gap at the end of the train.

'We've never seen that before,' I say, 'there's room for one more carriage.' It is however the only interesting thing about the station which is bland in the extreme. Cream tiles with pale green borders cover the platform side of the wall and the train side is nearly devoid of ads except for six all clustering around the area opposite exit. An announcer booms out from the loudspeaker. We cringe, cover our ears, and when she's stopped complain to each other about the volume. The next announcement is quieter.

'Do you think we might be being watched?' I ask Carole. 'Can they hear us?' Carole's more interested in the content of the last announcement which informs us of southbound delays due to a derailment at Morden.

'It might have been a rebel train that decided to jump the rails to escape from a subterranean life. Or a Northern Line saboteur?' she suggests. I know she's trying hard to make this an exciting station, but honestly, not even the knowledge that Jerry Springer was born down here can make it come to life.

We leave the platform and ride the seventy-seven APE escalator. This merely takes us to a large airy foyer and the exits where we pick up a mapette and do our usual head on one side, where shall we go act. The nice man on duty who is called Bryan suggests Highgate Cemetery.

'Been there, done that,' we mutter, mostly to ourselves. 'And it's very gloomy,' I add.

'I'll probably end up there,' Bryan says cheerfully, a big smile on his face, 'but I'd rather be next to my mother in Jamaica.'

'Well I'd rather be in Jamaica just at this moment, but alive,' Carole says, 'what do you do on an overcast cloudy autumn day with a chilly wind blowing?' Bryan recommends a visit to Highgate Woods and coffee in the café which sounds good to me. In order to exit the station we have to go up another escalator of 76 APE proportions.

'Gosh, this has got to be the deepest station,' I say to Carole and our subsequent research confirms that it is indeed the deepest on the London Underground. How thrilling.

Highgate Woods is delightful at this time of year. It's full on autumn and the leaves are beginning to turn and to fall. I am amazed that Carole doesn't know about leaf catching so I initiate her into the game which is as simple as the name suggests, you just have to catch leaves as they fall off the trees. It sounds very easy but is fiendishly difficult as leaves are light and flighty things and you can have one in your sight that's spiralling down and your hands are outstretched and then a puff of wind blows it in a completely unexpected direction.

'What to do on a cold windy autumn day,' Carole says once more, 'run about like a mad person ensuring that everyone gives you a wide berth because they think you're on an outing from the local MENCAP centre.' In order to encourage Carole and so she experiences the true beauty of the game, I turn it into a bet, first leaf caught wins, loser pays for coffee. I'm confident of my victory on account of being an experienced leaf catcher (I'm also a dab hand at catching falling snow on a wooden spoon, but that's another story), so when the novice Carole has an oak leaf drop straight into her hand I try to make it best of three but she's having none of it. I'll have to pay up.

We find the Pavilion in the park and I think it's charming, but Carole is less than impressed. Unfortunately there's really only room to sit outside. Carole looks grim.

'Look, this veranda is covered over,' I say pointing to the thick plastic cover attached to the overhanging roof.

'But it's not covered at each end so it's like sitting in a wind tunnel,' Carole complains. 'And I bet we'll have to wait forever to be served.' I have to admit that the wind has got up a little, but Carole's had her say and kindly agrees to stay.

'You see one of the differences between you and me is that I'm an outdoor type,' I say.

'Oh yes?' Carole says with raised eyebrows.

'Yes, I relish the idea of camping, living in a yurt, kipping in a wigwam or living in a caravan, which I did for two years as a teenager.'

'Well you'd hate it now. I bet that after the first cold night when you had to take a trip outside to the facilities you'd change your mind. I'd be hard put to say which you'd miss most, your washing machine, microwave, dishwasher, Hoover, central heating, oh, of course, it'd be your electric kettle.' I have to concede that she's got a

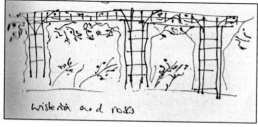

wisteria and roses

point. We sit at a table and I have my back to the pavilion so I'm in a position to admire the veranda with its wisteria which gently climbs the trellis, and the last remaining frail rose being blown about in the wind. I draw what I see and Carole watches me.

'We could include your drawings in our book,' she says and I'm thinking, well they're not that good, and she adds; 'Just for comic effect.'

The waitress takes our order and we have to have the pavilion toasted sandwich. Whilst we are waiting we are entertained by the man sitting next to us. He fusses about where he sits and changes his place three times. He asks for the heater to be put on which turns out to be one electric bar situated high up on the wall. I doubt if it has any effect at all and after all the disruption he's caused I hope it doesn't. He insists on giving the waitress his order before his companion has had time to look at the menu, and is generally a very diverting pain in the arse. I can't help thinking that Carole is enjoying this about as much as he is, but she's far too polite and considerate to make everyone else's life a misery by behaving as badly. The food comes quickly. The coffee is very good and the toastie is dead hot. Carole takes a bite and red hot tomato and liquid cheese oozes out burns her mouth.

'Have you noticed that the children have names like Oliver and Geraldine,' Carole says dabbing at her scorched lip. 'This place strikes me as being colonial, give or take a bit of sunshine, about twenty degrees Celsius and the odd elephant or camel.'

We watch as a mother ushers her young child onto a bench seat in front of one of the plastic windows, assuring him that, 'it's snug in here Sebastian.'

'That's a blatant lie,' Carole says quietly, 'it's a bloody wind tunnel.' Carole calls for the bill which comes quickly and so the shivering one is released from her torment. 'I thought my frostbitten bum might have become welded to the seat,' Carole says as we leave.

Our exit route takes us through the Flora and Fauna centre.

'It's like a huge nature table in here,' Carole says as we step inside. The centre, which is a wooden shed, is stuffed full to the gunnels with exhibits of the things that grow, live or feed in the park.

'This is just great for Primary school teachers,' I say and it's clear it's been visited by many as we can admire a variety of children's work on display around the room. I particularly like the centre's display of cut bits of wood which we can pick up and feel. The pieces of wood have labels so that we can identify the different species, but because nothing's fixed they've all been moved around from their proper places so we still can't tell a hornbeam from wild service tree or a rowan from a robina. Can I suggest Highgate Wood Information Shed that you stick the label onto the pieces of wood? We take some leaflets and would like to put something into a collecting box but there's none available – now there's another useful suggestion.

'How about another game of leaf catching?' I suggest as we walk back through the wood, I'm anxious to restore my reputation. Carole agrees, just so she can run about a bit and thaw out. I win with a plane tree leaf which Carole thinks was easy. 'Just because it's large doesn't mean a lack of skill,' I say. With a smug smile she delves into her pocket and holds up the tiny oak leaf that just happened to drop in her hand during the first game.

We wander down Archway Road past a parade of grand Dutch fronted shops. Most have seen better days, but the posh manicurists or hairdressers with the name of E. Scissor-Hands have undergone refurbishment in the modern minimalist style and look very swish, but they aren't doing much business, however, the other hairdressers with nothing like so grand premises called ROOTS is seething with activity with many customers waiting, chatting or having their hair plaited or put in to dreadlocks.

'There's a moral here somewhere,' Carole says indicating the contrasting two establishments. Next I spy a book shop called *Ripping Yarn.*

'Let's go in,' I say enthusiastically. 'It looks great.'

'It'll smell of mildew and wet dog.'

'My favourite perfume,' I say.

'That dates you, don't they say fragrance nowadays?' Carole asks. 'I've never really been one for fragrances,' she continues, 'but I found bottle of *Black Rose* in the deep dark depths of my make-up drawer, it's a perfume I used to wear when I was a teenager and with only one sniff I was transported back to 1959 and dances in the local church hall on a Saturday night.' She sighs wistfully as I steer her into the bookshop.

It's very well organised and I wander around the children's section finding an old *Girl* annual and ripping stories of *Jo and the Chalet School.* Carole mooches about picking up books with silly titles. She comes over and disturbs my almost transcendental state of deep concentration and insists on sharing them with me. We start with *Roundabouts from the Air* a book of completely uninspiring photographs which don't look as if they were taken from the air at all, but from the top of a bus. Next she shows me *A Year in Wales.*

'If this stuff can find a publisher we should certainly be able to too,' she says.

Leaving the delights of the second-hand bookshop behind, we continue on down Archway Road past an RSPCA shop. Our attention is drawn to a large yellow and black sign which says, NEUTERING STOPS AIDS IN CATS.

'It probably stops AIDS in people too,' Carole says. 'Funny how nobody ever suggests it as a cure for the spread of the disease in human society, isn't it.'

'Condoms for toms has a ring to it!'

We arrive at the entrance to our tube station in a side road full of trees and leaves, and find we have to descend four flights of steep steps to locate the foyer. It's the first station in the northern direction that has a really rural feel to it. Of course it occurs to me that Highgate must have been just that, a gate set on the top of a high hill. My research suggest that the name derives from a tollgate which was situated at the top of the hill to pay for the new road constructed under the orders of the Bishop of London in the fourteenth century. Imagine getting to the top and not being able to pay to carry on the journey – at least it would be all downhill on the way back.

'Why is Highgate station so far from Highgate village?' Carole asks.

'No idea,' I say, and with an unanswered question hanging in the air we descend back down for the onward journey.

'East Finchley next,' I observe studying the northern line map on the wall. 'Finchley must be big, it's got three stations to its name, East, West and Central'.

'It's north London's answer to Clapham', chirps up Carole. 'Do you think they're twinned? Tripleted even? Do you think students go on exchange visits and the mayors turn out to make grand welcoming speeches...' I ignore her.

'I think we ought to do them all together,' I say. 'But I don't think we've got time today'.

'A trilogy of Finchleys. Sounds like a saga.'

'Why don't we do Mill Hill today and the Finchley's next time,' I continue

'It's just a little spur' Carole says dismissively as we troop down the stairs.

'There were once plans to make another station at Mill Hill and then join the line up with Edgware. That would have made sense,' I add.

'Probably why it was never done,' she says.

Mill Hill East

Because Mill Hill East is an offshoot, a line all on its very own, we feel as if we are travelling into the unknown. We have to travel to Finchley Central and change trains. Our journey is now in the light of day and out of the window we can see wide-open green spaces and lots of trees.

'There seems to be quite a drop here,' Carole says, and I can see that she's right as we peer down at the road below, then we arrive at the station. We step out onto the single platform and walk to the front of the train to look at this end of the line place where we can see two red lights and then the buffers. We chat to the driver whose job it is to take the train backwards and forwards from Finchley Central to Mill Hill East. When he arrives at Finchley Central he gets out of the driver's cab and walks the length of the train and gets into the driver's cab at the other end of

the train. When he gets to Mill Hill East he gets out of the driver's cab and ....
Well, you know what's coming. He does this for two and a half hours. He likes it
because he gets some fresh air and exercise, but he's not so keen when it's pissing
with rain. He tells us to look at the Dollis Brook Viaduct, the highest point on the
Underground.

'We are enjoying extremes today,' Carole says, 'Highgate the deepest, the line to
Mill Hill East the highest.'

The station is very attractive in a quaint wooden weatherboarding way. We
admire the frieze at the edge of the roof which is cut into a pleasing medieval
banner shape, such detail normally associated with above ground stations, but of

course, this is an underground
above ground station. Funny that,
eh? There are trees aplenty here
and the platform is littered with
swirling leaves. There's a dear
little waiting room which we
promise to sit in if we have to
wait for a train when we get back.

Outside we look back at the
station building which is small
and neat. Walking down some
steps, we find ourselves on a wide road, opposite there's a sort of small factory site
all locked up behind high metal fences.

'It's rather rural here,' I say to Carole studying the mapette.

'God forsaken,' Carole mutters searching in vain for something of interest.
'There's no church in the square mile but plenty of golf courses, fields and some
allotments.'

We decide to take a wander in the direction of Dollis Brook and admire the
viaduct. It's not far away but it's just that, a viaduct and sadly the map's right, the
place is mostly residential and unremarkable. We pass a few shops, a vet with a Pets
Triage service, a Paint-a-Pot Coffee shop and come across a huge Waitrose. Carole
wants something for her tea so we pop inside. She goes in search of bananas and
comes back with a lemon yumyum which she eats, complaining that it's not lemony
or yummy enough to live up to its name.

As we leave it starts to rain quite heavily and I smugly produce my umbrella
whilst Carole puts up her hood.

'You look like a street-wise granny,' I say.

'You look like Mary Poppins,' she replies. We walk back to the station and Carole takes my picture in the rain, just to prove we've really been here as it's been a bit of a damp squib this visit.

'Well, if you like golf or gardening then Mill Hill East has its attractions,' Carole says.

'Not forgetting the size of the Waitrose.'

'And that maisonette we passed which had a notice on the door saying NO SPAM.'

'What's so good about that?'

'It just reminded me of the Monty Python sketch and it made me giggle.'

Much to our chagrin we find the waiting room locked. We look longingly at the seats and the shelter from the wind inside the waiting room. An elderly lady who has been waiting to meet her sister for the past two hours looks tired and in need of a seat. I suggest a mobile phone would have solved her problem, but she's having none of it. Fortunately her sister arrives on the incoming train. Carole and I wave to the driver as he transfers himself on his well trodden path from what is now the back to the front of the train, and he greets us like old friends. Then we're off, away from our diversion on the branch line and back to the main line.

Archway tower: built in 1963 and initially the property of the UK government, it was sold off in the late 60's and rented back on a 42year lease. It is currently an office block and its future hangs in the balance.

La Voute: There are a few reviews on the net and they are all five star. Well worth a visit if you're in the area: 10 Archway Close, N19 3TD

Highgate woods: Originally part of the Forest of Middlesex mentioned in the Domesday Book, this 70 acre area of ancient woodland is now 'managed' by the City of London. According to point 6 of the management plan:' Using Ratcliffe's systematic evaluation of Woodlands, Highgate Wood is of importance'. *The Pavilion Café is quite attractive and probably worth a visit on a sunny day. You can access the wood from Muswell Hill Road, N10 3JN.*

CHAPTER FIFTEEN

East Finchley

Half way between Highgate and East Finchley we pop out into the daylight. I don't know why it's so surprising but it's very welcome. It's a real pleasure to be able to look out of the window even though the scenery is unremarkable because initially we can only see the train track bank flanked by yellow railings. We arrive at a large, bright four platformed station.

'The train's not in a hurry to leave,' I say to Carole, 'and neither was the southbound train.'

'Ah, she says sagely, the driver's busy gathering his rods and cones and waiting for them to readjust.'

'And the train going in the opposite direction?'

'The southbound drivers are lingering before they enter the abyss.' She's in poetical mood today.

We look about us and notice the architecture of the station which dates from the 1930s, with metal framed windows and circular glass stair wells with architraves forming a neat circular effect.

'So pleasing,' I murmur.

'That's one of your favourite words,' Carole says and I instantly resolve never to use it again as it's obvious I'm overusing it. 'This station looks as if it's the product of a deliberate design process rather than something that was tacked on as an afterthought,' Carole says, and she's quite right, its effect is harmonious, and well, pleasing, oops no, that's really the last time, I promise.

We sit on the seats that are under a little shelter in two rows that face each other. It's nice and chummy from a social point of view, but it's a dull day and we look longingly at the waiting room which is on the other platform – isn't it always? We listen to the announcements.

'She's got a lovely warm voice,' I say to Carole.

'Yes, but it's edging on being patronising. I can almost hear her say: *The train arriving at platform 2 will terminate at Morden, because there's no more line left, but you wouldn't know that you bunch of morons and I don't suppose you can read Morden on the sign at the front of the train or on the digital display where it's been clearly visible for the last five minutes. Please mind the gap because we think you're all so stupid you won't notice and won't extend your foot far enough to get into or off the train you half-wits.'* Oh, if only they would broadcast such a message, what a shock we'd get.

We fall into conversation with two northern line railwaymen who are on their way to another job and they ask if we've noticed *Robin Hood* who they refer to as the emblem of the Northern Line. It's a statue of an archer sculpted in Art Deco style; he kneels on a plinth on top of the main entrance to the station, and with his bow drawn, he appears to be aiming with some concentration as if he has just pulled, or is pulling that stringy bit.

'Where's the arrow gone?' Carole asks and the men explain that the Archer is supposed to have shot the arrow down the tunnel to Morden.

'There was an arrow put up on a plinth at Morden when this statue was erected,' one of the men tells us, 'but it was nicked after a couple of weeks.'

'Good old Londoners,' Carole says. It's clear that our two new mates are in no hurry to get to their next job because they continue waxing lyrical about the statue.

'The Archer's symbol of the Northern Line representing speed and precision,' we are told without a trace of irony, well I suppose we can't argue. We've spent a lot of time on the tube by now, and it's been speedy and so far gone straight to the places it says it's going to. 'The statue's called Archie by the locals around here. It was unveiled in July 1940 and cost £240 pounds,' the talkative one of the pair continues.

'If the current financial crisis isn't solved by St David and St Nick we'll all end up paying that for a tube ticket,' Carole says as I begin to back away from the men, the demands of my bladder calling an end to the conversation.

We exit via the steps under the platform leaving me wondering what the stairs above ground are for. We head for *The Old White Lion* turning right out of the station which gets not so much as a cursory glance from me, my steps are getting shorter by the minute. Much to my distress, we find the pub shut which is a shame as it's very attractive with pointy roofs and white paintwork. The pub used to be called *The Dirt House* because much of the manure deposited by the horses in London was sold in East Finchley to the local farmers who consequently were renowned for producing magnificent hay crops. Well I never, but that doesn't solve my current difficulty.

We turn round and retrace our steps walking up the High Street which is in fact the Great North Road. It's a curious mixture of affluent suburbia containing an Italian trattoria, a fish restaurant and an upmarket shoe shop called *Koko* next to derelict shops and offices, betting shops and greasy Joe cafes. We walk briskly up the hill and for once not wanting coffee or anything to eat I go to Costa and beg a favour from a nice black woman who doesn't at all mind me using the facilities in spite of no purchase.

We've picked up a mapette which comprises a meagre single sheet but concerns about my continence have prevented us from its perusal.

'There's not much here,' Carole says, 'other than a synagogue and a convent.'

'And Archie,' I add. 'I'm sure it's a very nice place to live, its tube station is remarkably airy giving a great service into central London.' I'm always the one who looks on the bright side, sees the positive.

'But as for things to do and places to visit there's not an awful lot,' Carole says dismissively.

We walk on past some very pleasant shops and go into a second-hand bookshop where we both buy children's books. Carole's is hilarious. It shows how children think machines work on one page and on the next explains how they really work. I am particularly taken by an illustration of cats licking plates clean inside a dishwasher. We go into the Hospice shop which smells of mothballs and second hand clothes and leave quite quickly.

'Look at that,' I say pointing at a very attractive green grocer's shop. My attention is riveted by an exotic looking green vegetable with pointy florets all patterned in smaller pointy spirals. 'I bet those patterns follow the Fibbonacci sequence,' I tell Carole. She nods wisely as if she knows what I'm talking about and I'm impressed.

We stare down at the vegetable whose label tells me is a Romanesco and I decide to buy one and eat it, which I did. It was very tasty, much better than cauliflower to whom it is related. Carole takes a picture of the window of a very smart shoe shop which has a mirror on its back wall so we're in it too. She's funny like that.

On our return to the station, we bump into two more railwaymen waiting for a train. A particularly voluble Irishman called Chris proceeds to regale us with statistics. All trains are 120m long, comprising six 20m coaches and can achieve speeds of up to 45mph. The open air section of the line is between East Finchley and High Barnet and he assures us that there is abundant wildlife in the grassy banks on either side of the tracks. The distance between East Finchley and Finchley Central is 2300m but between Finchley Central and Finchley West, a mere 800m. Our new friends' train arrives and we wave them off whilst contemplating the information they had imparted. Carole starts.

'So, what they told us suggests that Finchley Central has been misnamed since if it were central, it would be equidistant from East and West Finchley. By rights it should be called Finchley West of Centre, or Westish,' she says, but then our train arrives and hopping on board, contemplating our long haul to Finchley Westish, and subsequent short haul to Finchley West proper, we travel onwards. During our 2300m journey I ponder the next question Carole poses.

'Why does the direction come first in East and West Finchley, but the name of the town takes precedence in Finchley Central? Could this possibly be a subtle recognition of the fact that Finchley Central isn't actually located in the centre? Think on.'

Finchley Central

With the question of Finchley's centrality still unresolved, we arrive passing by sidings where we can see trains waiting repair. The station is very similar in design to East Finchley except for the modern, out of keeping lift.

'Hideous,' Carole says looking at its stone cladding. 'Prince Charles would condemn that as the carbuncle of the Northern Line.' It doesn't stop us using it to go up to ground level to exit the station.

'All this Finchleying is making me hungry,' I tell Carole, so we walk up the side road to the main drag and come across *Bites* which serves wonderful mushroom soup.

'Only three measly slices of bread from an anorexic baguette to accompany your potage, will that be enough?' Carole asks, but I'm too busy soup spooning to reply. The place is scrupulously clean and the only oddity is the stepladder which is stored in the ladies toilet, but it's all right as it's a clean stepladder.

We've decided not only from our perusal of the mapette, but also from an advertisement at East Finchley to visit Avenue House where there is a museum dedicated to the history of Stephen's Ink.

'Finchley is actually quite rural,' Carole says looking at the mapette, 'generously endowed with sports grounds, playing fields, allotments, a park and a golf course.' From the comfort of the café we plan our route unsure if we can get into the grounds of Avenue House via Glenhill Close. Determined to live dangerously we set off. It turns out we can't, but I'm glad we paid a visit there as it's a road of 1930s style housing with the same consistency of décor and design that so delighted us on East Finchley's station. The houses are painted white and have curved bay windows, and all have turquoise blue paint on the window frames and doors. It's a very quiet cul-de-sac and there are plenty of trees and piles of leaves to kick our way through.

Finally reaching the grounds of Avenue House we see a Victorian mansion set in beautifully landscaped gardens incorporating an impressive arboretum. It looks particularly stunning as the autumn red of the leaves and brilliant well-watered green of the grass provide a striking contrast to the white and cream of the building.

'I could live here,' Carole says
'Yes, imagine summer parties on
the lawn. All the family could come
and stay and I could hide when
they all started to argue,' I say
wistfully. I imagine my
grandchildren playing amongst the
pendulous branches of the huge
weeping beech, so large they have
to be propped up by two substantial metal poles.

We enter via the front of the building and admire the proportions of the hallway and look towards the large reception room where weddings are held. We are directed to a smallish room which is stuffed full of museum exhibits tracing the life of Dr Stephens who invented the original indelible ink, and his son Henry who developed it into a lucrative business. We are greeted enthusiastically by a highly articulate volunteer curator who is delighted to share her extensive knowledge of the history of the area in general, and of the Stephens family in particular. Ink is arguably not the most fascinating subject, but the combination of the social and economic concomitants of its development, interwoven with the family history made for a fascinating story.

Whilst admiring documents that were written more than 150 years ago which are still clearly legible, we learn that the inventor of indelible ink, and founder of the company was a medical doctor, Henry Stephens who trained with the poet John Keats. Dr Stephens was fed up with the time he had to spend mixing inks which quickly faded so he invented a new fluid which became the basis for the founding of the family business and cemented the family's fortune. His ink looked blue when being used, but dried black. Being superior to other inks on account of its indelibility, it became the ink used for ship's logs and legal documents, and this is still the case today as a legal requirement. His son Henry Stephens, known colloquially as Inky, built a factory in Finchley and expanded the business considerably. He bought Avenue House and grounds which on his death he willed to the people of Finchley.

'They knew how to philanthropise those Victorians,' Carole observes looking at a picture of the inventor Laszlo Biro in the part of the museum dedicated to the development of writing. 'I bet he didn't leave anything to his community except a load of empty ball point pens,' she said clutching the biro that she intended to buy - oh the irony.

We walk back through the woods revelling in the autumn sunshine. .

'That woman was so well informed,' I say.

'I can imagine her on Mastermind, specialist subject: Stephens Ink 1832 – 1918.'
With this thought lingering we reach the tube station and set off on our adventures
again, ready for the final Finchley.

West Finchley

We have been warned by the lady curator that there is nothing of interest to see
here. Undaunted we alight at a much smaller station than East Finchley comprising
only two platforms. Sitting on the platform I can hear birdsong and a dog barking.
This is the most rural station so far, a comment I make to Carole.

'Positively bucolic,' she says. The southbound platform boasts a pretty white
wooden building.

'I'm expecting Bernard Cribbins to emerge from there,' I say to Carole pointing
in its direction. She catches my drift immediately.

'Yes and Jenny Agguter to appear in a pinny clutching a red flag made from her
underthings,' she says.

'Funny that such an attractive woman should have such an odd name, I mean it's
really Jenny A Gutter isn't it?'

We are both distracted by the noise of the rails which twitch and vibrate as a train
approaches. That's a first; another first is toilets on the platform.

'There's a plethora of facilities in the Finchleys,' I observe.

'It does rather suggest an ageing population,' Carole says.

'And a local council mindful of their micturative needs?' Carole nods in
agreement as we leave via an attractive metal latticework bridge over the line which
is painted white and green.

Wandering down from the station towards a row of shops we stop to look at our
mapettes. A man in his early 30s holding the hand of small child stops and asks us
if he can help us. He's breathtakingly attractive with a wonderful head of wavy hair
and the tiniest beard on his chin. The boy is a diminutive version of himself. We
say we want to go somewhere of interest and he laughs. Carole suggests the Scout
Hut – yes, we are that desperate. He says it's just a wooden building behind the
shops. He says if we do find anything of interest to put it on the internet and he'll
pick it up, but he's right, we don't.

'Well that encounter was a testament to the power of nature over nurture,' Carole
says, 'especially where hair is concerned.'

'Yes, that kid couldn't have been anyone else's, even his hair was like his Dad's,' I
say ruefully.

'I get my inferior pilosity from my parents,' Carole says, 'thinness from my mother and softness from my father.'

'My hair's like my Dad's, thin, greasy, double crown, widow's peak, cow's lick.' If anyone deserves sympathy for the short straw in the hair department it's me, I'm not having her stealing my thunder.

We make for the parade of shops but rarely have we seen such an uninspiring collection of retail outlets. There's nothing to capture the imagination. Taking the road bridge over the railway line we discover that there is nothing of interest here either and we can't gain access to what looks like the 'pretty' entrance to the station as this one is only open during the rush hour. The only notable artefact we encounter on our tramp through the suburban streets is a cracked mirror left out for the dustmen.

'Stand there,' Carole says and I do as I am told whilst she takes an arty picture of the mirror reflecting my naughty pink shoes, those of the recalcitrant laces. 'It's small miracle that you haven't tripped over them,' Carole says, 'I don't know why you persist in wearing those shoes.'

'They score ten out of ten for comfort. I like the colour and it's given us a talking point and countless opportunities to stop.' Well that's my story and I'm sticking to it. 'It's a good job that mirror is on the ground,' I say, 'I'm sure my hair looks a mess.'

'After our encounter with the West Finchley angel of wavy locks it's not surprising that you feel that way. Three Finchley's is enough for anyone,' Carole says stifling a yawn, and so we cross the footbridge, pausing only for me to retie my laces. Sorry West Finchley, we wandered round your streets but only found unremarkable suburbia. It was worth it though to meet that attractive man.

Finchley East: Originally a Great Northern Railway station in 1867, the original building was demolished and rebuilt to an Art Deco/Streamline Modern design by Charles Holden in the late 1930's. Eric Aumonier created the 10ft kneeling statue known as The Archer, *also the name of the local community newspaper.*

Stephen's Ink Museum: Avenue House is situated in East End Road, a short walk from Finchley Central station. It shows aspects of Henry Stephens life, as well as the history of the Stephens Ink Company, Avenue House and the development of writing materials. It is open from 2pm – 4.30pm on Tuesday, Wednesday and Thursday and is free. www.london-northwest.com/sites/Stephens

CHAPTER SIXTEEN

Woodside Park

'It can't be any more boring than West Finchley, can it?' Carole asks as we step off the train at the very rural Woodside Park station.

'I like that nice pointy valence hanging down from the canopy which covers the platform,' I say looking about me, enjoying the view of the trees and admiring the wooden buildings which complement the station's rustic charm. There's a chill breeze blowing.

'I like the look of that waiting room,' Carole says.

'But will it be open?' I ask.

'Most we've come across so far have been locked, haven't they. Perhaps that's why they're called Waiting Rooms, you have to wait for them to be opened.' We try the door. It opens. We step into warmth and a room which still smells of fresh paint. We sit on the newly varnished bench and admire the colour scheme, the pale green walls with contrasting dark green skirting boards, windows and door panels. It's scrupulously clean. We use the facilities and here we find a fault. The ladies lavatory needs a jolly good dose of bleach, and then several more doses.

'Let's not be hypercritical,' Carole says, 'this waiting room is definitely four star, even if the toilet facilities are only two.'

We strike out prepared to brave the heart of darkest Woodside Park, our exploratory zeal undiminished by the bland West Finchley experience. We leave via the covered bridge over the line. As we are on the bridge a train approaches the station so Carole whips out her camera and takes a photograph.

'It looks so small,' I say.

'What does?' Carole asks.

'The train. In the confines of a tunnel as it comes roaring onto the platform the tube train makes quite an impression, but out here it is sort of diminished.'

'I know what you mean,' Carole says. 'Look at that little signal box,' and we admire its pointed roof and as the wind swirls around our legs we imagine ourselves snugly ensconced inside, enjoying a cup of tea whilst worrying about changing the points every so often.

'Oh come on,' Carole says, 'I had enough of *The Railway Children* at West Finchley.'

Leaving the station we ignore the charms of a bijou coffee stall in the open, sure that we'll find something better all warm and cosy with seating. This does prove to be foolish fancy. We walk up the road and round the block seeing large Victorian houses, in-filled with small blocks of modern flats, some more attractive and in keeping than others.

'This place is quite deserted,' Carole says.

'We haven't passed a single shop, cafe or pub,' I say forlornly.

'Well unless you're an architect or an estate agent, there's not much to excite at Woodside Park.' I look at the mapette.

'The place is well provided with schools and churches,' I say.

'And there's a park,' Carole says, but the wind remains chill and we're in no mood for wandering about in the damp getting our shoes muddy. 'Spike Milligan lived in Holden Road for quite a long time,' Carole says and I brighten visibly.

'We'll go there.'

'The house was demolished some time ago,' Carole says. Just then a leaf floats past my face and I make a grab for it. Carole starts singing the Ying Tong song, and that's it.

'I'm not sure we've done this place justice,' I say as we return to the station.

'Let's get out of it,' Carole says. 'I'm sure it's a pleasant place but to live, but the good thing about the tube is that you seldom have to wait more than five minutes to leave for your next, and potentially, more exciting destination.'

So we do.

Totteridge and Whetstone

'I'm looking forward to this station,' I say as the train rumbles through the leafy suburbs.

'Why?'

'Because the curator lady in the Stephen's Ink Museum mentioned the whetstone as a place where men used to sharpen their swords in days of yore.'

'How long ago is yore?' Carole asks.

'I don't know, let's find out.'

The station is strikingly similar to Woodside Park except for the waiting room.

'The step's slippery,' Carole says as we go inside.

'This is horribly Spartan,' I say looking round at two scratched wooden benches, a bare concrete floor, walls in need of a coat of paint, and it's unheated. We don't linger. Crossing a rusty bridge to the exit we arrive at the ticket office which sports the notice, CLOSED. We can see the mapettes inside as well as several men milling about. Carole is unabashed, knocks and asks nicely so we are given the vital information. How else will we know where to go?

'We need coffee and food,' I say and Carole agrees. We are spoilt for choice, just within sight of the junction between Totteridge Lane and High Road we can see Pizza Express, Ask, The Griffin Pub and The Popular Café.

'Where do you want to go?' Carole asks.

'Well there's only one choice really, it's got to be The Popular Café.'

'Why?'

'We need to check out the accuracy of its title.'

Inside we see why the café is so named. It's not so much the number of clientele, rather the proximity of the tables. In an effort to maximise profit the proprietors have seen fit to cram as many tables and chairs as is humanly possible in a space no bigger than the average lounge. Carole orders at the counter as I weave my way to a free table by the far wall terrified that my fat arse will sweep someone's coffee onto the floor. I arrive safely and cautiously slide into my seat in an effort not to disturb the man sitting at the table behind me. Carole joins me. The waitress brings our order and we watch nervously as she has too little room to manoeuvre. It is also impossible to have a discreet conversation, this, however, suits the man at the table behind who wants to share his views and recent life experiences with anyone within listening distance, which is in this case, everyone in the cafe. It's not only that his voice is loud, the pitch is penetrating. He talks incessantly and even his friends look bored. On a more positive side, the café's service is good, the coffee and food very pleasant. I reach down to feel in the pocket of my coat which is hung over the back of my chair and realise that I've put my hand into the pocket of the coat of the man sitting behind me, that's how close our chairs are. Fortunately he doesn't notice, he's too busy telling his friends some appallingly dull tale of something he did that was absolutely fascinating to nobody but him. We are delighted when he and his cronies leave and shortly after we follow their example. It's a pleasant place, but fewer tables would make it more popular with me.

We set off in search of the whetstone and find it about 200 yards up the road in front of an attractive pub called The Griffin. The stone is rather unremarkable, being square in shape, about 18 inches in height and that's all. I've been hanging on to a slender thread of excitement which is very nearly dashed when Carole says the stone looks more like a mounting block.

'But then if that were the case the tube station would have been called Totteridge and Moutingstone wouldn't it? So I'm going to believe in the whetstone theory,' I say in a huffy sort of voice.

'All right,' Carole says, and I think I hear her mutter, 'keep your hair on', under her breath. 'Stand there,' Carole orders whipping out her trusty camera in an attempt to lighten the atmosphere. 'I can turn this into an arty picture by including your shoes. How many times have the laces come undone today so far?'

'Twice,' I say and thaw as I watch Carole's crazy contortions in finding the right place to snap the picture.

'I'm going to have to take the whetstone from a particularly interesting angle in order to avoid the parked cars and miscellaneous traffic signs. They'll detract from its historical authenticity.'

'And the shoes?' I ask.

'Will add a surreally whimsical chronological counterpoint to the grey, grounded solidity of the stone.'

'Gosh! That's a load of pretentious nonsense,' I say.

'Yea, well think yourself lucky I don't want to amputate your feet and preserve them in formaldehyde,' she replies, coming over all Damien Hirst

We go inside the pub and look at the menu which makes us wish we'd chosen it instead of the overcrowded café with its boring one man show. The bar staff are pleasant and helpful and direct us to read all sorts of information about the whetstone.

'That writing's quite difficult to read,' Carole says peering at the pleasantly olde worlde script chalked onto a blackboard hanging on the wall.

'It probably came from days of yore.' We learn that the stone outside is only a *chunk* of the original. Soldiers would use it to sharpen their swords, and it proved particularly useful for the men en route to the Battle of Barnet who could hone their weapons on the way to the fray.

'As well as dropping in for a quickie to fortify their courage,' Carole adds. 'I suppose the Battle of Barnet was fought in the civil war?' Carole asks, but having read Henry VI, I tell her that it's one of the battles of the Wars of the Roses.

'They all came from the north the people who had an interest in fighting in the Wars of the Roses, and they all seemed to be related to each other in some way or other. It just goes to show that royal families are as dysfunctional as the rest of us.'

'We knew that already.' Carole says.

'Shakespeare's play Henry VI part 3 mentions the Battle of Barnet.'

'Oh yea,' Carole says in that please don't tell me any more voice.

'Most of the characters other than the two kings, Edward IV and Henry VI are places. There's Oxford, Exeter, Somerset, Northumberland, Westmoreland, York of course, Norfolk, Pembroke and Clarence.'

'They all had a long way to travel to get to Barnet just for a battle. Probably took them all of parts one and two to get there,' Carole muses.

'Do you want me to tell you about this play or not?' I demand shirtily.

'Not. Definitely not. Absolutely and categorically not!'

'That's a 'no' then?' I ask, trying not to look or sound hurt

'Affirmative. Just tell me who won the battle.' I still haven't managed to convert her to my way of thinking about Shakespeare and I might have to draw my sword on her yet.

'The Battle of Barnet was a victory for the Yorkists but they had to go and have another battle at Tewksbury.'

'Was it a rematch? Or maybe like in a football tournament where they have two legs? '

'I don't know,' I admit humbly.

'When was the battle fought,' Carole asks as we wend our way back to the station.

'Easter Day, 14th April, 1471.'

'And the Yorkies won?'

'That's right, and returned Edward IV to the throne. This battle was a bit silly because it took place for the most part in thick fog which caused the Lancastrians to attack their own troops.'

'Well it obviously needed a rematch then. They should have gone to a Battle Tribunal and claimed unfair victory because of fog on the pitch'.

'Uhuh.' By this time we have reached the station and it is with some relief we leave long lost battles and long dead playwrights behind.

On to the end of the line.

High Barnet

'What do you reckon will be waiting for us when alight at High Barnet?' Carole asks. 'A drum roll, red carpet and admiring London Transport staff holding out glasses of champagne?' she continues. We get just what I expect at this north-eastern end of the branch of the Northern Line, nothing.

We alight to look at where the rails cease and view the space into which they might have continued which is filled with bales of stones, small dry ones that is, in contrast to the single large whet one we saw at the last station. The bales form a sort of protective fence, I suppose in case the train fails to stop, overshoot the buffers and plough into the no-man's land beyond. The end of the line is a strange sight where the natural landscape takes over from the artificially constructed line, comprising an overgrown bank covered by shrubs and young trees. It reminds me that nature always wins and our attempts to keep it at bay are but temporary.

Carole stares at the sign warning passengers not to pass beyond the barrier or they will be prosecuted.

'The grass and stone beyond the gate are not electrified surely?' Carole says so I point to the sign that says: **Danger. High Voltage.** 'Well if it's that high there wouldn't be much left of any recalcitrant passengers who fail to heed the warning,' she says. I think she's feeling stroppy because we have both a sense of achievement, but also of sadness at the end of the line, even though we've still all of the Edgware branch of the line to visit.

'Stand there,' Carole orders and I stand to one side on the platform, pink shoe laces tied at the ready. 'Look wistful,' she says. I put my head on one side trying to attempt to carry out her instructions. 'I said wistful, not stupid,' I think I hear her mutter as she clicks away.

'Perhaps the barrier is there to stop passengers jumping the gate and disappearing up the hill?' I suggest.

'I'd like to leap over the gate and kiss the hallowed earth,' Carole says.

'Forgive me for pointing it out, but aren't your leaping days over?' Carole nods glumly.

'Yea, and I'd probably get a huge fine, not to mention miscellaneous sprains and strains, for what I suppose would be a pointless gesture of defiance.'

'But you do rather relish those gestures of defiance, don't you,' I reply.

'Mmm, and the older I get the easier it is to get away with it. I just adopt a vacant stare and look bemused.'

'When asked your name say 'Matron knows that,' in a feeble voice and wander off. Works for me every time,' I say. I am of course lying I've never said this, but she's not to know.

We head for the waiting room which is unheated but has its original fireplace. The weather outside is drizzly and unpleasant. Carole looks around.

'Now who would light and tend a fire in this day and age?' she asks. It's a rhetorical question. She's not expecting an answer. Of course no one would carry a bucket of coal to a waiting room to light and tend a fire. Thoroughly disappointed with the waiting room we leave and climb some steps and go over a rusty bridge that is desperately in need of a coat of paint. As so often happens as we look at our mapettes a very pleasant tube employee asks us if we need some help and mistaking us for walkers, offers to direct us to Hackney.

'Now why would you go to Barnet if you really wanted to walk to Hackney?' Carole says as we walk away from the station. 'Is there a secret tunnel?' I shake my head and hold up my hands in the gesture that means search me. 'Are the two places twinned?' Carole asks. 'Would you walk in those shoes? How long would it take us and how many times would your laces come undone?'

'He was trying to be helpful,' I explain, 'and being ladies of a certain age we offer neither threat nor promise to men and because they feel safe with us they proffer advice.'

'Don't they just,' Carole said, 'Next thing you know he'll be telling us Stalin's tomb is in Hackney.' I am left thinking that in my case they are right to view me as neither threat nor promise, but I'm not at all sure about Carole................

Misunderstanding cleared up, we are directed to the Museum of Barnet as a place of interest. Taking the steep footpath out of the station, Carole has an idea.

'Perhaps the Battle of Barnet was really fought between two groups of warlike hairdressers, charging each other with scissors and teasing combs over the rights to set up a chain of salons in the area.'

'Not so much the War of the Roses as The Cut and Blow dry Campaign.' We walk up the Great North Road, past pleasant shops and Barnet College which is in the process of being rebuilt and all we can see are the tower cranes looming over the site. Ahead is a huge church dedicated to St. John the Baptist. We stop to admire Hatherley House which was formerly a school in Tudor times.

We find the museum.

'Great!' Carole says, but she doesn't mean great at all because the museum is shut today. She's really disappointed. 'Just when my curiosity was aroused. I wanted to find out about the myriad manifestations of Barnet including High, Chipping, Friem, etc.'

High Barnet is a very pleasant place so we wander about a bit but then it starts to spit with rain so we take refuge in our usual haunt, a café in the park which is in a decent sized shed. The park is small but perfectly formed to use a cliché and everything is very well cared for.

'It's much neater than that scruffy display we came across in Finsbury Park,' I say.

'Eh?' says Carole absent mindedly.

'You know, the one commemorating 700 years of the worshipful company of barbers.'

'Perhaps it takes a battle to bring a little military discipline to floral displays,' she suggests. We look at the award-winning park having been given recognition for neatness and careful planting in 2008. Carole thinks it's a bit too uniform with its beautifully trimmed grass and neat pansied flower beds, but I like the regimentation suggesting order and control. There perhaps you have us in essence, she's a wild child at heart and me? I'm a Virgo, in need of a sense of order and control even though I know it's futile. Phew, what finding a cup of coffee can do for you.

Carole says we must have champagne when we get to Edgware and it's stopped raining when we leave. Off to pastures new as we say farewell, adieu to the northern most point of the Northern Line.

The Griffin: Situated in Whetstone, there has been an inn on the site of the present Griffin pub for centuries but the current building dates from 1928. The buildings to the left of it are late 15th century. Whetstone's name may derive from the stone in front of the pub but it is debatable whether this was used for sharpening swords and knives or as a mounting block. According to Wikipedia, Totteridge and Whetstone is the 63rd richest area in the UK on account of the number of multi-millionaires who live on Totteridge Lane.

Battle of Barnet: An important battle in the Wars of the Roses fought on Easter Day, April 14th 1471 between the Yorkist king, Edward IV and the Lancastrian Earl of Warwick who had changed his allegiance. Like most wars it was all about greed and power and the usual chaos of the battlefield exacerbated by the foggy conditions which resulted in one of Warwick's commanders attacking his own side. Twit.

Barnet Museum: opened in 1938 to house the collection of Barnet and District local history society. It houses archives, objects, prints, photographs, paintings and maps reflecting the development of High Barnet and the surrounding area and a collection of period costumes, accessories and domestic items. However it is likely that, from April 2011 both this and the Church Farmhouse Museum will have its funding withdrawn, so may not exist by the time this reaches print. www.barnetmuseum.co.uk

CHAPTER SEVENTEEN

Mornington Crescent

'I've washed my hair,' I tell Carole. She looks at me critically. 'Why didn't you comb it?' I refuse to answer. I don't want her to know that I got up late this morning, but not even the mess that is my hair, on this quite spectacularly bad hair day can curb my mounting excitement as the train pulls in to the Xanadu of the Northern Line.

'Legendary,' is all I can say as I step off the train into this iconic station. 'We should kneel,' I whisper reverently.

'Nah,' Carole says out loud, 'my knees are too old for all that malarkey.'

You will only understand our excitement and reverence, well mine, I'm not so sure about her reverence, it seems to me that Carole doesn't do reverence – gosh, you'd think we'd had a bet about how many times I can get reverence into one sentence, oops, losing the sense of the sentence now. I repeat, you will only understand if you listen to Radio 4's, *I'm Sorry I Haven't a Clue*. If you've never heard of it skip the next paragraph as it will be meaningless to you, and I really don't want to waste your time.

The programme *I'm Sorry I Haven't a Clue* has for many years been one of the very few broadcast comedy programmes that has had me consistently weeping with laughter into my washing up water. An essential part of every programme is the playing of Mornington Crescent, a game whose rules have either been lost in the mists of time or there has never been a standardised version, who knows the truth of the matter? There is little agreement about their origin, some asserting that this game involving players in turn naming over-ground and underground stations in the environs of London, in a particular order, should conform to those published in NF Stovold's 'Mornington Crescent: Rules and Origins' but, like many other aficionados, Carole and I have firmly held opinions. For example, when playing the game we always adhere to the Armitage rules, no doubles, no shuffles and no Nid. Neither of us will tolerate the Old Etonian version where a player can be caught In Pop, but we do use Burlington's original rules where a WC postcode counts double, crescents are wild as rule 42 is suspended until Tooting Broadway is played, appropriate for us, as it's one of our stations, on the Northern Line.

So here we really are, on the station and we're not disappointed. Beautifully tiled walls in cream with a dark blue border and the words MORNINGTON CRESCENT picked out in claret; a paved gleaming platform; solid wood platform furniture in mahogany, including a glass fronted cabinet which holds the fire extinguisher all exude class. The announcer is female with a slightly patronising tone.

'Not many passengers are there,' Carole says.

'This is the most select of stations,' I observe.

'A palace of subterranean transport,' she adds.

'Look, there isn't even a gap to mind,' I say.

'Trains and platforms evolved to symbiotic perfection.' I mentally decide to take back my comments about her lacking in reverence.

Tearing ourselves away from the platform we find that there is a lift and the 66 steps up to the ticket foyer are only to be used in a real emergency.

'Why?' Carole asks, but I don't know any more than she does, and I don't encourage her otherwise she'll start going on about what constitutes a *real* emergency as opposed to a pretend one. The lift takes us to the ticket foyer which has splendid old-fashioned green tiles topped by a big agapanthus frieze. There's huge trunking on the ceiling for the wiring of the security cameras.

'Perhaps this is to prevent Mornington Crescent fans from trying to chip away a bit of the station to keep as a souvenir,' I say.

'There's about one camera per passenger,' Carole notices.

'I remember when this station was closed,' I tell Carole.

'Yea, it was shut for most of the 1990's and there was talk of it closing permanently. Mornington Crescent fans got a campaign going so they gave it a complete refurbishment.'

We stand under the plaque on the wall telling us that the station was reopened by members of the cast of *I'm Sorry I Haven't a Clue*, including the late Humphrey Littleton. Next to it is a commemorative plaque in memory of the late Willie Rushton.

'He was my favourite,' I tell Carole as we have a quiet moment.

Outside we notice the date of the opening of the station in 1902, and admire the exterior which has the same brown tiled façade and arched windows as the Elephant and Castle. Having emerged into the sunlight on the Hampstead Road we consult our mapettes for the eponymous crescent but our eyes are immediately drawn to the left to a very large white art deco building. It's imposing by virtue of its size, symmetry and the Egyptian decoration on the pillars with two large black panthers flanking the steps up to the entrance. We walk towards it and Carole notices the word Carreras on the façade which she tells me used to be a brand of cigarettes.

'Let's go in and find out what goes on here,' Carole says as we approach the doorway and I trail behind her hoping we don't get thrown out. As we step inside the door the fire alarm goes off and we are almost bowled over by the rush of retreating employees who sweep us back down the steps onto the street. Anxious to learn more about the building I approach a man in a pink cardigan who is standing by a pillar lighting a cigarette – not a Carreras one. He turns out to be a good choice of interlocutor and tells me about the history of the building now known as Greater London House, which was formerly the Carreras cigarette factory.

'Ironic that you now have to leave to have a smoke,' Carole says and the man nods ruefully.

Carreras was the name of the Spanish nobleman who set up the company. He had a shop in Wardour Street known as The Black Cat shop because his cat used to sit in the window and the name was transferred to his brand of cigarettes

'So that's why the building has eight foot tall black cats as statues,' Carole says.

'Yes and cats' faces along the frieze at the top,' the man points out.

'We're really here to see Mornington Crescent,' I say.

'Ah, now that's why the planning laws were passed,' Mr. Pink Cardigan tells me. My word he's a veritable Stephen Fry of information. 'When the factory was being built the residents objected strongly, the building being sited on their communal gardens, and spoiling their view of the corresponding crescent and park opposite. It didn't stop this factory from being built but it ensured that permission had to be granted in future.'

'Yea, so ugly buildings were only built in working class areas,' Carole mutters. We thank the man and bid adieu, making our way round the back of the old Carreras factory where we see Mornington Crescent in all its glory. 'It's a shadow of its former self, isn't it,' Carole says and I nod.

'It's certainly seen better days.' We can see why the residents objected to losing their garden and their view being wrecked. They would formerly have had an expansive view over parkland, now their horizons are limited to the ugly back of a former factory. The only consolation is that it's painted pristine white. We look at the crescent.

'It's like the curate's egg,' Carole says. 'Good in parts.' We wander along trying to peer into people's windows. I point out a nice duvet cover to her, she shows me a dining table elegantly laid for eight. We come to Clarksons Row and peer down the small cul-de-sac, then set off to explore. We come to a dead end - a tall brick wall.

'Wonder what's over there?' I say. It's my day for asking questions I know that Carole can't answer. Again, Carole doesn't reply, she just climbs up and peers over the top so I have to do it too. 'Oh!' I exclaim in disappointment.

'What were you expecting?' Carole asks as we cling precariously to the wall looking down at the mass of railway lines below. 'Daniel Craig filming the next James Bond movie?' We climb down and are glad to return to the second half of Mornington Crescent which is much like the other half. I point out a large house with a huge porch and an old faded sign with HOT showing.

'What was hot that was on offer?'

'It was probably a hotel,' Carol says looking at me in that sympathetic you can't help being so thick sort of way and I smile ruefully.

'It's the worse house in the crescent,' I say. 'Look at that balcony sticking out from the first floor, it looks dead dangerous and crumbly to me.' Carole looks up and moves away.

Reaching the end of the Crescent we cross the road to a large central island and look up at the statue of William Cobden.

'What did he do?' Carole asks.

'He was responsible for the repeal of the Corn Laws,' I say.

'You're a mine of information today,' she says.

'It's written here,' I point out on the statue, 'but I do know a bit about the Corn Laws thanks to a remarkable history teacher.'

'Oh yes, what made her so remarkable?' Carole asks.

'She was very thin, and physically frail but she was completely terrifying. She was truly the most formidable teacher I ever came across. I used to spend history lessons thinking of ways to kill her.' Carole is shocked so I have to reassure her I was only day-dreaming; the poor woman died from cancer a year before she was due to retire, not by my hand.

'And the corn laws?' she asks.

'Well they were terrible for the poor keeping the price of bread artificially high and benefiting wealthy landowners. Cobden championed the cause of the poor.'

'So he was a philanthropist,' Carole says, 'and he's carrying on his philanthropic work by providing a perch for sunbathing pigeons.'

We walk about a bit more and go into the local library.

'This is like taking a child into a sweet shop and saying, help yourself,' I say to Carole as I look about me overwhelmed by the opportunities on offer for the local residents. I'll give you a flavour. You can enter the Bedford Open Poetry Competition and win £300 if you come first. You can go to Bethnal Green, to the Museum of Childhood, and do a fascinating variety of free activities. You can visit UCL's Museums and see their science and medical collections or their Ethnographical collection or bits of rock in the Geology display. Carole and I study the leaflet.

'That does look like fossilised vomit,' Carole points out.

'Look,' I say drawing Carole's attention to a series of events to bring together practitioners from the worlds of psychoanalysis. She raises her eyebrows and I'm not sure if she's interested or not but see she has been distracted by an Age Concern leaflet entitled: *Later life as an older lesbian, gay or bisexual person.* I spot *Nordic Walking in London and Surrey.* The cost of these escapades is quite reasonable at £5 for an hour, £7 for half a day or £12 for a full day. But the most mystifying aspect of the leaflet is the reminder to *bring your own poles* (with a small 'p').

I leaf through a free paper, the Camden Gazette, but Carole tries to drag me out of the library. Desperately I point out a competition to win tickets to a Cliff Richard concert and Carole is ecstatic.

'Thank goodness, it's too late to enter,' she says.

'What about Hampstead Comedy Club? They're offering a gig with a comedian who is described as being *post humour.*'

'Probably works for the Royal Mail,' Carole says. We stop at the counter and ask the librarian on duty if there's a leaflet which enables people to praise the facilities on offer. He smiles ruefully and shakes his head.

'We've got these though,' he grins apologetically indicating a *DO YOU WANT TO COMPLAIN ABOUT US?* leaflet which is prominently displayed. The leaflet is available in Bengali , Somali, French, Farsi, Chinese, Lingala, Albanian/Kosovan and can be obtained in Braille, in large print or on a CD. Carole takes one as we walk out muttering:

'I'm gonna complain about the lack of praise and commendation forms'.

Chalk Farm

'Oh yes,' Carole says as she steps off the train, 'this is worth a visit.' She's admiring the tiles which are red and cream with the name of the station picked out in brown.

'Do you think that's red ochre?' I ask Carole, and for once, she agrees that they are. I admire the wall panelling on the non-platform side which is red.

'I'm not so keen on the standard moulded iron seating,' Carole says and I have to agree. Gosh, we're getting on well at this station.

'Those Mornington Crescent wooden benches were much more comfy on the bottom,' I add.

'But sitters can't be choosers,' Carole says, and as we're in the habit of waiting until the alighting passengers have departed so we can sit and make notes I take her point. We listen to a man making an announcement and can't understand one single word but the warm patronising woman is very clear when it's her turn to perform. Here the ads are only at one end of the platform.

We have to go onto the other platform with trains taking passengers in a southerly direction in order to exit. We take the 20 steps up to the lifts. Here there are 53 steps that are only to be used in an emergency.

'Why?' Carole starts, but I hurry her into a waiting lift. There are more green tiles in the foyer area and a newsagent inside the station. Mapettes are easily accessible and we come out clutching ours and looking at them earnestly. Carole has been busy doing some research and it's her turn to be Stephen Fry. She draws my attention to the familiar brown glazed tiled façade with arched windows.

'Leslie Green was the architect responsible for the design of many stations on the Northern Line.'

'Eh?' is my considered response.

'Yes,' she warms to her topic, 'he worked in the early 1900's and this station has the longest frontage of all his stations.'

'Well they are very attractive,' I say.

'Even though they're brown,' Carole says, 'and brown isn't one of my favourite colours, in fact I doubt it it's anyone's favourite colour, except I suppose the odd pig.' We look around and find not a trace of chalk, or a farm in sight.

'Why Chalk Farm?' I ask aloud, not expecting an answer.

'It's Anglo Saxon meaning cold cottages,' Carole says.

'Bloody Wikipedia,' I mutter under my breath.

'Not a very appealing name is it,' Carole says, 'obviously not dreamt up by an estate agent.'

We study our mapettes and a passing lady asks if she can help us. We are hungry we explain and so she directs us to what she says is the best local café called *Truly Scrumptious*. She might also have mentioned that it's the smallest café in the world and we sit in the doorway. I expect the food is very good but I make a bad choice in ordering and don't really fancy what I've picked and look at it steaming in front of me wishing for something different. Carole has been much more sensible and tucks in to her tuna and sweet-corn sandwich with relish – I mean enjoyment not the other sort of relish.

After our lunch we go to the Round House which is a music venue. Carole has been here before as she likes modern music and is very well informed about performers I've never heard of. I'm too ill informed to gauge whether the acts on offer are of any quality so I keep quiet. I peer at the list of financial contributors to the building of the Round House.

'Look Carole,' I say pointing at the inscription on the wall. Not only is there The Worshipful Company of Clothmakers, Tallow and Candle Makers, but our old friends, THE WORSHIPFUL COMPANY OF GROCERS. Since our abortive visit to their headquarters, we have noticed that they have featured on every list of worthwhile charitable projects on the Northern Line.

'The name, Primrose Hill is much more appealing than *cold cottages*,' Carole says and so we make our way over the bridge that spans the railway lines towards the posher end of Regent's Park Road. The bridge is decorated with work by local artists and Carole takes a picture of fish and flowers on one side and the city scape in pink and black showing the silhouette of the Round House on the other. Once across the bridge we enter a different world with its selection of exclusive small shops and restaurants and elegant Victorian terraces.

'Not a Starbucks in sight,' Carole says.

'Far too common for this area.'

'You can go into one shop,' Carole says knowing I'd like to go into all of them.

'Okay, as there's no book shop in sight, I'll choose this,' I say pointing to a bijou culinary emporium which is bursting at the seams with very expensive designer cooking utensils. After much ooohing and aaahing and inspecting our distorted faces in the gleaming stainless steel saucepans, and flicking through the cookbooks we make our choices. Carole holds up two soft green rubber cups which look as if they've been stolen from a teenager's bra.

'What are they for?' I ask.

'Poaching eggs,' Carole says. I hold up a pink potato peeler that I'm going to buy as a present for my youngest daughter who collects pink kitchen objects; perhaps one day she'll learn how to use them. We leave the shop.

'Did you see the price of that box that had four or five different coloured chopping boards with pictures on them?' Carole shakes her head. 'Well there's one for fish, another vegetables, another meat and so on.'

'Go on,' Carole says. 'How much?'

My impression of hairy Engels

'£36.' Carole whistles.

'Hardly cut price.'

On the way back to the station we pass a house with a blue plaque telling us that it was the residence of Frederick Engels, he who bankrolled Karl Marx and collaborated on some of his writing. At home I find a striking picture of him with a beard and moustache on Wikipedia. He's another hairy one, the picture looks as if he's had a small terrier stuck on the bottom half of his face.

Back at the station Carole points, her face a picture of distaste. My attention is directed to a strikingly ugly building, so, loath to leave any stone of Chalk Farm unturned, we investigate. It's Haverstock Hill School and the frontispiece looks as if bits of the cladding have fallen off, but no, it's been designed to look like that. Just think, someone was paid for that, we mutter in disgust. Usually keen to photograph anything, whether it moves or not, Carole tucks her camera firmly into its case and secretes it away in her bag.

'I'm not taking a picture of **that!**' Disgusted of the Northern Line, we leave.

Mornington Crescent: *Originally named* Seymour Street *before its opening in 1907, the station was little used and for many years only opened on weekdays. In 1992 it closed temporarily to refurbish the lifts and remained so for much of the 90's as permanent closure was considered. A successful campaign to retain it culminated in its reopening in 1998 by the regular cast of the radio programme* I'm Sorry I Haven't a Clue *—Barry Cryer, Tim Brooke-Taylor and Graeme Garden and the late Humphrey Lyttleton. They had immortalized it, and the plaque to Willie Rushton, an original member of the cast who died in December 1996, was unveiled in 2002.*

Carreras Building: *Designed by ME and OH Collins, completed in 1926 on what was the Crescent's communal gardens, this is one of the best known Art deco buildings in London. It was converted into offices in 1961, but the Egyptian detail, including the two large black cats either side of the main entrance, were reinstated during a restoration in the late 1990's.*

The Roundhouse: *Built in 1847 as a turntable engine shed, the building was only used as such for 10 years by which time the engines were too large for it. It was used as a warehouse for some time, finally becoming a cultural centre in 1966. This closed in 1983 through lack of funds and remained so until it was purchased by the philanthropist Torquil Norman for £6million in 1996. He formed the Roundhouse Trust which raised the money for its redevelopment. The Roundhouse currently houses a performance area which can hold an audience of up to 3000 standing or 1700 seated spectators, a café/bar and an art gallery.*

Primrose Hill: *This 78m hill is located on the north side of Regents Park and offers a clear view of central London. The built up part consists mainly of Victorian terraces and has always been a fashionable (and expensive) part of London. Wikipedia shows a list of its former and current notable residents.*

CHAPTER EIGHTEEN

Belsize Park

'There's no name on the wall tiles,' I gasp as we pull into the station.

'It's your favourite flooring, great slabs of smooth sparkly stone, the sort for tap dancing,' Carole says kindly, softening the blow of no tiles picking out the name of the station on the wall. I look at the floor, biting back the tears and admire its sparkly dark black appearance. I think about going into a Dylan Thomas moment, *bible black, sloeblack, slow black, crow back*, but it's not a good idea with Carole in tow.

'I'd take a picture, but you're not wearing your pink shoes,' she says, and it's true I'm not.

'We'll get on faster without the normal stops for lace tying,' I explain. We turn our attention to the wall tiles. 'Brown against regulation cream,' I say noting it down in my book.

'A study in cream and claret,' Carole says admiring the ceiling tiles and noting it down in her book. A female announcer gives us the clearest message. 'Positively Angela Ripponesque,' Carole says, 'and look at the clarity of the digital display, the stationmaster's been on an effective communication course.'

'Well that's how we like our underground stations to be. Modestly tasteful,' I say.

'Yes, and with so few ads all bunched up at one end of the platform, we don't have to look at *beautiful people* engaged in *cool* activities.'

'Is this platform convex or concave?' I ask Carole as I can never remember which is which.

'Concave,' she says decisively, 'convex sticks out. It's thoughtfully engineered, without the gaping void into which sylphlike beings might easily disappear if an eager passenger pushed too hard or sneezed too violently.' Carole shudders at the thought she's just voiced.

'I wouldn't fit down there,' I say to Carole.

'Why do you think some stations have bigger gaps than others?' I can see that this is purely a rhetorical question and I'm not required to answer. 'Do you think that it was once fashionable, like the young men these days who insist on wearing their trousers so loose that you can see most of their underpants?'

'You wouldn't be likely to fall down the back of somebody's trousers,' I point out.

'Ah but, the overall impression is the same, one of general slovenliness which is almost de rigueur in young men,' Carole says.

'But not in underground stations,' I say. I'm trying to be the voice of reason today, but clearly the odds are stacked against me.

'I used not to mind, *mind the gap* but as I grow older, it seems to get bigger and I sometimes feel like Alice in Wonderland, totally overwhelmed by throngs of larger than life commuter lemmings jostling me towards a crevasse.'

'You're exaggerating,' I say unsympathetically, 'You're thin, but not that thin.'

'It's all right for you,' she says, and I can hear her mutter under her breath, 'they don't make gaps that big.'

We have to leave by accessing the southbound platform and I am embarrassed to see that there it is, Belsize Park in big brown letters, but really, it wasn't on our arrival side, honest. Whilst Carole takes a picture I admire the view through the half-moon window at floor level on the bridge that spans the platform. I can see legs and feet where people are walking towards the steps down to the platform. I

do a little drawing just to amuse myself. It's no masterpiece and still the case that my hypothetical cat could do better.

We arrive at the lift.

'219 steps,' Carole says, 'well we could climb them if we were step aerobics fans.'

'Or, we were in training for some life threateningly exhausting sponsored 'run up the monument and abseil down' event.'

'We'll take the lift,' Carole says and I agree.

'It'll be effortless.'

'Unless there are galley slaves winding the handles of the capstan in the basement,' she says.

We search for the mapette which is found for us by a very helpful man and we begin to plan our visit. We're expecting a park, I mean the name has led us to believe there'll be one, but no, not a park in sight. Close scrutiny reveals miscellaneous green bits but not much of interest. We can't make out what six lozenge shaped grey blobs are but we can see that they're off Dunborne Road. Carole thinks they might be bomb shelters but I don't think so, so we decide to check them out, but first toilets and coffee, in that order. Addressing these twin needs in reverse order could result in embarrassment.

'There are two public conveniences,' I say.

'Yea, both at opposite ends of the map.'

'We can walk that far.'

'What, with legs crossed praying that our pelvic floor muscles are stronger than our stomach muscles. Being an OAP under these circumstance is equivalent to one of the labours of Hercules.'

'Do you mean Steptoe's horse?'

'No you daft thing, the bloke in the Greek myth. Horses can drop their load wherever they like.'

Outside we step into a busy wide street with a huge pavement area lined by shops. A little way up the hill on the opposite side there's a very attractive building labelled on the map 'Hampstead Town Hall', so with more hope than judgement we head straight for it. It turns out to be an Arts Centre and a pleasant lady clutching a large coffee from a nearby shop, doubtless inferring our plight from our somewhat bizarre posture, peculiar gait and generally desperate body language, takes us in to the pass controlled building and escorts us to the loo. On the way she regales us with a brief history of the building which indeed, used to be the Town Hall, as evidenced by the grandiose entrance hall and stairway that Carole resolves to photograph. The place is now called the Interchange Studios and has been rescued from demolition by its friends. We are left to wander about, and much relieved, we stop to admire the staircase.

'I can imagine Cinderella rushing down and losing her glass slipper,' I sigh romantically.

'Because she had to catch the last train from Belsize Park,' Carole says.

'It's a lovely building,' I say.

'With friends, who stood up to the big bad Camden Council who threatened to huff and puff and blow the place down so that evil developers could have their wicked way.'

'That lady was good to let us in, and right prevailed here so life's not all bad,' I moralise.

'Yea, well done friends of Hampstead Town Hall.'

We've made up our minds to motor on today, so decide to have coffee on the hoof and repair to an adjacent bakers shop and here we come across another clue to the auspiciously artistic nature of Belsize. We spot a man whom we recognize and nudge each other.

'Who is he?' Carole whispers.

'I don't know, I'm trying to think,' I say, 'he's definitely an actor.'

'Yea, I think I saw him play Uncle Ralph in *Nicholas Nickleby* in the early 80s.'

'I wanted to see that but couldn't get a ticket.' We're still whispering and so drawing attention to ourselves.

'They were like gold dust, a friend got me a pair for midweek. Our seats were up in the gods and incredibly uncomfortable. We watched both halves of the performance which lasted eight hours in total; I had a numb bum and a painful back ache by the time it finished, but it was riveting. It's the only time I pulled a sickie in my long teaching career.'

'He's very good, I know that, I'm sure he's done loads of Shakespeare.' Carole pulls a face, we get our coffee and leave the shop and the name pops into my head. 'John Woodvine,' I say out loud and much to my embarrassment find that he's right behind us.

'I'm glad we didn't ask for his autograph,' Carole says when he's out of ear shot, 'such a sycophantic pastime.'

'To the bomb shelters?' I say.

'Onwards,' she says and sipping our piping hot coffee we set off.

We begin walking down suburban streets and come across the house once lived in by Piet Mondrian.

'I like his stuff,' Carole says, 'all those thick black lines with simple bright colours filling some of the gaps.'

'Very symmetrical work,' is all I can think of to say.

We come across some white flats that look very stylish and modern and so stand out from the rest of the surrounding area. They spark a chord with me and I recognise them as the Isokon block, built early in the 1930s intended to be the last word in modern living. With small kitchens and a communal restaurant they signalled a new and more modern way of living attracting many writers, most notably, Agatha Christie. We learn that the building is now Grade 1 listed, refurbished recently by Camden Council and provides housing for some of their key workers.

'I expect they did it to placate Isokon's friends,' Carole says.

'Maybe Camden Council have redeemed themselves by restoring the Isokon building and using it for such a laudable purpose,' I say.

'Building befriending seems to be rife in this area.'

'So if you had to chose one building to befriend, which one would it be?' I ask.

'Oh, easy question, I'd have Liberty's in London because I go there to worship, not to buy. You?' she asks.

'You mean ever? In the world?' I need clarification here.

'No, just in the UK.' So I think and think.

'Bore Place, a sixteenth century country house at the bottom of the weald of Kent. Used to be owned by a family who left it as an educational trust.' Carole nods, she's been there and likes the grub, all organic and lentils and that sort of thing.

'Good choice, a bit isolated though? I like Liberties in part because it's teeming with people.'

'Ah but the countryside of Kent is deep in my soul.' Carole sniffs in a dismissive way knowing I'm talking rubbish.

Sadly the elegant simplicity of Isokon is a one-off as we realize when we come across a building with more security than Fort Knox. It's an ugly estate of flats all imprisoned behind tall black metal bars. We are unable to walk through it which is our shortest route and have to circumnavigate it and it doesn't improve from any angle. We come across a local resident and ask why it's so protected. He shrugs his shoulders and says that it's how we all live now. We don't agree. Unfortunately we think it's where the lozenges are situated and we are forced to abandon our quest as the place has proved to be impenetrable to the casual visitor. We move on. Carole takes a picture of a road bridge with a six foot chain link fence topped with barbed wire.

'Belsize derives from bel asis meaning 'beautifully situated." (She's got a house in France you know).

'Oh yea,' I say, 'well it might have been in the past, but I don't think much of it now.'

For the first time on our travels Carole gets us lost. I blame Carole because she is always in charge of the map. I have no sense of direction and little talent for map reading so she shoves me, metaphorically speaking, in the right direction. We pass Crecy Road and which reminds me of the battle fought in 1346. I can't help admiring King John of Bohemia who fought against the English even though he was far too old and nearly blind so I tell Carole. When the Prince of Wales came across his dead body he was so moved he adopted his shield with three white feathers and his motto, Ich Dien, out of respect for his bravery.

'Bet he never had a baby though and would have kicked off bigtime if Queen Lizzie had asked him to pick the kids up from school,' is Carole's only comment. Next we pass a restaurant which Michael Palin frequents and the window shows an extract from Russel Brand's silly *Booky Wook* which refers to some outrageous behaviour on the premises. Carole refuses to stop to read any of it. Then we're back on track and headed for the book shop. Hurrah!

In the bookshop I buy a copy of Virginia Woolf's *The London Scene* and Carole drags me out wanting more, saying it's time to leave. We never locate those mysterious grey lozenges and are glad to move on to Hampstead, it has to be better than this, but the station has one last surprise for us, another Cinderella moment.

'Look at that,' Carole says holding her camera up and clicking away at a magnificent flight of steps that lead down to the platform. 'Just imagine Cinderella running down there.'

'She could have broken her bloody neck,' I say.

'Yea, why didn't her Fairy Godmother tell her to take a pair of trainers secreted in her handbag?'

'What was she thinking of?' and with those thoughts we're off to Hampstead.

Hampstead

'Oh another convex platform,' I say as we step off the train.

'Excuse me,' Carole says, 'you're right, but this is totally misleading.' We walk up the platform and stand staring at the name spelt out in the tiles on the wall which announces the station as HEATH STREET, but the roundels and standard underground dado all bear the expected inscription

of HAMPSTEAD. Carole shakes her head.

'It's too much. We might come up on the Yorkshire Moors,' she says. I tell her she's exaggerating.

'If the tardis can do it, why not an Alstom underground train.' I debate whether to tell her that Dr. Who isn't real and decide against it.

'Alstom? What's Alstom?'

'The make of the train,' Carole says. Oh, she's been doing her homework this week.

We sit on the platform and take notes. The floor is tiled in those awful dull yellow jobs with ingrained dirt as standard, my least favourite tube floor covering option. The ads have been scraped off and the wall opposite just looks a mess. I concede that warm coloured claret tiles against cream do somewhat ameliorate the effect even if they are giving us the wrong name of the station. A London Underground employee approaches and asks what we're doing so we tell him. He's called Ian, *aka* Tichmarsh because he was responsible for the oddly named *Underground in Bloom* competition's award winning garden at Hendon.

'You must have green fingers,' Carole says; 'how do you get flowers to grow underground?' He knows she's teasing him but patiently explains that Hendon is an over ground station and we promise to look out for it.

'How come this station's called Heath Street?' I ask.

'That's what it was called when it was opened in 1907, and then it was renamed in the 1920s, long after the tiling was done.' We've released the trigger and like so many underground employees he's both knowledgeable and enthusiastic about his work. 'Hampstead is the deepest station on the London underground,' he's about to get into his stride but then his train comes in and with a cheery wave this mine of information is lost to us. Never mind, Carole's taken his picture.

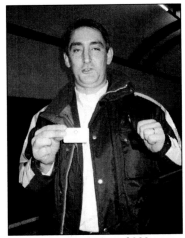

We leave and make our way to the exit. We are offered the choice of 320 steps or one of four lifts.

'Not a difficult call,' Carole says pressing the lift button but finds that the lift doors are impatient and unforgiving as they readily spring into action. Stepping out at the foyer Carole says it's surprising we didn't get the bends on the way up, the ascent being long and speedy.

I admire the ticket office which is framed in green tiles and sports a brass ledge. It looks like something from a different era, one from a past which was less frantic than the pace of life today.

'Nice,' I say pointing it out to Carole whose seen it for herself anyway.

'Well you'd expect it at Hampstead wouldn't you, given the neighbourhood, it probably has its own *Friends of Hampstead Underground Ticket Office.*'

'They couldn't have Kate Winslet buying her ticket from any old office,' I say. 'I wonder where she might go for lunch?' Carole knows me of old, this is my signal that it's time a little something. Collecting our mapettes and emerging onto a busy street on the side of a hill with plenty of interesting shops, we walk downwards, it being the easier option. I glance down Flask Walk and see a café called *Simply Scrumptious.*

'We've got to go there.'

'You've really got a thing about cafes with silly names,' Carole says, but having tried *Truly Scrumptious* at Chalk farm, we have to try *Simply*; it's only fair. After vegetable soup we compare notes.

'No contest,' Carole declares firmly, '*Simply* wins hands down being considerably more scrumptious than *Truly*,' and I have to agree.

'We could adopt this adjective when signing off letters,' Carole says, 'what do you think of Yours Simply?'

'How about Yours Scrumptiously?'

'Nah, it sounds like an invitation to cannibals so best avoided,' she advises.

'But on the café stakes, La Voute is still simply, truly, the best,' I say.

Suitably, nay scrumptiously fortified, we set off into darkest Hampstead in search of Burgh House. We admire the charming terraced houses that line Flask Walk and lead into Gardner Road. We stand in front of a large building with *Wells and Campden Baths and Wash House 1888* emblazoned over its ground floor windows.

'Is that a mistake do you think?' I ask Carole.

'Perhaps the gentry thought if Hampstead had a 'p' in it then Camden should too.'

'I bet people had a pee in the bath.' She doesn't laugh.

'My Dad was born in the back streets of Greenwich, once a poor neighbourhood, now occupied by trendy artists,' Carole says looking about her and I'm sure it's a valid comparison.

We've arrived at chucking out time at the local primary school.

'Natives,' Carole whispers as we turn to see the all the litte Arabellas, Melissas, Galahads and Silases making their way to the waiting rows of 4 x 4s, clutching Mummy or Nanny's hand and gabbling excitedly. We think about the poor folk with no running water who used to live in those charming terrace houses and use the baths and how their lives contrast with these children in their designer clothes.

'I wonder what the building is used for now?' I say. Carole doesn't know either but she bets it's got lots of friends.

Arriving at the listed Queen Anne House which is Burgh House we find it's got lots of friends, so many buddies it could win a popularity contest in Harpers. Inside we find a reception manned, or to be more accurate, ladied by a very well groomed person of the female gender. It's obvious that she's a volunteer and Carole's encounter with her reminds me that there are two sorts of them; the chatty I'd like to help you, delighted to see you variety who we encountered at the Stephen's Ink Museum, and the other sort. Carole picks up a guide and begins leafing through it. Without looking up from the paper the woman is reading she says in a haughty tone,

'Do you want to buy it?' Carole does, but later tells me she wished she'd said:

'No, I just want to finger it a bit and leave it shop soiled.' I blame Carole for having pink hair which either makes her look interesting and individual, or an elderly reprobate; take your pick; I know which view I choose. I suggest returning to the museum when she's wearing her Hell's Granny leather jacket with spikes and studs, and yes, it really does have Hell's Granny spelt out on the back.

Burgh House houses Hampstead Museum which is both an historical treasure trove and a monument to the rich and famous who have lived and are still living in the area. We could buy a map showing the whereabouts of the prominent people.

'Look, the English equivalent of Hollywood,' I say to Carole.

'Do you think they run bus tours?' she asks.

'Certainly not, far too vulgar, you have to wander about finding those blue plaques for yourself.' We both admire the cartoon on the back of the guide showing a postman approaching a house with a blue plaque which reads, 'Only house in Hampstead where nobody famous has lived.'

We repair to the exhibitions and visit a room full of paintings and drawings by Constable from the period when he lived in Hampstead. Carole's not that interested.

'We had the Haywain on our sitting room wall and I was never that impressed,' she says. I'm very interested having recently come back from a visit to East Bergholt in Suffolk and seen for myself the pond which shows the Haywain up to its spokes in water. Poor old Constable moved to Hampstead because of its elevated position for the sake of his wife's health. It was here that she died leaving him after twelve years of marriage with seven children. So sad.

Upstairs we find two rooms with exhibits relating to Hampstead in the past including information about the London Underground. We learn that local people slept in Hampstead station during the Second World War. I read an account by a man who said how terrible the tube smelt when there were so many people on the platform and the sanitary arrangements were a bucket at the end of the platform. Carole's reading it too.

'I don't see Kate Winslet putting up with that,' she says.

Also of note is an Isokon chair and pictures of the Isokon building before Camden Council did it up. I like the story about a hollow tree on Hampstead Heath which is reputed to have contained a winding staircase comprising forty-two steps leading to an octagonal room which could hold up to twenty people. Carole shakes her head.

'You've been reading too much Rupert Bear; all that stuff set in Nutwood Forest with Rupert finding a door opening in a hollow tree and a pixie with spiked hair peering out.' I admit it, I'm a Rupert Bear aficionado.

'What's not to like?' I ask.

It's time to move on and resisting the urge to finger some postcards to annoy the snooty receptionist, we emerge back on to the street. We want to visit the heath and after a brief stop to identify Constable's surprisingly modest house, we only

spend a short time admiring the trees, enjoying the elevated position and distant views before the gathering gloom renders the woods creepily uninviting. Unheathed, we pass some beautiful houses on the way back to the station. It's nearly dark when we come across the Chalybeate Well. I peer at the inscription which tells me that the well was given together with six acres of land to the poor.

'I don't see many poor, do you?' I ask Carole.

'No, and I was looking in the estate agent's window and I don't think they'll be moving in here in a hurry.'

'I bet that water tastes foul,' I say.

'Isn't it odd that people came to drink it in the past, but what's new? Nowadays people pay for plastic bottles of water from Buxton or that foul tasting Badoit.'

'Give me a glass of tap water any day,' I say.

'Far more ecologically healthy,' Carole adds. We agree that life is strange. 'The human race is illogical,' Carole says. 'We construct beautiful buildings and befriend them. We pay to drink something that tastes strikingly unpleasant. We make up fairy stories about women in unsuitable shoes, and we think we are rational.'

'What's the shoe reference?' I ask wondering if she is having another dig at my preferred pink boat shoes of the recalcitrant laces.

'Cinderella,' Carole says.

'Oh gosh yes, glass isn't really the right material for shoes is it.' Carole gives me a sympathetic glance. I'm not giving her my full attention because the lights are on in the houses and I can peer into basement kitchens; they are uniformly minimalist with no clutter, no basil on the window ledge, no food splattered cookery books messing the place up, but have acres of empty plain black granite work tops. I sigh in envy. Carole shivers a little, it's really chilly now. Time to go back underground.

Hampstead Town Hall: Built in 1886 as the Vestry Hall of Hampstead parish, it became Hampstead Town Hall after the 1910 reorganisation of local government. When Hampstead became part of the new super-borough of Camden in 1964, the hall continued to be used for council services but became run-down and Camden Council tried to close it in 1994. A campaign by local residents resulted in the Hall becoming a Grade II listed building and a partnership with the Interchange Trust enabled them to secure Lottery and Arts Council funding to refurbish and maintain it for community use.

Isokon flats: The modernist building was constructed between 1933-1934 containing 34 flats and designed as an experiment in communal living. It was granted Grade I listed status in 2000 when Camden held a competition to select architects to carry out the renovation which was completed in 2005.

Underground in Bloom: This yearly competition may sound bizarre but in fact over half of London Underground stations are actually above ground and the tube owns approximately 10% of the overall wildlife habitat in London. Judging takes place in August each year covering categories such as Tubs, Hanging baskets and Fruit and vegetables. Underground staff plant and tend these in their own time.

Burgh House: Built in 1704 and used mostly as a private residence, the house was taken over and refurbished by Hampstead Borough Council in 1946. A charitable trust formed by local residents managed to lease the building from Camden Council and raised the funds necessary for further refurbishment and in September 1979 the house and museum was first opened to the public,
http://www.burghhouse.org.uk/home

CHAPTER NINETEEN

Golders Green

The sun is out, the sky is blue, there's not a cloud to spoil the view but we have never until now, noticed how particularly annoying the air-conditioning outlet is as we rattle along the tracks in the direction of Golders Green. We've been here before, on a damp miserable day and lacked the energy to counter the cold dreariness of the weather. This time we are in luck. It's hot, hot, hot.

'It's as noisy as one of those high powered hand driers," Carole says. 'You know, the Dyson ones, like the one in the Ladies at the Oval cricket ground.'

'I do, it had the velocity of a wind tunnel. But this,' I say indicating the air-con unit just behind my right ear'ole, 'is just as noisy but without the accompanying blast of air.'

'Um, more like a dying hamster's last breath.' If its sole purpose is to discourage conversation it doesn't work, we just shout at each other. When that becomes wearisome and as we have a long journey we move to seats adjacent to an equally ineffective but much quieter outlet.

'Golders Green here we come again,' I say with enthusiasm 'and then it's Brent Cross shopping mall which I'm looking forward to,' I say rubbing my hands together in anticipation.

'Why do you want to go there?' Carole asks.

'It's the sort of shopping mall that comes up from time to time in the news so it will be interesting to see what it's like.'

We pop out of the tunnel into the daylight and the sunshine floods the carriage, because the sun is out, the sky is blue, there's not a cloud to spoil the view… We pass a terminus on our way in to Golders Green and Carole thinks we should visit it, and then we are pulling into the station.

'Do you remember that on our last visit there was a scrappy piece of paper warning us that the New York self-winding clock wasn't working?' Carole asks and indeed I do. We are delighted to report it is now fully functioning. The station is very well provided with timepieces both traditional and digital, and it has five platforms, four in use and one that seems to be reserved for staff only.

'Perhaps it's the staff picnic platform, a place where they can have their lunch in the sunshine,' I suggest.

'I like that idea, but in a truly egalitarian society everyone should use the picnic platform, open to passengers, staff and train spotters alike. Maybe local enthusiasts could start a *Friends of Platform 1 Society* and meet once a month.'

'Share their pork pies and wagons wheels,' I add.

In addition to the multiple clocks, the platforms boast an abundance of benches, some old and granular from repeated coats of paint, others newly constructed from steel and hardwood, so there are plenty of places to park the bum when the legs are craving respite. Sitting we admire this delightful outdoor station with its wood friezes fringing the roof canopy making a decorative pattern. Looking up we see the canopy is supported by wrought iron structures which have been painted green and look very attractive. We are very conscious of being close to the end of the line because of the exposed wires that line the sides of the end of the platform. The waiting room provides a jarring note being a totally incongruous glass box looking for all the world like a prop for a double-glazing company's campaign. Carole tries the door which is very stiff and we can only open it if we both pull hard on the door handle. Carole goes in and perches on the strip of metal that passes for a seat. She mouths something I can only make out distinctly.

'You look like a goldfish in a goldfish bowl, I say as we struggle with the door to let her out but she can't hear me. 'What were you saying in there?' I ask.

'I feel like a goldfish in a goldfish bowl.'

The announcer comes on and seduces us with his silky sexy voice, addressing us as *ladies and gentlemen* and telling us that there or no major delays because the sun is out, the sky is blue, oh stop it I hear you say.

We exit the platform and here's the weird thing about this station, a first for us, we have to go **down** to the exit. There's a state of the art lift that has recently been installed and we get in together with an old man who hears we are planning a visit to Brent Cross Shopping Mall and recommends we go by bus from this station. When he's out of earshot I say to Carole:

'I had enough of buses at Tuffnel Park. If we're not careful it'll be Stalin's tomb all over again.'

We emerge from the station to be faced by a bus terminus and watch as they circumnavigate the clock tower. Beyond there's a busy intersection and in all it has more sets of traffic lights than we have ever seen in close proximity. Those not in use are hidden under bright orange plastic covers like a budgie's cage at bedtime. A walk past the news stand reveals just how multi-cultural this part of London is since it carries newspapers and magazines from all over the world. Our first destination however is the underground train terminus just up the busy Finchley Road and under the railway bridge. We turn into a small road following two people who are walking purposefully towards the huge blue and yellow automatic gates I can clearly see their official passes dangling from their lapels.

'Come on,' Carole says, grabbing my arm. 'We can snuck in behind them.' Carole doesn't have a care in the world.

'But what if...?' I begin to quaver as the big gates respond to the approaching workers and slowly slide open. 'What if they won't let us out?'

'Or we're transported to a parallel universe where hobbits are forced to crawl around under trains armed with grease guns effecting necessary repairs.' I smile weakly and relax as I see that Carole is making towards the Visitors Centre.

'I've been reading John McCarthy's book about his five year imprisonment and it's made me jumpy,' I say, now ashamed of my wimpishness. We muster all the charm at our disposal and approach the security guard and ask to be shown around the depot which doesn't seem an unreasonable request to make in a Visitors Centre. The man on reception makes a phone call and we don't wait long before Derek the Depot Director with his delightfully alliterating name and title, comes down to speak to us. We can be shown round but we need to make an appointment. He says there are many people working in the depot who have been employed by TfL for a long time, are very knowledgeable and would be only too delighted to give us a tour round. We are fortified by this successful encounter, and promising ourselves to write a letter we leave.

The sun is out, the sky is ... well you know the rest, so we decide to visit the animals in Golders Hill Park and find the coffee shop. After traipsing about for a bit we're getting nowhere, Carole's visuo-spatial skills having completely deserted her.

'Another false start,' I say.

'More like a false middle,' Carole says grumpily, but soon we can hear the thwack of tennis balls and the gates to the park are just round the corner. The numbers of people on court demonstrating more enthusiasm than ability remind us that Wimbledon week is fast approaching.

'We should have a game one day,' I suggest.

'Not likely,' Carole says dismissively. 'I'm Mrs. Can't Hit a Ball for Toffee.' I secretly suspected as much which is why I want to play her, I'm not much cop myself and it would be good to win.

'Shame.'

'I went to Wimbledon once. It took me hours to get there driving through London in the rush hour and play was rained off in the middle of the third game and the strawberries were well over-priced. How stupid is that?' I know that Carole's on a roll. 'Until global warming really kicks in it seems pretty daft to play a sport which can't be played in the rain. It's also my objection to cricket and playing in white sports gear when you're likely to get very sweaty and wipe your hands on your clothing leaving grubby marks also strikes me as none too bright. I bet it was men's idea as most of them don't do the washing.' I'm listening but not really taking in what she's saying because as we've moved into the park which is undulating and beautiful my attention is riveted by a man dressed only in his underpants.

'Look,' I say pointing in the most vulgar of fashions, 'that man is nearly naked.'

'Isn't this a lovely park with amenities for the young and old, the sporty and the languid,' Carole says attempting to raise the tone by ignoring my obvious fascination by the scantily dressed chap.

'Let's get a closer look,' I suggest.

'I've never been a big fan of the Y-fronts page of the Littlewoods Catalogue,' she says loftily and steers me towards the animal pens.

'I only wanted to wander past casually. I wouldn't stare,' I claim as Carole walks  me up to an enclosure containing the Greater Rhea, an emu sort of bird with long legs, a big body and a small neck. We read the blurb and admire the emancipation of the male of the species who sit on the nests of eggs of several different females. Next we spot some Patagonian Maras, a sort of rabbit look alike with the ears of Dr. Spock. We admire the fallow deer and a couple of donkeys that graze peacefully in a distant enclosure. Children are playing in a nearby adventure playground and a beautifully landscaped water garden is home to a few ducks and a moorhen.

Carole agrees we must return and we do pass MUP (man in underpants) who turns out to be MIST (man in swimming trunks). Sadly he looked so much better from a distance, the proximity not only revealing the truth behind his sartorial choice, but also his bald patch and spare tyre. Nature catches up and I realize I need the facilities. Carole suggests that returning to the station would be the better choice but as I set off in the direction indicated by a sign I thought I'd seen earlier, she sits on the grass to wait in the sun (which, incidentally is still out and the sky still blue). She turns out to be right as I have to walk half way across the park. She is too concerned by the length of my absence to gloat.

'Were you kidnapped by a marauding group of men in their underpants?'

'No, I had to beat the bounds of the park. I found the café, which was heaving with people enjoying their lunch in the sunshine, and I've seen flowerbeds and ponds and pretty bridges. It's so beautifully kept,' I enthuse as we wend our way back to the tube without getting lost once. We admire the Hippodrome which is a Grade II listed building adjacent to the station.

'Queen played there in their early days,' Carole says wistfully.

'Did she?' A notice tells us that the building is now on lease to the El Shaddi Christian Group. I hear Carole humming, *Another one bites the dust.*

Brent Cross

On the tube between Golders Green and Brent Cross I take my feet out of my shoes.

'They're a big improvement,' Carole says nodding at my smart white slip-ons. 'No laces to come undone and hold us up.'

'They're quite uncomfortable,' I complain, 'especially after that marathon trek looking for the loo in park.'

Stepping off the train we can immediately see that this station is much smaller than Golders Green having only two island platforms. The platforms are covered by a wooden awning but the wrought iron supporting the canopy is not as ornate and it's painted black. What is an improvement is the larger glass waiting room with two doors, proper sized seats and a heater.

'What's the point of that?' Carole asks indicating the heater, 'seeing as there's the

 gap of several centimetres between the bottom of the walls and the floor.'

Having seen grander things we leave, but gasp in amazement at the size of the foyer which springs to view as a light airy chequer boarded space of dance floor proportions. Carole holds out her hand to me.

'A military two step or we've got

space to strip the willow and swing our partners,' she says but I point to my feet which are already sore oppressed. I'm not to be deterred, Brent Cross Shopping Centre is beckoning me.

Collecting our mapettes we see it in glorious technicolour, well it's actually that weird lavender colour they use for places of interest on these dear little maps. There's little else that catches our eye at Brent Cross apart from Clitterhouse Playing Fields which lends itself to amusingly obvious mispronunciation, but is otherwise we suspect lacking in significance. Exiting into Heathfield Gardens we admire the pleasant suburban ambience. A local resident points us in the right direction reassuring us that the shopping mall is no more than a mere five minutes stroll away. As we walk down the road the sound of traffic becomes increasingly apparent.

'It's the North Circular,' Carole shouts as we're faced by the incessant roar of lanes of traffic all speeding along the road. We turn left and walk parallel with the busy road heading towards a ramp which will take us up to a walkway running adjacent to the railway line. This will take us to the other side of the road above the torrent of traffic. The access is littered with KFC and MacDonald's wrappers and the beer cans nestle amongst the weeds. It's a very unpleasant experience traversing this bridge as we can feel the vibration caused by the traffic speeding under us and the trains thundering just above our heads making us feel very insecure. I'd like to say we stop to admire the view, but the truth of the matter is, we stop to despise the view. To the left there's a derelict house with a tree growing through its middle, with branches well above what used to be the roof of the house. It's both repellent and fascinating. We spy what we think is the shopping mall in the distance but since the Brent Cross flyover with its maelstrom of traffic lies between us and it, we have no idea of how we are going to get there.

'What are we doing here?' Carole asks. 'This is so alien,' she shouts indicating the traffic and the surrounding urban junkyard. 'We're not even that keen on shopping,' she says. When we're in a quieter place having reached the far side of the road we decide it's the almost mythical status of being one of the first 'malls' to be opened in the UK.

'So we're not so much shoppers as retail archaeologists,' I decide.

'By 2050 it'll probably be a listed building with *friends,'* retorts Carole gazing down at the River Brent, a shallow sluggish polluted stretch of dull murky water with rubbish-strewn banks.

'Who would want to live here?' I ask. Carole knows the answer.

'A rat.' I grimace as I see a fire extinguisher lying on its side on the opposite bank of the river which barely deserves the name. I wonder how it got there looking so strikingly out of place, and that is part and parcel of the total feeling of neglect, of being in a no man's land that is the pedestrian's milieu.

We continue to follow the infrequent signposts and we pass safely under the flyover but then risk life and limb crossing a roundabout eventually emerging at the back of the Brent Cross Shopping Centre.

'That man in the lift in Golders Green was right about getting a bus,' I gasp as I limp into Fenwicks like someone who has just run the London Marathon in glass slippers. Carole nods.

'I need coffee and a paracetamol,' she says, 'that traffic pollution has given me a splitting headache.' We wander about a bit rather underwhelmed by the place being rather small and ordinary in comparison to recent developments such as Bluewater in Kent and Westfield in London. We find a place and sit down for coffee and cake. Carole looks quite miserable and I cheer up as I've got my shoes off under the table.

'What's the matter pet?' I ask.

'I don't like shopping malls,' she says.

'What's not to like?'

'They overwhelm me with their glossy trendy opulence and false promises of eternal happiness.' Now I just see them as rather convenient places to shop in warmth and comfort and never had any illusion of eternal happiness but Carole looks pale so I keep my thoughts to myself. 'This place hasn't even been allowed to age and become retro,' Carole says. 'If it had aged it would have gained character, but no, it's got to be trendy or die,' she says.

'That's the nature of a retail business, keep up or go under.'

Carole urges me to share her pain au raisin; I refuse. She insists. I carry on refusing but finally I agree to a quarter. She cuts it in four, eats two bits, I eat one and then she cuts the remaining quarter in two so we eat half of that each. It keeps us entertained on our walk back to the station as we struggle to work out what fraction of the cake we've each consumed. She thinks it was three eighths to five eighths.

'That's thirty six and a half percent to sixty three and a half percent and I did it all my head,' Carole says cheerfully. I'm quite happy, I've bought pink socks to go with my

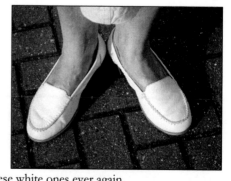

pink shoes and I won't be wearing these white ones ever again.

Golders Hill Park: Managed by the City of London Corporation as part of the Hampstead Heath Local Nature Reserve, the park is situated on a site formerly occupied by a large house which was destroyed by bombing in World War 2. The park has large expanses of grass, a well tended flower garden, ponds and a water garden as well as a small zoo, restaurant, tennis courts and a putting green.

Golders Green Hippodrome: Built in 1913 as a 3000 seat Music Hall it later became a theatre and was taken over by the BBC in 1969 as a television studio/concert hall. In 2003 the BBC left the Grade II listed building vacant and in early 2007, Christian group El Shaddai International Christian Centre purchased the hippodrome for £5million.

Brent Cross: Is actually in the London Borough of Barnet and takes its name from an old crossroads near the River Brent. The shopping centre, opened in 1976, was the first stand-alone shopping mall to be built in the UK. Although smaller than more recent shopping centres such as the MetroCentre and Bluewater, it has one of the largest incomes per unit area of retail space in the UK.

CHAPTER TWENTY

Hendon Central

'It's a long way,' I remark looking at my watch.

'To Tipperary?' Carole adds and my heart sinks. It's going to be one of those days.

'It's taken us nearly an hour and a half to get here,' I tell Carole.

'There are people who spend more time that that travelling to work every day, but as far as I'm concerned they're either certifiable or have a sad home life.' Having spent much of our time recently travelling about I'm wondering which we are and plump for certifiable.

'I like that seat,' Carole says as we hop off the tube onto the island platform. We sit on the attractive bespoke bench which is tucked discreetly under the stairs and look about us.

'Most of this is original,' I observe.

'Except for the new lift and the glass waiting room,' Carole says. Above us, the green steel supports for the wooden canopy are not as attractive as the wrought iron ones at Golders Green, but there are the by now very familiar extensive anti-pigeon devices. On both sides of the platform there's leafy green stuff, trees and shrubs, waving gently in the summer breeze.

'Another one,' Carole says pointing to the ubiquitous New York self-winding clock which is telling us it's coffee time so we climb the broad steps in the middle of the platform to the chequer board floor foyer. 'What a bizarre mixture of modern fixtures and fittings right next to the original Art Deco tiling and woodwork,' Carole says and whilst I look around at the square foyer with windows high up in the ceiling to let in light, she waxes lyrical about the charms of the large French style wooden doors with art deco decorations. I admire a curved tiled bay opposite the ticket office tastefully clad in white tiles with green, then darker green and black border. 'I like this,' Carole says looking about her, and I have to agree, it's clean, light, airy and tasteful.

Tucked within the entrance to the foyer is a coffee bar, Barista, which boasts *award-winning coffee* so we decide to give a try. The waitress brings us our beverages.

'Lots of froth,' Carole says slurping hers from the cup.

'I'm not sure that the coffee is quite as good as the froth.'

'Funny word froth,' Carole says.

'Okay, what else would you call it?'

'Spume?' she offers.

'Oh no, that's a horrible word and has all the wrong connotations.'

'What about lather?'

'No, that's not right either. How about effervescence or suds?'

'Suds, like lather is too soapy, but I like effervescence. How about you?' I like it too I tell her but that froth is the best.

Because it's Hendon I'm rather hoping to be knocking on the door of the police training academy, but it's not to be; rules is rules; it's not on the mapette, and if it's not there, it's off limits. We've deviated once looking for Stalin's tomb and that led us into a whole heap of trouble. Carole suggests visiting the British Hernia Centre, but although I think it's an amusing option we probably won't be allowed over the threshold and neither of us want to see one close to.

'I wonder if they're managed by a Primary Care Truss,' Carole says waggishly and I have to laugh.

'What do you think the Institute of Psychosynthesis gets up to?' I ask as it's marked on the mapette

'It sounds like an electro pop group specializing in songs about serial killers, or it might be just a lot of psychobbable a la Assagioli.'

'Assagioli sounds like a type of pasta to me. All will be revealed somewhere past the War Memorial,' I say.

'Is that the Hendon equivalent of *over the rainbow*?' Carole asks. It's hot so we decide to take a wander in the direction of The Church House Museum and see what else comes up.

We walk up past the dual carriageway road which is busy with traffic. I'm wearing Jesus boots, those leather sandals with straps that fit round the big toe, and they're very comfortable. Carole clutches her map and leads the way.

'We need to turn right here,' she says as I examine an attractive house, probably built in the nineteenth century on the corner of a very busy junction. It's a sad sight as the location is appalling, noisy and dusty. We turn into a cul-de-sac and find that the Institute we are looking for seems to have morphed into a gated block of boring old offices housing a few small businesses.

It's too hot to linger so we push on up The Burroughs in search of the Church Farmhouse Museum and come across what used to be Hendon Town Hall which is in the process of being revamped to become part of Middlesex University.

'That's a magnificent building,' I say stating the very obvious.

'I wonder who it could be friends with?' Carole asks. She's got a thing about buildings having friends of a similar stature, ugly ones go together, attractive ones have suitable friends.

'It's got a nasty dose of the builders with all the mess and disruption that entails,' I say. Carole looks sad.

'Yup, and you can't ring NHS Direct, there's no medication, it's an infestation  that takes its time.'

'And there's no knowing how long it will take,' I add.

Whilst admiring the immaculate flower beds we peruse the strategically placed notice-board which shows that Hendon must be the most twinned town in the UK having links with towns in France, Germany, Cyprus, Israel and somewhere in Uganda that sports a hippopotamus on its coat of arms. I count them.

'That's eight twins in all,' I point out to Carole, still stating the obvious.

'Excuse me for being pedantic, but isn't that octuplets, so it's octupleted, not twinned.' She's right, I can't argue.

We make for the cool of the local library grateful for its comfortable air-conditioning. The library's shade and shelter is not the only welcoming aspect as we run into a friendly lady sitting behind a desk who offers to help us. We're not really sure what we're looking for and get involved in a conversation about the new building and the hi-tec self check out system. I foolishly ask her if she loses many books and she admits some go missing, but no more than before.

'Let's face it,' Carole says, 'if you really want to steal a book it's not that difficult but most people are honest.' I blush to my roots and in a fit of guilt confess to my outstanding library book, due back at the Holborn Library on 16th March, 1965. I try to cover my embarrassment with excuses.

'I did think of returning the book in the 1980s but found that the original library had been knocked down, and rather lost heart after that.'

'Just imagine the fine,' Carole gasps.

'I could probably fund a new wing, they could name it after me, the Worham Wing, it's got a ring to it, don't you think?'

'Rogues Gallery more like,' Carole mutters. The librarian points to the security measure of barriers that sound an alarm if a book is being taken out without being checked out.

'What if someone was to hold their arms up in the air with a book in their hand as the barriers are only shoulder high?' Carole asks.

'That's why I've a good view of the exit so I can keep an eye on those *reach for the sky* offenders,' she says giving me a suspicious glance. We opt for the local history section and Carole suggests testing the security system out to see if it works, so I give her one of my withering glances to deter her. We go up the glass lift to the next level and Carole mutters under her breath. I think I can hear her saying, *hypocrisy* and *long-standing book thief.*

We both find books on the local area and sit to read at our leisure. I go straight for Hendon's famous residents, first alighting on Mark Lemon who lived at the house that is now the Museum we are heading for. He was the first editor of Punch. Other local luminaries are Richard Llewlyn, surprisingly born here in 1906 as he is the author of *How Green Was My Valley* and always claimed to have been born in Wales. Two of my favourite sportsmen lived here, the great Sir Henry Cooper and Dennis Compton, the cricketer. From the world of entertainment came Marie Lloyd and Eric Merriman, scriptwriter of that wonderful radio show *Beyond Our Ken.* The only other person of note is Peter Mandelson who went to Hendon's County School and later joined the local communist party.

'I've found a reference to that Clitterhouse Place you were talking about a station ago,' I say interrupting Carole who looks up from the book she's perusing. 'Clite takes its meaning from the Anglo Saxon word for clay, so there must have been an ancient pottery on that site.'

'Look,' Carole says and points me in the direction of a paragraph that mentions Church End as the oldest settlement in Hendon and the house we are about to visit as the oldest in the area. It's time to move on, back into the sun. It's warm out but the museum is easy to find being well signposted. It shuts for lunch and so we go the Claddagh Ring, an Irish pub and consume a very good sandwich at a reasonable price as we watch Roger Federer wop some poor player in an early

round of Wimbledon. Well, I watch it and pass comment with a lady sitting at an adjacent table who is also absorbed whilst Carole reads the Irish Times.

I can't tell you how disappointed I am to arrive at Church Farmhouse Museum to find that it's closed. There's a notice in the window saying it's due to *unforeseen circumstances.* It's

a beautiful house dating from the mid seventeenth century and we walk into the front garden, peer in the windows and creep round to the back garden. A man comes out and I apologise profusely for our intrusion, but he's fine. He's keen to share the reason for closing the museum. On Saturday night Hendon experienced a fall of rain so torrential that it stopped the traffic; it also poured through the light fittings of the museum. Things had got damp and smelt and they were spending the day clearing up. I was so sorry, I really wanted to go inside that museum and the next time I'm in Hendon I'm making straight for it.

In the spirit of adventure, we make our way back to the tube station using a series of footpaths marked by a green line on the map. Carole is expecting to be tramping across greensward but we're traversing along tarmac paths which run between very expensive and well-kept detached houses. It all has an air of prosperity about it.

'Posh alley ways,' I say, but Carole is disappointed about the lack of grass and mud underfoot so I snatch a couple of leaves off an evergreen hedge and toss them on the path in front of her.

'It's not the same,' she says disconsolately.

We are soon back to the circus that is the intersection by the tube and we're off to Colindale.

Colindale

'I didn't expect that,' Carole says as we pass into a long tunnel which runs between Hendon and Colindale, as we've almost forgotten we're on the underground. We pop back out into the daylight and catch sight of the Police Academy in the distance. It's a large college type building with acres of playing fields around it. 'Do you think the foyer will be crawling with trainee police persons?' Carole asks as we pull into the station. We're expecting bands of them ready to direct us or stop and search us but none of this happens. As we emerge onto the platform Carole reminds me we've seen more policemen at Stockwell than we have here.

About a third of the platform is under a road bridge and there are only two platforms. The canopy needs a lick of paint. Carole and I both admire the brick built waiting room, acknowledge our friendly old clock and the regularly spaced benches, but it's pretty bland so we take the steps up from the platform to a small foyer clad in pale grey tiles. This unremarkable station doesn't prepare us for what awaits us. We're ready for the RAF Museum having seen the notices at Hendon that Colindale is where to alight for onwards transmission, and we're going there, but having found our mapettes, we are aghast to see how it just fringes the right hand side of the map with only a fraction of its building showing. Carole looks at me. I look at her. We both look at my feet, mainly because they can be revolting. On this occasion they are clad in the most sensible of sandals suitable for hot weather travel.

'I must have a picture,' Carole says, anxious to continue documenting my footwear on account its role of hampering our journey with its frequent incidents of 'recalcitrant laces'. Today the footwear is fortuitously benevolent but in spite of my comfortable sandals we plump for the British Library Newspapers store, mainly because it's only spitting distance from the tube station and the day has not got any cooler, and we've already walked around Hendon in the heat.

We set off along a miserable road, with miserable shops, set opposite an uninspiring field and see a building which is imposing in a Colditz sort of way,

which is our destination of choice, a utilitarian building constructed in 1932.

I insert a word of warning, there's no obvious welcome for the casual visitor to the British Newspaper Library. We pass several doors that look firmly shut, until we arrive at the front entrance. Pitching up in the very small foyer we are greeted by two jolly security men who are amused by the fact that we travel around on the Northern Line looking for places of interest. They'd like to issue us with entry passes, all we need to do is to produce two items that prove our identity. One has to have proof of address. Carole does this is thirty seconds flat and as I frantically scrabble through my cards, I can see myself sitting outside sobbing quietly into my hanky. I've my Legoland pass with my picture on it; my Boots reward card, local library card, National Trust Membership, English Heritage, Waterstones rewards card, membership of the RAC, old lady rail card and various cards for video shops, but not a single thing with my address on. I have proof of being old, middle class and a person who likes reading, but it's not enough. The security guard phones upstairs. We're getting used to this routine. Surly curly bossman Christian arrives from above to question my sincerity, am I a flippant upstart granny who just might be trying to gain access under false pretences?

'What are you doing?' he asks. Cripes, that's a good question, now how to answer? Wasting my time and yours I'm tempted to say, but that wouldn't get me in. I explain about the Northern Line, about travelling its length, about getting on and getting off at every station, seeing what we see, writing about what we see. I realise he doesn't understand and I can't blame him, I don't either. This is a crazy idea after all, but the sight of my library card seems to reassure him, libraries and librarians must be taken seriously and he agrees to issue me with a temporary pass. As and when I return with my driving license, I like Carole, could be the proud possessor of the 'full monty'.

Carole and I put our essentials into a clear plastic bag, hand over our handbags, and armed only with a pencil we go upstairs. We find ourselves in a large airy reading room with tall windows and large desks with stands to hold the huge books of bound newspapers so that they can be read in comfort. There are about twenty people scattered about, all intent on their research. They hardly speak at all, and if they do it's in the hushed tones reserved for libraries and funerals. We are greeted by two very quiet young librarians who get us to fill out a comprehensive form, and then, we're issued with passes, mine a piece of paper valid for one day only. Carole smugly waves her small plastic pass in my direction which entitles her to use the facilities until December 2012. Huh! We're sent to find surly curly Christian but upstairs he's a changed man and gives us the red carpet treatment by initiating us into some of the mysteries of how to use the library. He's extremely knowledgeable and rather serious until I ask about comics. He then shows his human side by giving an amusing account of the avid collectors who attempt to steal the rarest items. He grins widely whilst explaining that comics are kept in the most secure place, readers are supervised at a special desk whilst having access to them and searched on exit. A line from Shakespeare springs to mind, *Lord, what fools these mortals be.*

I order a collection of newspapers and after about ten minutes I am presented with all the papers of the Chislehurst and Kentish Times for the year 1946. I'm well impressed. We look up March, which is when Carole was born and chuckle over the advertisements, announcements and articles. Carole's order comes up and she leaves me alone as she has to read hers on microfiche. Left to my own devices, I turn to September, the month of my birth hoping to find some article relating to me. Yes, it's narcissistic and you may be surprised to imagine that any child born in 1946 is worthy of comment in any paper, it being baby-boomer times, but my birth was just a bit different taking place in the main operating theatre of what was then known as Farnborough Hospital because my mother was carrying triplets. Turning the pages I see that in 1946 Chislehurst is lagging behind in the

Chancellor's drive for the people of Britain to save money; the good people are urged to avoid buying goods because all the effort of the country must now focus on exports. I would laugh out loud at the contrast with today's spend, spend, spend philosophy in order to stimulate the economy, in a time when prosperity is so prevalent, but this is not a laugh out loud place. It's a place of silent study, thoughts inwardly digested and not shared, but taken home for private use. Next I notice that the Liberals are to debate an important issue. Will the threat of atomic warfare abolish future war? We still don't know that answer. I'm ashamed of myself, but I'm drawn to the divorce columns. Now, the dirty deeds and mistakes of couples are no longer a source of news and entertainment unless they are people who have appeared on television, but here it's Ruby and Edward's trouble that catches my eye. He's suing for divorce. She's not contesting it. He claims a divorce on account of her misconduct in a flat in Kidbrooke with Ernie. It's only a few lines, but there's a family's story there for all to see.

The wonderful thing about newspapers is the proximity of diverse information. My eye is drawn away from Ruby and her adulterous carryings on in Kidbrooke, to the report of a tragic accident. I am one (of many) who has complained about the over zealousness of Health and Safety legislation. As a teacher I had to asses the risks of taking a group of consenting adults to the theatre, all of whom were making their own travel arrangements. I ask you, how would I know what might befall them as a consequence of a trip to see *The Winter's Tale* at the Globe Theatre? Might they become irrationally jealous? Might they try to live in an unrealistic rural idyll? It was so silly, but reading here of the tragic death of an ex army captain who was killed trying to board a bus struck a chord. Here's a man who has gone through the second world war, come out at the end unscathed only to meet his maker prematurely because he tries to get on the 61 in the direction of Orpington whilst the bus was moving. Continuing with the notion of stark contrasts I see more juxtaposition of this tragic story with the trivial; on the same page there is an illustrated advertisement for a brand of biscuits. There's a dialogue and it goes like this accompanied by a sweet picture of an innocent child with her pretty curls framing her perfect face, and her mother looking slim, well groomed and oh so happy in her domestic bliss.

'What are biscuits made of Mummy?' lisps the child.

'Sugar and spice and all things nice, just like you,' Mummy says gazing fondly, or smugly, down at her perfect child.

'Then I'm a proper biscuit of a little girl,' the child says.

Oh, please.

I found no report of my birth, but I did come across references to familiar names from my childhood which sprang out of the paper. The newspaper has returned me to a past I haven't completely forgotten. So absorbed am I that I don't notice Carole's approach.

'The big hand's on the six and the little hand's half way between the four and the five,' Carole whispers in my ear, and I get the message, it is time to leave.

'It's all right for you,' I grumble, 'you can come back any time.'

'True, but it's a long way to go to read a newspaper.'

We return to the station crossing a bridge which is decked out with Union Jack bunting.

'Are they expecting a coronation soon?' I ask, but we don't know the answer.

'Weird place Colindale,' Carole says. It is to move on, back to the future so to speak.

Hendon Town Hall: *Hendon became an Urban District in 1895 and the new town hall was built in 1901 from designs by T H Watson. It was made famous as the place where Margaret Thatcher made her first appearance and speech as Prime Minister in 1979. The building has now re-opened after the refurbishment which was in progress when we visited and offers a range of council services as well as the Citizenship and Naturalisation service.*

Middlesex University: *The Hendon Campus has been refurbished and redeveloped and is home to the university's Business School and The School of Engineering and Information Sciences. Most of the courses from the School of Health and Social Sciences are also held here and in 2011 their art, design and media courses will move to a new purpose-built building in Hendon.*

Church Farmhouse Museum: *The Church Farmhouse was built around 1660 and was a working farm until the early 20th century. The most famous person to live at the farm was Mark Lemon, co-founder of Punch, to whom there is a blue plaque. It was opened as a museum by Hendon Borough in 1955 and had three furnished Victorian period rooms and a continuing exhibition of 20th century toys and games. Unfortunately it closes from 31st March 2011 – a victim of council budget cuts but let's hope it has enough friends to ensure its future.* www.churchfarmhousemuseum.co.uk

British Library Newspaper Store: *originally a repository for regional newspapers, Colindale now holds the entire British Library newspaper collection, except for pre 1801 London newspapers. Reading rooms are available for visitors who wish to read the newspapers. An online newspapers catalogue of 52,000 items is available at the library's* newspaper catalogue *from which items can be ordered by credit card – go to:*
www.bl.uk/reshelp/findhelprestype/catblhold/all/allcat.html

CHAPTER TWENTY-ONE

Burnt Oak

We're excited as we step off the train at our penultimate station, Burnt Oak which boasts two sets of platforms, but it's a short-lived emotion as it's very similar to Colindale. It's another platform part of which is under the road with good old metal girders supporting the platform's protective canopy, but it all needs a lick of paint. We enter the now familiar glass box waiting room and park our bums on the aluminium shelf which pretends to be a seat.

'These end of the line stations do suffer from a bit of neglect,' Carole says as we look out at scenes of urban blight. The sagging corrugated roofs of an old market, a tatty car park with a peeling wooden advertising hoarding bearing an out of date 0181 number, and the depressing looking back to a row of shops with their mess of discarded boxes and general rubbish creates an air of neglect and decay.

We are cheered to learn that there is a good service on all underground trains at this point in time as the male announcer joyfully tells us as we trudge up the steps taking us to the by now familiar square foyer with its chequer board floor and high windows creating feelings of warmth and affection. My elevated mood is rapidly dispelled as I desperately search for my ticket and I am flooded with relief when I locate it. I stuff it in the barrier but it won't go in to let me through in spite of my repeated attempts to force it into the slot. Indignantly I present it to the man on the gate who politely points out that it's out of date. It's last week's ticket and I undertake another frantic search and finally find the miscreant. Phew! I'm through the barrier, waving my mapette like a triumphant runner crossing the finish line.

Carole and I emerge onto a street lined with small shops on both sides of the road which reflect the vibrant multi-cultural diversity of the area. There are many shops selling exotic ethnic food with a disproportionate number of greengrocers, each trying to outdo its neighbour with the extent and attractiveness of its pavement display. The fruit and veg are piled up in plastic bowls and their lovely colours and simple freshness demonstrate their good quality. We walk up the hill towards the main road in search of a coffee shop, it's been a long journey and we are in need of refreshment, so at the top of the hill we take a right turn and saunter along the

Burnt Oak Broadway. Now for nearly every other station we've been to, we've had our choice of coffee shops within spitting distance of the station, but not here. We pass a Registry Office. I ask Carole if she'll marry me, but she declines which is a bit of a relief as she's a rubbish cook.

We cross the road having spotted a café which turns out to be the Turkish equivalent of a greasy Joe's café. Carole ascends to use the facilities whilst I order the cheapest coffee so far at 58p per cup, and when we taste it, we know why, it's like dishwater. Carole returns from the facilities with dire warnings.

'You have to walk through the tiny washing up area to get to the loo which is notable for the grubbiness of its hand-towel. None but the brave would venture to dry their hands on it, come to think of it, I'd think twice about wiping my feet on it – **with** my shoes on.' Being both curious and desperate I can confirm from my own visit that everything she said is true.

The café is full of white people eating chips and burgers and there's not a fresh (or frozen) vegetable in sight. This is in stark contrast with the excellent range and choice of healthy food we have seen for sale on display on our way here. Everything on offer in this café is fattening, greasy and bad for the health and comes with chips. I'm surprised we weren't offered a chip to stir our coffee. The clientele seem to be consuming the food with some enthusiasm. To distract ourselves from the unedifying sight of one section of the local populace hardening their arteries, we peruse the mapette. We had hoped the local swimming pool would feature, but it doesn't and I'm sticking to the rules, so no going outside the area.

'The only swimming we're likely to do today then is if we get caught in one of the torrential downpours,' Carole says watching the water streaming down the café window. 'I wish I was a weather witch,' she continues.

'Do what?' I ask.

'A winsome weather witch casting sunny spells to turn grey clouds into white ones. I'd direct downpours into crystal rivers that we could bathe in.'

'Crikey,' is all I can think of to say, what's she been taking? I continue looking at the mapette. The only thing of interest that appears is a footpath running between the train track and Silk Stream.

'I'm not sure how we can access it,' Carole says, but never daunted, leaving half the coffee behind, we set off as the rain has stopped.

'Silk Stream sounds quite magical,' I say, it's my turn to wax lyrical.

Our mapette seems to suggest that we might be able to enter the footpath from a new building development so we traipse about, only to be met by temporary steel fencing. We retrace our steps and end up in a housing estate meeting with another blank wall barring our way. We walk around the Edgeware Community Hospital grounds which puts us in mind of our friend Jeanie who has just had surgery on her knee elsewhere, so we sit on a low wall and send her a text. Various hospital staff walk past giving us sympathetic looks and we realise we're close to the brain damage rehabilitation centre.

'The entrance to this must be guarded by some evil wizard,' Carole says, but that's not really the case as we find it when we emerge onto Deansbrook Road. We've tried to bunk in at the middle, but it can only be accessed from either end since it is sandwiched between iron railings and barbed wire with the stream on one side and the underground line on the other. Looking down it I can see it's another tarmac path with all the summer's growth of weeds, brambles and trees enclosed behind concrete poles and wire meshing, topped off with barbed wire.

'It's like a prison exercise yard,' Carole says.

'Isn't it supposed to be an inner city nature trail?' I ask.

'I think so. I suppose all of this,' Carole says waving her hand about indicating the acres of vicious fencing, 'is to deter hooligans.'

'Well it hasn't worked,' I say and point out the nature trail sign which has been ripped off and sprayed with graffiti and sits poking out from the nettles.

'We're trapped,' I say when we're halfway along the path looking at the green metal fencing, which is about eight feet tall, that lines one side of the pathway and the barbed wire topped wire mesh fence on the other side.

'I wouldn't care to be here late at night,' Carole says. On the right-hand side of us there is the hospital car park where we forlornly traipsed about; this is followed by the housing estate and the building site.

'Why the over the top fences when we've just walked on the other side?' Carole asks. I understand the need to protect the railway lines but I can't make any more sense of the expensive fencing than she can.

We wander along the path, catching the occasional glimpse of the tube rushing past but we are too far away from Silk Stream to see it. It's a bit disappointing and leads us to yet another example of urban detritus being dumped in a no-man's land. As we turn the corner at the end of the trail which will take us back to the road and the tube station we are greeted by a disgusting smelly rubbish dump. A wire mesh fence has been pulled down so that people can throw their unwanted goods onto the banks of Silk Stream. Some items are in the water where they've been left to moulder and decay and form a scene of squalid neglect.   'You wouldn't want to be a duck round here would you,' I say.

'No self-respecting mallard would regard this as des res,' Carole agrees. There's a shopping trolley piled high with more urban detritus, a brandy glass, beer cans and

McDonald wrappers mingling with other items of rubbish and it cements our view of Burnt Oak as shabby and dirty. This small neglected corner is unnecessarily disgusting, it could be so attractive.

'Silk Stream? I don't think so,' Carole says, 'they should call it Shit Stream.' We hurry back to the tube hoping that our final frontier is better than this.

Edgware

'It's the end of the line,' I say to Carole as we pull in across a complicated set of points, the wheels grinding as we take a sharp turn to the left to our platform. She knows this as well as I do so she ignores me, but I feel as if I should kiss the platform as I descend from the train. It's been a long time since our very first station, London Bridge, followed by the memorable flashing incident at Borough which began our quest. Was it to see if all London Underground employees were as handsome as Dave? Was it to see how many stations Carole could behave badly at? No, it was the love of the line, the challenge of the journey, the thrill of the adventure, the coffee in unexpected places, the sense of discovery and danger. I'm lying about the danger, there really wasn't any; I'm just getting a bit carried away.

It's a toytown terminus of a station with a high arched roof covering the two main platforms leaving the third in the open. We alight onto a covered platform that is under the semi-circular girders that support a pointy perspex roof. We've never seen anything like it, and its effect is pleasing. It's not quite in the Golders Green, Morden or East Finchley league, but it's homely and welcoming for the end of our journey. We sit and watch for a while as the trains arrive and their drivers emerge making for the little cubbyhole at the far end of the platform which constitutes a staffroom or office. They disappear only to re-emerge some time later.

'What do you think they do in there?' I ask Carole.

'I suppose they have a cuppa, eat their sandwiches and go to the loo before they've got to head off in a southerly direction.' I nod. I'm sure she's right.

'We could ask one of them,' Carole suggests looking at a balding bespectacled driver walking past us dressed in shorts that show his very unattractive hairy legs. I shake my head and am just about to pour cold water on the idea, when the next train disgorges its passengers and a positive Brad Pitt of a driver emerges walking towards us.

'Good idea,' I say, and we're in luck, he's a good natured as he is good looking. His name is Steve and no, he doesn't mind if we ask him some questions or take his photograph. He confirms that the Edgware turn-around is like the Mill Hill one in that the train is able to make its return journey because it has a cab at either end.

'Makes sense,' Carole says. 'Imagine trying to do a three point turn or having a huge carousel, it'd make the driver dizzy.' Steve tells us he's a relief driver and driving back to Golders Green after his break where he'll wait in case he's needed. He likes driving and when we tell him of our quest and our desire to visit the depot at Golders Green he gives us an address to write to. What a star. With a cheery wave he disappears into the cubbyhole.

'We've met so many helpful people, interested in their jobs,' Carole says, and I have to agree, we've met a few grumps but the vast majority have been approachable, affable, well informed and easy to talk to.

'Not sure about shorts man though,' I say to Carole.

'No, they're not standard issue but even if they are he shouldn't be frightening the passengers with legs like that.'

The station is busy with trains coming and going and pulling out to rejoin the tide of tubes ebbing and flowing along the length of the Northern Line, ready to collect the multiplicity of humanity that is swept up and deposited every day. We can't quite believe that we've got to the end and wander up and down the platform with its wealth of benches, just a little reluctant to leave it behind. We peer into the empty driver's cab.

'It's hardly the bridge of the starship Enterprise,' Carole says.

'Well I don't suppose there's much call for *boldly going* if you're an underground driver.'

'I suppose Steve is already on his way to Golders Green,' Carole says and we both know the steps are there waiting for us to make the final exit. It's time.

The foyer has an ordinarily sandy coloured floor, is square with high windows and boasts a repair shop belonging to Madame George who will undertake alterations. My attention is drawn to a gentleman in a suit with a hat and his prayer shawl fringe hanging just beneath his jacket. My eye is not drawn to him because he is in the standard costume expected of an orthodox Jew, but because he is talking on his mobile telephone and gesticulating in a theatrical way that I really like. I'd like to follow him and talk to him and find out about his life, but my own journey doesn't lead in his direction.

Outside there's a small turn around road for taxis and a bus station to the left so it's a well connected station from a transport point of view. Carole has said all along that we must have champagne and a slap up meal when we reach the north pole of the Northern Line, avoiding snacks in greasy cafés and we won't go to anywhere with scrumptious in the title. We'll do ourselves proud which is just as well.

'I'm hungry,' Carole says. 'My tummy's rumbling.'

'Not as much as mine I bet.'

'Mine's about 0.5 on the tummy Richter scale.

'Mine's about 3.'

We turn left up Station Road and looking about see that this area is far more prosperous than Burnt Oak. The shops comprise the usual suspects, the road wider, the pavement tidier. We walk past the Broakwalk Shopping centre

something of a toytown mall offering little more in the way of comestibles than a garnished supermac.

'Hardly cordon bleu,' Carole says dismissively. Fifty yards up the road we have the choice between Chinese, Indian and Italian food. We plump for the Italian which is called Mascalzone, is not part of a chain or a franchise and no offence to the cuisine of China or India, find we've made an excellent choice.

The menu is interesting and the surroundings pleasant so we settle down to a very palatable meal accompanied by a bottle of sparkling, fruity red wine called Fragolino Rosso.

'It sounds like a down-market floor covering,' Carole says, but it doesn't taste like it, it's really appetizing and turns out to be a great accompaniment to our delicious food. I order calves liver in a white wine sauce with mash and Carole orders something that doesn't involve the slaughter of small innocent animals. My meal is perfectly cooked and delicious and I enjoy every mouthful. We are then offered a taste of iced coffee that appears to be on tap. It's very refreshing, but too sweet for my palette and so I have ordinary coffee, but Carole, always one to try something new slurps her way through a thick glass of the stuff. People come and go, sitting at tables, all talking Italian. It begins to rain and we watch the inhabitants of Edgware rush about covering their heads with free London newspapers, running and ducking into doorways. It's only a shower and then sleepy and replete we have to leave the wonderfully relaxing atmosphere of the restaurant.

We've determined on a visit to a pond which appears on the corner of the map. I'm not sure it's the best that Edgware has to offer, but after a very satisfying lunch and half a bottle of red fizz I'm in no mood to argue with Carole's choice.

'Look,' says Carole, 'the lake goes off the edge of the mapette – who knows, it could be the edge of the world. Why else would the Northern Line stop here when it could have continued on to Inverness?' It's a question that stimulates so many thoughts I'm unable to give her a coherent answer, or is the effect of the booze?

To access the big pond/small lake we have to pass through Cannons gate pillars which mark the entrance to the estate owned by the first Duke of Chandos. The house, built in 1713, took eleven years to complete at a cost of £200,000.

'What's the modern equivalent of £200,000?' Carole asks.

'I think it's about £27,000,000.'

'Tidy sum of money then.'

'It was all gone by 1747,' I say. 'Everything except these pillars was sold off to pay the family's debts.' Carole shakes her head.

'All is vanity, all vanity,' she says. 'These residences are still pretty desirable though,' she says gesturing towards the large detached houses that sit back in the tree-lined road. It begins to drizzle as we reflect on changed times and how the excessive wealth of one person has now been replaced by the affluence of many. We locate the pond. Well, it's an expanse of water with a small island in the middle.

'The residents jointly own these green spaces,' I point out to Carole who is taking pictures and not reading the notices.

'That's why they're so many notices, don't feed the ducks, don't fish, don't leave rubbish. If only some of them moved to Burnt Oak they could encourage it to clean up its act.'

We watch a family of pushy moorhens mooching about with their heads nodding forwards for our entertainment.

'Where's that stale bit of bread you had in your pocket?' Carole asks.

'I chucked it away earlier,' I say. 'I

didn't want to litter, I saw the notices.'

'Blame the residents association,' Carole says addressing the moorhens, 'that's why we've nothing to give you.'

'The moorhens don't look convinced,' I say.

'Next thing they'll be hanging around at traffic lights in the Edgware Road threatening to poo on the windscreens of unsuspecting motorists unless they're given left over ciabatta. Bloody middle class moorhens.' We admire the trees fringing the pond which are enormous and well established so probably left over from the Duke's day. The disconsolate moorhens return to the water regarding us disdainfully and we don out kagouls as it begins to drizzle in earnest.

We leave the wet area behind us and make our way back to the station via a synagogue that has a distinctly run down look to it. We'd like to go in and talk to someone about the Jewish religion, about the Eruv that allows the faithful to move about on the Sabbath, but it's locked and our final time wasting opportunity is lost.

'How would you recognise an Eruv?' Carole asks, but I don't know the answer.

'We could ask a rabbi if we see one,' I suggest, but we don't see one. We wander past the semi-detached houses of Edgware and admire the neatness of the gardens and our final fling is a visit to the very over-heated Broadwalk Mall which has become more attractive now the drizzle has turned to real rain. Carole buys a bottle of water and offers me some. The heat of the place has made me thirsty and in my enthusiasm I manage to shower myself with water.

'A fitting end to an unremarkable, but nonetheless interesting journey,' Carole says.

Burnt Oak: *the name was originally used in 1754 and referred to a large field in which a burnt oak tree was situated. The original station opened in 1924 but as the area developed it was replaced by a larger one in 1928. The areas main claim to fame is that in 1929 Jack Cohen used the name Tesco for the first time and founded the chain of stores.* **Silk stream** *is the name of a brook, a tributary of the river Brent which joins at Brent Reservoir and is part of the Blue Ribbon network of waterways in London.*

Cannons Gate: *Cannons was the stately home built for James Brydges, first Duke of Chandos between 1713 and 1724 at a cost in present day terms of around £28 million. The grounds of Cannons extending to 105 acres were renowned for their magnificence and included a pleasure garden, water garden, orchard and a grand terrace opening on to a parterre with gilded statues. The house became famous, featuring in various travel guides of that time and attracting many visitors. Its majesty was short-lived, however since the Brydges lost a significant part of their fortune when the South Sea Bubble burst and the second Duke, Henry, auctioned off the very fabric of the building, as well as all its contents, fixtures and fittings in 1747 to satisfy debtors. The colonnade can be seen in front of the National Gallery in London. The estate was purchased by William Hallett, a cabinet maker who built a large villa on the sit which is today the North London Collegiate School.*

Final reflections

It's been a wonderful journey, not only for the things we've seen but for the shared experience. We've had highlights and low lights. The outer lying stations have occasionally been thin on the ground as regards interest, but here I must exempt Colindale and the wonderful British Library Newspaper store. We returned to the museum at High Barnet and learnt more about the Battle of Barnet, especially through the wall map charting the progress of the two armies. We were slightly underwhelmed by the rest of the museum. We also visited the Church Farmhouse Museum at Hendon. This place is very child friendly with various teddies tucked away in unexpected places just to give the children an activity in spotting and counting them. Some of the exhibits were interactive and upstairs we found an extensive display of various editions of the London Tube Map and how it changed over a period of time. We stared long and hard at Harry Beck's innovative diagrammatic view and admired its clarity. What a hero.

We've had some great inner London experiences, the British Library at Euston, The British Museum at Tottenham Court Road, the museum at Bank. We've visited some strange and unexpected places, in particular the Stephen's Ink Museum sticks in my mind, not only for its exhibits but also for the personality and enthusiasm of its attendant on the day of our visit. We've met some interesting people who have given up their time to us, to talk to us, to steer us in the right direction. Strangers have approached and offered to help us as we stare at our mapettes. We've experienced the generosity of people. We've also encountered some rotters, those who have shown us they hold us in contempt but we bear them no ill will. They have been so very much a small minority of the people that we are left with warm feelings for the friendliness and kindness of our fellow human beings. We have found an overwhelming number of London Underground staff to be polite, knowledgeable, efficient and helpful and many have chatted to us at length, showing their interest in their work and in our project. This book is dedicated to them, to the men and women who work day and night without praise and thanks from a general travelling public who take them for granted.

Best of all, has been Carole's company, her humorous take on places, people and events and her unavailing good humour. She has been a truly, good companion.